Adoption in the
United States

Also Available from Lyceum Books, Inc.

Advisory Editors: Thomas M. Meenaghan, *New York University*
Ira C. Colby, *University of Houston*
Wynne Korr, *University of Illinois at Urbana-Champaign*

Straight Talk About Professional Ethics
Kim Strom-Gottfried

Empowering Vulnerable Populations:
Cognitive-Behavioral Interventions
Mary Keegan Eamon

Cross-Cultural Practice: Social Work with Diverse Populations, 2E
Karen Harper-Dorton and Jim Lantz

Social Work with Volunteers
Michael E. Sherr, foreword by John G. McNutt

Diversity, Oppression, and Change: Culturally Grounded Social Work
Flavio Francisco Marsiglia and Stephen Kulis

Social Work in a Sustainable World
Nancy L. Mary

The Ethics of Practice with Minors
Kim Strom-Gottfried

Theory and Practice with Adolescents
Fred R. McKenzie

Adoption in the United States
A Reference for Families, Professionals, and Students

MARTHA J. HENRY
CENTER FOR ADOPTION RESEARCH,
UNIVERSITY OF MASSACHUSETTS MEDICAL SCHOOL

DANIEL POLLACK
YESHIVA UNIVERSITY

LYCEUM
BOOKS, INC.

Chicago, Illinois

© Lyceum Books, Inc., 2009

Published by

LYCEUM BOOKS, INC.
5758 S. Blackstone Ave.
Chicago, Illinois 60637
773+643-1903 (Fax)
773+643-1902 (Phone)
lyceum@lyceumbooks.com
http://www.lyceumbooks.com

All rights reserved under International and Pan-American Copyright
Conventions. No part of the publication may be reproduced, stored in a
retrieval system, copied, or transmitted in any form or by any means without
written permission from the publisher.

6 5 4 3 2 1   08 09 10 11

ISBN 978-1-933478-20-3

Library of Congress Cataloging-in-Publication Data

Henry, Martha J.
    Adoption in the United States : a reference for families, professionals, and
students / by Martha J. Henry, Daniel Pollack.
       p. cm.
    ISBN 978-1-933478-20-3
    1. Adoption—United States—Handbooks, manuals, etc. I. Pollack, Daniel. II. Title.
    HV875.55.H46   2008
    362.7340973—dc22
                                                        2008017148

To Aaron Lazare, MD, a man of infinite warmth and wisdom

Contents

Boxes and Tables

About the Authors

Martha J. Henry, PhD, is director of the Center for Adoption Research at the University of Massachusetts Medical School. Her background in developmental psychology informs her work creating adoption and foster care curricula and trainings for medical, social service, legal, and educational professionals, as well as for families. She has developed a course and seminars for medical students regarding health care practice and considerations for adoption and foster care.

Daniel Pollack, MSW, JD, is professor at Wurzweiler School of Social Work, Yeshiva University, New York City. He is also senior fellow at the Center for Adoption Research, University of Massachusetts Medical School in Worcester, MA.

Preface

It is our belief that the people whose contributions make an adoption possible must understand that the success of that adoption depends on their ability to work together as a team. Members of that team include the child, the birth parents, and the adoptive parents, as well as representatives of the legal system, the social services system, and the medical and behavioral health systems. Professionals involved in an adoption placement may include social workers, lawyers, doctors, nurses, allied health professionals, educators, court personnel, and human services personnel. These laypeople and professionals come together to develop a comprehensive plan to ensure that the adoption will be a success. Each member of the team is important; collectively, they fulfill a variety of functions. They promote coordination between agencies, ensure that the interests and rights of all concerned parties are addressed, and identify problems in coordination or communication between individuals and agencies.

Multidisciplinary teams are not a new concept. It is not sufficient for each professional to perform his or her own professional activity. All professional members of the team work cooperatively to deliver coordinated and integrated services to each member of the adoption triad (child, birth parents, and adoptive family). Thus, professionals need to worry less about professional boundaries and more about making sure that the needs of all members of the adoptive triad are addressed. A sense of interdependence and shared purpose ensures a successful adoption and results in a stronger family.

Each section of this book is important for every reader. For instance, regardless of whether or not you are a lawyer, be sure to read the section that provides information on legal issues; likewise, even if you are not a doctor, you should read the section on medical issues. This is especially important for professionals, because understanding the work done by one's colleagues on the adoption team supports one's work as a member of that team. Likewise, it is important for birth and adoptive parents to have this knowledge because it can help them recognize the professionals who are available as resources during the adoption process.

In general, adoption of children in the United States is not regulated by federal law; rather, it is governed by state laws. Regulations, procedures, and professionals involved in adoption vary from state to state. This reference book provides information about all aspects of adoption, whether it is private or public, domestic or intercountry. Although other reference books have been written regarding adoption, to date, no comprehensive guide has brought together information relevant to so many professional disciplines. This text provides both a wide range of information about adoption and a developmental perspective on basic medical and behavioral health information to educate parents, professionals, and students about issues relevant to children who were or will be adopted or who have experienced foster care. It will also help readers understand the different types of adoptions and the professionals who are involved in the process, the laws regarding adoption in their state and other states, and the requirements to adopt children from other countries. Because it provides information on the legal, educational, medical, behavioral, and developmental aspects of adoption, social workers, teachers and students of social work, lawyers, and educators who work with children will also find the information in this book useful.

For prospective adoptive parents, the experience of adopting a child can be both wonderful and intense. For the adoption professional whose work involves bringing a child who needs a loving home together with a family who wants to care for a child, the experience is both challenging and rewarding. It is imperative to recognize that for the birth mother or birth parents, this is a difficult and painful decision. The adoption process can seem overwhelming for birth parents and prospective adoptive parents, as they must sort through the procedural aspects while managing a wide array of emotions. Well-informed professionals in the fields of social work, psychology, law, and medicine can guide and support parents and children throughout the process.

Prospective adoptive parents, birth parents, and professionals can all use the information in this book to understand their rights and responsibilities when making an adoption plan for a child, considering adoption as an option to create or expand a family, or ensuring that a spouse or partner has the right to bear legal responsibility for a child. Furthermore, prospective adoptive parents can use this book to prepare for all the stages of the adoption journey, from selecting a professional with whom to work and undergoing a home study through bringing the child home and living as a family for a lifetime. Choosing adoption as a way to create or expand a family requires thoughtful consideration of the options available and the type of family one wants to create, as well as the leap of faith that is necessary for parenting, regardless of how children come into one's family. People who consider adoption often have an array of concerns. This book is meant to be a resource about the various aspects of adoption and to provide information about what is currently known regarding outcomes for members of the adoption triad.

In the United States, there were 513,000 children in foster care in 2005 (Adoption and Foster Care Reporting and Analysis System, 2007). Approximately 20 percent, or 101,000 of these children, are legally free for adoption. More than 20,000 children from other countries have been adopted into the

United States each year since 2002. Thousands more children are adopted through private domestic adoptions each year. A few of these children have only been waiting days; others have been waiting years. All of them share the need for a caring and committed family who can give them a chance at the future they deserve.

Adopting a child is a rewarding yet demanding undertaking. Prospective adoptive parents must maintain a positive attitude and be willing to take the time to understand the difficulties to be faced and to make a firm commitment to the welfare of their child. With any legal or professional undertaking, corruption and fraud can occur. Unfortunately, adoption is no different; members of the adoption triad do not always experience the process of adoption within the guidelines of the legal requirements, state laws, and appropriate and ethical professional practice for child adoption identified in this book. Parties engaged in the adoption process—both those making adoption plans for children they are unable to parent and those seeking to parent children through legal adoption—should be aware that they may encounter unscrupulous people, including licensed professionals, during the process. Being an informed consumer of professional adoption services is vital to a successful adoption experience. Thus it is critical that expectant parents and adoptive parents understand their rights, the applicable state and federal laws, and the standards for professional practice regarding child adoption. Making an adoption plan or creating a family through adoption is one of the most important decisions a person can make. It is strongly advised that members of the adoption triad work with licensed and well-informed professionals throughout the process and take advantage of their expertise. Attempting an adoption with little or no professional help can lead to an unlawful adoption process, inappropriate and illegal exchanges of monies or gifts, excessive and unnecessary expenses, and, most of all, avoidable emotional anguish.

Acknowledgments

Our sincerest appreciation goes to all those who contributed to this effort, whether it was in writing, editing, conceptualizing, typing, or many other supportive roles. You gave generously of your time and knowledge. Truly, your efforts and encouragement exceeded our expectations. We would like to acknowledge Rose Reith for her hard work, long hours, and dedication to editing and preparing the manuscript. Her tremendous commitment has made this book possible and we are grateful for all her efforts. We wish to thank Sonia Elizabeth Fulop, our editor from Lyceum Books, whose efforts tightened and clarified the text. We express immense gratitude to our families. Without their constant love, we would not have been able give this work the devotion and concentration it needed. It is with great pleasure that we acknowledge them.

We would also like to acknowledge everyone who shared so willingly of their time and expertise by contributing sections of the book. We extend our sincere thanks to Jodi Adams, who contributed to the research spotlight on birth parents; Heather C. Forkey, who contributed to the research spotlights on physical, developmental, and mental health issues in foster care and health care for children in foster care; Wendy Guyker, who contributed to the sections on the history of adoption, transracial adoption, and outcomes of transracial adoption; Gretchen Hall, who contributed the section on special education services for adopted children; Richard Moriarty, who contributed the section on intercountry adoption; Cassandra Perry, who contributed the section on adoption in cases of fetal anomaly and genetic risks; Rose Reith, who contributed the section on openness in adoption; and Linda Sagor and Peter Toscano, who contributed to chapter 7.

Finally, the authors wish to thank each other. We were fortunate to share an encouraging, inspirational, and supportive relationship throughout this endeavor. May it continue for many years!

A Note on Language: Accuracy and Respect for Children, Parents, and Families

Language is a powerful tool that allows us to share our perspectives. The choice of one word or phrase over another can convey very different meanings or highlight different aspects of a situation and can actually be hurtful rather than helpful. Values and beliefs can be conveyed unintentionally when people do not appreciate the history or meaning behind phrases describing adoption or foster care experiences. The use of accurate and sensitive language concerning adoption and foster care is important because it is essential to show respect for different people, perspectives, and experiences. It acknowledges the equality between adoptive and birth relationships, and the thoughtful consideration and lifelong choices involved with child adoption. Sensitive language shows respect for adoption as a choice for people unable to parent, people seeking to create or expand a family, and people who have remarried or are part of a same-sex couple and are seeking to ensure stability for their children, but most importantly it respects adoption as a wonderful way for children to become part of a family.

Historically, language describing foster care, adoption, and children without parental care has highlighted the negative aspects of these experiences and has reinforced negative stereotypes. These descriptions may lead to implicit or explicit bias toward children and families in these situations.

Children who have experienced foster care have experienced significant loss. Like most children, they have usually developed some form of attachment with their birth parents. It can be very confusing for children when hurtful language is used to describe their birth parents or their situation, and this can make it difficult for them to understand why their perceptions of the situation are so different from those expressed by others. Furthermore, children who are older at the time of adoption may often have memories of good times spent with their birth parents or families. Using appropriate and sensitive language allows children to make distinctions between what their parents were able to do for them and the circumstances that resulted in their placement in foster care.

One way to eliminate potential bias and help children who have experienced foster care or have been adopted understand their situation is to model the use of sensitive and appropriate language.[1] For example, it is important to recognize that the use of phrases such as "gave up," "given up," "put up," and "surrendered" to describe an adoption may imply that the birth parent discarded or wanted to dispose of the child or rejected responsibility for the child. People "give up" bad habits and dispose of belongings they no longer want by "putting them up" for sale. Words like "put up" may also bring to mind the orphan trains that ran from the mid-nineteenth century through the early twentieth century.

Thus a better choice than saying, "She put her baby up for adoption," would be to say that a birth parent "chose" or "made" an adoption plan, or to describe a child as one "for whom an adoption plan was made." These are better choices because they recognize that the decision to make an adoption plan is extremely difficult and requires a great deal of thought on the part of the birth parents. Using this language also recognizes the right of the birth parents to make that decision for their child. Describing an adoption as an event that has been planned acknowledges that birth parents love their children and are trying to ensure that they will have good lives. It helps to eliminate any suggestion that the child is unwanted or that the birth mother was unable or unwilling to be responsible for the child. Using accurate descriptive language when one is speaking or writing about adoption relationships can avoid any suggestion that adoptive families are artificial or second best and that the birth family should feel shame and disgrace.

Other words that are inaccurate are those that make note of the distinction between children born into a family or adopted into a family, and those that reference the legitimacy of a child with respect to his or her parents' marital status. Words such as "real" or "natural" that are used to distinguish between children who are born into a family and one who was adopted into a family unfairly label the child and are inaccurate. The use of the phrase "own children" to describe birth children is also inaccurate. All children are real and natural. Lack of a genetic link does not make a child unnatural, nor does it prevent a child from really belonging to his or her parents, whether birth or adoptive. When one is speaking of the child of an unmarried couple, it is more appropriate to describe the child as having been born to unwed parents than it is to refer to the child as illegitimate. Table 1 provides some examples of hurtful language and alternate language choices, with an explanation of why the alternatives are more appropriate.

---

[1]Positive adoption language has been discussed by others in connection with adoption, education, and social work. Marietta Spencer, a social worker from Minneapolis, first introduced the concept (Stroud, Stroud, & Staley, 1997). Subsequently, authors like Pat Johnston (2001) have written on the need for respectful adoption language in an effort to acknowledge that families formed by adopting a child are equal to families formed by birth.

TABLE 1   Respectful and Accurate Language

Hurtful choice	Wise choice	Explanation
Gave up Given up Put up Surrendered for adoption	Chose or made an adoption plan A child for whom an adoption plan was made	The decision to make an adoption plan is extremely difficult and requires a great deal of thought. Children who were sent on the orphan trains from New York to rural areas in the West, Midwest, and South beginning in the mid-1800s were displayed or "put up" on a platform so that prospective adoptive parents could see them and decide which child they wished to adopt.
Keep the child	Parent the child	People who choose adoption are not discarding their children but are unable to parent them.
Real or natural parents	Birth parents	There are no imaginary or unnatural parents.
Real or natural child Illegitimate child	Birth child Child born to unwed parents	All children are real, natural, and legitimate. Lack of a genetic link does not make someone unnatural or illegitimate, nor does the status of the marriage of one's birth parents confer legitimacy.
Your own children	Birth children	All parents consider their children their own regardless of how they came together to be a family.
Is Adopted Adoptee	Was Adopted Person Who Was Adopted	Adoption describes a process, but it is not an enduring quality of a person. Adoption is not a diagnosis or a condition. For some people, adoption is a significant part of their identity, and for others it is not. A person who was adopted may choose to refer to him- or herself as an adoptee but others should not assume that the person who was adopted is comfortable with this identifier.
Foster child Foster youth	Child or youth who is living with a foster family or who has experienced foster care	The emphasis should be on the child or youth, not his or her foster status.
Your mom and dad	Parents Guardians Family Caregivers	It is important for children to have their families validated. Referring to a child's "mom and dad" can make kids who don't have a mother or father or both feel invisible. The better alternative is inclu-

TABLE 1   Respectful and Accurate Language—(*continued*)

Hurtful choice	Wise choice	Explanation
		sive of different kinds of caregivers and does not assume a mother-father pair (e.g., children may live with a single parent, grandparents, an aunt, an uncle, foster parents, two moms, or two dads).
Girlfriend Wife Boyfriend Husband	Partner Spouse Significant other	The assumption of heterosexuality excludes lesbian, gay, and bisexual people and relationships. The use of neutral language opens the door to better communication.
Alternative families	Nontraditional families	The word "alternative" implies that there is such a thing as a standard or normal family and implies value judgment on the non-standard or "alternative" family. People in non-traditional families are usually ordinary people.
Neglectful parent	Parent who is unable to meet the needs of a child	Children who have experienced foster care or adoption do not want or need to hear their birth parents criticized. However, it is important for children to understand what their parents were unable to do that resulted in their separation.
Abusive parent	Parent who is unable to manage his or her own behavior	Children who have experienced foster care do not want or need to hear their birth parents criticized. However, it is important for children to understand what their parents were unable to do that brought them into state custody.
Drug addict Alcoholic parent	Parent whose abuse of substances affects his or her decision making and ability to be responsive and responsible	Children who have experienced foster care do not want or need to hear their birth parents criticized. However, it is important for children to understand what their parents were unable to do that brought them into state custody.
Unfit parent	Parent who is unable to meet the needs of a child	There are many reasons that parents are not able to adequately care for children. Children benefit from having a clear sense of those reasons.

TABLE 1   Respectful and Accurate Language—(*continued*)

Hurtful choice	Wise choice	Explanation
Unwanted	Unable to be parented by a birth parent	There are a variety of reasons people may be unable to parent their children. Desire is usually not a reason, and describing a child as "unwanted" is detrimental to his or her sense of self and may very well be inaccurate.
Taken away	Placed in state custody	The state, guided by law, has decided to remove the child from his or her home for specific reasons. "Taken away" suggests that the decision to remove the child was arbitrary and unreasonable and does not recognize that the focus is actually the child's well-being.
Track down relatives	Search for information or relatives	"Tracking down relatives" could suggest that they are unwilling to be found. Conducting a search can take many forms and can mean searching for information, people, or both.
Reunion	Making or keeping in contact with a birth parent	Having contact with birth parents and relatives can take many forms and does not always lead to reunification.
Adopt a highway Adopt a whale Adopt a playground Adopt a school	Sponsor a highway Sponsor a whale Sponsor a playground Sponsor a school	The use of the word "adopt" to describe temporary relationships and fund-raising activities may make parents uncomfortable and may be confusing or hurtful to children.

In order to avoid misunderstandings and hurt feelings, and to reduce stigma for members of the adoption triad and their families, it is important for professionals and parents to understand the impact their word choices can have on a person's experience or understanding of adoption and foster care. The hurt feelings engendered by the use of inappropriate and inaccurate language can linger indefinitely. Thus, parents, professionals, and students can benefit from understanding the impact of choosing one word over another when discussing adoption or foster care. Children and families also benefit from the sensitivity and awareness of the professionals who work with them.

Chapter 1

Adopting in the United States

Adoption is the permanent legal transfer of full parental rights from one parent or set of parents to another parent or set of parents. This legal transfer ensures that adoptive parents are afforded the same rights and responsibilities that giving birth to a child would provide them. Children who are adopted receive all the legal, emotional, social, and kinship benefits of birth children. Each state has its own laws regarding the various aspects of adoption. For instance, in some states the only entity legally able to place a child for adoption is a licensed public or private adoption agency, while in other states, lawyers or other individuals are permitted to place a child for adoption. In addition, each state has laws regarding timeframes for relinquishing the child and rescinding parental rights, as well as specifications on allowable birth parent expenses. Since adoption agreements can be arranged when birth parents reside in one state and the prospective adoptive parents reside in another, it is important that the laws of both states be understood and followed. Federal policies also inform adoption practice, particularly in public adoption from foster care, in cases when the child is of Native American heritage, and in intercountry adoptions.

History of Adoption in the United States

Massachusetts was the first state to pass a modern adoption law, the 1851 Adoption of Children Act, which recognized adoption as a social and legal contract based on children's welfare, rather than on adult interests. This law marked a significant turning point because it directed judges to ensure that adoption decrees were "fit and proper," though the definition of "fit and proper" was left to judicial discretion.

In 1854, reformer Charles Loring Brace, supervisor of the New York Children's Aid Society, implemented the orphan trains. Brace proposed that children from New York City who were homeless or neglected and living on the streets be sent by train to live and work on farms in the Midwest, South, and West. Children would be placed in homes for free, but they would serve as an extra pair of hands to help with chores around the farm (Children's Aid Society, 2008). Today, the still-operating Children's Aid Society describes Brace's orphan trains as the inception of foster care in the United States. In 1868, the practice of foster care, or "placing out," was strengthened when the Massachusetts Board of State Charities began paying for children to board in private family homes. In 1869, the board assigned an agent to visit homes to check on the children's well-being. The movement to care for children in families rather than institutions continued to develop.

Congress established the U.S. Children's Bureau in the Department of Labor in 1912. The goal of the Children's Bureau was to supervise issues relative to children's lives and their well-being in the United States, without regard to their social status or class. The Children's Bureau was led by Julia Lathrop, who was also the first woman to head a federal agency.

Requirements that adoptive parents be qualified to adopt through social investigation and home studies were passed into Minnesota law in 1917. This law also included provisions for the confidentiality of adoption records. Twenty years later, the Child Welfare League of America put forth an initiative that set minimum standards for permanent (adoptive) and temporary (foster) placements.

In 1948 the first recorded transracial adoption of an African American child by white parents took place, also in Minnesota, and in 1957, in response to the increasing numbers of international adoptions that resulted from the effects of World War II and the Korean conflict, as well as other international events that brought children in need of care to the attention of adults who were interested in meeting their needs, the International Conference on Intercountry Adoptions issued a report on the problems observed with international adoptions. Also that year, adoption agencies in the United States sponsored legislation to prohibit or control proxy adoptions.

Concern for children with special needs, who were considered to be hard to place, led the Los Angeles County Bureau of Adoptions to launch the first organized program promoting adoptions by single parents in 1965. It was anticipated that this practice would help public agencies find loving homes for these children.

Sealed adoption records, secrecy in adoption, and adopted individuals' struggles to access their original birth records were brought to the attention of the public in 1971 when Florence Fisher founded the Adoptees' Liberty Movement Association, which had two goals. The first was to end the standard practice of sealing adoption records once an adoption was finalized. The second was to make it possible for any adopted individual over age eighteen to see his or her birth and adoption records. The struggle for adopted individuals to access their original adoption records continues to the present day. Some states have established laws that permit access to original records after adopted individuals reach adulthood. Other states still require that the person who was adopted petition the court for permission to see his or her original birth certificate (see Appendix A for state-specific information regarding access to original birth records).

In 1978, the United States Congress passed the Indian Child Welfare Act in response to the "alarmingly high number of Indian children being removed from their homes by both public and private agencies" (National Indian Child Welfare Association, 2008). The intent of the Indian Child Welfare

Act is to defend the right of Indian children to remain with their tribes and families whenever possible. The law requires that the priority in cases involving Indian children be the child's best interests, particularly with respect to stability for their families and the tribes to which they belong.

The Adoption Assistance and Child Welfare Act was passed in 1980. It promised adoption assistance monies to states in which adoptions of children with special needs were made a funding priority. The act also allocated funding for programs that work to strengthen and keep families together and prevent child abuse and child neglect, with the goal that children in foster care can return home or do not need to be removed from their homes in the first place.

The Hague Convention on the Protection of Children and Co-operation in Respect of Intercountry Adoption was approved by sixty-six nations in 1993. A year later, the United States signed the convention, and it was approved by Congress in 2000.

The first federal legislation that focused on race in connection with adoption was the Multiethnic Placement Act of 1994. According to the act, if an agency received funding from the federal government, it could not prevent the adoptive or foster care placement of a child with parents of a different race, color, or nationality. There was still some leeway in that race could be considered as one aspect of a family's suitability for a particular child; however, it could not be the only factor against a placement. The law was revised in 1996 by the Interethnic Adoption Provision Act, which completely eliminated the ability of agencies to consider race, color, or nationality when planning a child's placement.

In 1997, the Adoption and Safe Families Act recognized that the federally mandated policy of working only toward strengthening and reunifying families did not necessarily serve all children in care. The Adoption and Safe Families Act was put in place to emphasize that children benefit from permanency planning. In some cases adoption may be a more appropriate goal. This act represented a change in child welfare policy with respect to family reunification and helped promote consideration of adoption as an option for permanency.

In response to ever-increasing numbers of children being adopted into the United States, the Child Citizenship Act of 2000 made it possible for children born outside the United States who were being adopted by U.S. citizens to receive United States citizenship automatically when they entered the country with their adoptive parents. This act eliminated the formal legal naturalization process for children adopted through intercountry adoption. Also in 2000, for the first time in the history of the United States, the option to select "adopted son/daughter" was included on the U.S. census form as a category of kinship relationship.

Each of these events in United States adoption history happened as a response to people's perceptions of children in need of care and families. Each led to further changes in the way adoption has been viewed by the public. These events all played a role in helping to bring adoption to the place it currently holds in the fabric of American society. Without them, the remarkable number of public, domestic infant, private, and intercountry adoptions occurring each year in the United States might never have come to happen.[1]

Views of Adoption in the United States

While many people view adoption as a successful and acceptable way to incorporate new members into a family, it once was seen as a second-best option to having a child by birth, and people who were infertile were perceived to be defective (Diamond, Diamond, & Jaffe, 1999; Miall, 1987). Women who chose to make adoption plans for unplanned pregnancies or were encouraged to make that decision by parents or clergy were often viewed in a negative light and shamed by society (Schooler & Norris, 2002). A complex interplay of historical, social, and cultural events and forces, as well as public policy and law, has shaped adoption over time. Although the roots of adoption practice in the United States had been formed both in a legal and social sense by the late 1800s, recent cultural and political trends have been most critical in shaping contemporary adoption practices. Historically, mental health professionals paid little attention to adoption (Brodzinsky & Schechter, 1990), which was simply seen as a successful social service solution for the three parties of the adoption triad: birth parents, adoptive parents, and child. It was assumed that all parties involved would go on with their lives, without care or worry once the adoption placement was finalized (Brodzinsky & Schechter, 1990). During the first half of the twentieth century, secrecy in adoption was prevalent. The belief that children and families were best served by the strict observance of confidentiality resulted in adoption practices that encouraged parents to allow others to believe that their adopted children had been born to them. In fact, before the 1950s, families with adopted children were often told not to tell their children that they had been adopted (Krueger-Jago & Hanna, 1997).

Activism on the part of birth parents and individuals who were adopted during the 1960s and 1970s has challenged traditional notions regarding the importance of secrecy in adoption and has increased demand for more forthright exchanges of information between members of the adoption triad (Zamostny, O'Brien, Baden, & Wiley, 2003). Today, the majority of domestic adoptions have some degree of openness, meaning that they involve at least a basic amount of communication and contact between the members of the adoption triad. Still, some adoptions are closed. In a closed adoption, a birth mother or birth parents might receive minimal information to help select

---

[1]This discussion of the history of adoption was adapted from the History of Adoption Project Web site (Herman, 2003).

adoptive parents for the child, but complete names and other identifying information are not shared by either set of parents, and no plans for contact are made.

Adoption is now viewed as an acceptable way to form a family that has lifelong implications for members of the adoptive triad (Zamostny et al., 2003). In other words, the conceptualization of the adoption experience has changed over time as more people have chosen to build their families through adoption.

Considering Adoption

Many issues arise when people consider adoption as a way to create or add to a family. Often, when people first begin to think about adoption, it may not seem right for them. For couples, it is normal for each partner to feel differently about the idea of adopting, especially at the beginning of the process. Over time, as people explore and learn more about adoption, they may become more comfortable with the idea of being adoptive parents. Adoption is not right for everybody; there may be a long winding path to travel before one can decide whether it is the right choice. Adoption is a lifelong family commitment that begins as a very involved process requiring immense emotional and, in some instances, financial dedication.

There are many reasons people choose adoption as a way to create or add to a family. For example, some people choose to adopt because of a previous family experience with adoption, because they are taking on the responsibility of caring for the child of a relative who is unable to parent (i.e., kinship placement), or because they have always known they wanted to adopt a child. Stepparents may want to adopt their spouse's child or children from a previous marriage to help the custodial parent with his or her responsibilities or in order to provide the family with greater stability, love, and care. Some people adopt a child before or instead of having a child by birth, while others may adopt after having children by birth or even after having raised a family to adulthood. Other people believe that if they have the ability and the means to raise a child, then they should become parents to children who need them, rather than bringing new children into the world. Some people have genetic conditions they do not want to pass on or medical conditions that make having a child by birth very risky. Single people may want to have a child and believe adoption is the best approach to parenting. In addition, same-sex couples may want to create a family through adoption.

Sometimes people who would like to create or add to their family turn to adoption when they find that because of a diagnosis of infertility they are not able to have a child by birth. For people experiencing infertility, there are a few important things to think about in deciding whether adoption is the right choice. For instance, how do you feel about your infertility? It is normal to have a wide range of feelings, such as shame, despair, feelings of inferiority, and anger. If a person is often angry and preoccupied by the unfairness of infertility, he or she may need some time before being ready to adopt. It is important for people to recognize and resolve their feelings about infertility before pursuing adoption. Some people feel a strong desire to have children who resemble them or feel a need to have children who carry their genes. In these cases, adoption may not be the right choice. If, after reflection, people conclude that being a parent is more important than how one becomes a parent, then they should actively explore the possibility of adopting. Adoption may fulfill a desire to be a parent, but it should be understood that it is not a solution for infertility.

As a person determines whether adoption is appropriate for him or her, it is important to consider how one's extended family might react to having a child join the family through adoption. Will family members be welcoming or apprehensive? What, if anything, might need to be discussed among the family to help them support the adoption decision? Prospective adoptive parents may want to consider taking a parenting course before their child arrives. No child is born with an instruction manual, and during the course of our formal education, we receive virtually no training regarding how to raise children. Learning techniques that will help adults to shape their child's behavior can add a tremendous amount to the rewards of parenting and can make the task of parenting much easier.

Adoptions in the United States are primarily handled in one of two ways: either through licensed agencies or privately, often with the assistance of an adoption attorney. Each state has different laws regarding who is allowed to place children for adoption. Certain states only allow state-approved and licensed adoption agencies to make adoption placements, while other states permit attorneys and some may permit an adoption facilitator to do so. In addition, each state has a social services agency responsible for adoption placement services for children in foster care who need permanent families (see Appendix B).

Agency Adoptions

Adoption agencies are licensed by the state in which they are located, and in states in which they have satellite offices or are approved to practice. Agencies can be either public nonprofit organizations affiliated with a government agency or private for-profit or nonprofit entities affiliated with a religious or other social services organization. The licensing and procedural standards that govern adoption agencies provide some assurance of supervision and oversight regarding how these organizations operate and conduct business.

In agency adoptions, state-licensed social workers assist birth parents and adoptive parents throughout the adoption process. Agencies offer prospective adoptive parents a variety of services; they conduct the mandatory home study or pre-adoption certification, collect medical and biographical information, place the child with the adoptive parents, and supervise the placement process prior to the legal finalization of the adoption. They also offer services to birth parents, including the screening of prospective adoptive parents, collection of medical and biographical information, counseling and emotional support prior to and after the birth and placement of the child with an adoptive family, and provision of financial assistance throughout pregnancy and post-placement. Licensed adoption agencies can be found through each state's licensing authority.

Independent Adoptions

Independent adoptions, also referred to as private adoptions, are conducted by attorneys who specialize in the legal issues of adoption, or by adoption facilitators, who are usually self-educated and possess knowledge about adoption from personal experience. Adoption agencies are not involved in independent adoptions. Attorneys are licensed and regulated by the states in which they practice. The American Academy of Adoption Attorneys (see Selected Resources for contact information) is a national association of approximately 330 attorneys from the United States and Canada who have distinguished themselves in the field of adoption law. The Academy's work includes promoting the reform of adoption laws and disseminating information on ethical adoption practices (see Appendix C for their code of ethics). Members must meet strict affiliation requirements and can provide valuable assistance in processing interstate or intercountry adoptions. Some adoption attorneys act much as an agency would, working to help locate a child or expectant mother or to connect prospective adoptive parents with a birth mother who has expressed an interest in planning an adoption for her child. However, attorneys are not qualified to perform home studies, which must be completed by a licensed social worker.

Other aspects of the complex role of an adoption attorney can include arranging the initial steps of the adoption process and finalizing the adoption through the court process. As mentioned previously, laws governing adoption vary from state to state and country to country. An adoption attorney should understand complex adoption laws and be able to review financial matters with prospective adoptive parents so they can take advantage of all adoption benefits and assistance available. If prospective adoptive parents choose to use an adoption agency, an independent adoption attorney can review the agency contract to make sure it is legally valid.

The best way to find a qualified adoption attorney is to ask other adoptive parents who have had positive experiences with particular attorneys. In addition to the American Academy of Adoption Attorneys, another resource is each state's bar association. It is important to select an attorney for whom adoption is a central focus. Costs for the services of an adoption attorney can range from $15,000 to $25,000, so it may be helpful for those who are seeking the services of an attorney to compare the costs and services offered to be sure they arrange to work with an attorney who can meet their needs. Overall, an adoption attorney can be a useful advocate for the client at every stage in the adoption process, from the initial inquiry through postplacement concerns.

In a very small minority of states (see Appendix D), it is legal for prospective adoptive parents to hire an adoption facilitator, whose role is to locate an expectant birth parent for a fee. In other states, an individual may assist prospective adoptive parents in their search for a child to adopt but may not charge a fee for this service. Facilitators are not qualified to conduct home studies. Other expenses such as the birth mother's medical, counseling, and living expenses; the adoptive parent's legal fees; and home study fees must be paid in addition to the facilitator's fee. Adoption facilitators usually operate independently of any professional organization and therefore are not under the authority of an oversight or supervising body. It is important to note that facilitators are not licensed, do not have to meet educational or licensing requirements (e.g., they are not required to be insured), and do not fall under the jurisdiction of state or federal agencies. Facilitators are never required for an adoption, whereas attorneys or licensed agencies may be.

Approaches to Adoption

There are three types of adoptions: adoption of a waiting child from public foster care, domestic adoption, and intercountry adoption. Before deciding which of the three types of adoption is best for them, prospective adoptive parents should consider their own resources and abilities as well as what characteristics they are looking for or are willing to accept in the child who will become part of their family. Parents need to consider how a child will fit into their extended family. They may also want to consider how a child of another race may experience their neighborhood or school system. Many people find it helpful to talk to people who have adopted children and consult with professionals who are knowledgeable about the different types of adoption. Seeking out community groups that are not affiliated with agencies or professionals who provide placement services can also be helpful, as some people feel more comfortable asking questions in a setting in which the professionals who may facilitate their adoption are not present. These groups often offer information sessions that provide an overview of the processes, children available, and outcomes of different types of adoption. For prospective adoptive parents, conducting research about local licensed adoption agencies and professionals should be the first step in finding an agency or professional. Talking to families formed through adoption is also helpful. Parents who have adopted can share the lessons they have learned about the adoption process and may be able to provide a reference for or express concern about a particular agency or professional.

As prospective adoptive parents begin to understand the different approaches to adoption, they may begin to contact adoption agencies and professionals to request information packets. Agencies generally include information about their programs, fees, and application requirements in addition to their contact information and stories and pictures of families they have brought together. Choosing an agency or adoption professional is one of the most important decisions to make in the adoption journey. The organization or person chosen is involved throughout the adoption process and post-placement period. Prospective adoptive parents should be sure they are comfortable with the style and philosophy of the agency or professional with whom they decide to work. It is important to keep in mind that parents and professionals need to work together throughout the adoption process. Through orientation sessions, prospective adoptive parents can learn about the agency, its programs and services, the children served by the agency, legal requirements, the rights and responsibilities of adopting parents, matching procedures, and the time line for completing an adoption (table 2

TABLE 2   General Questions for Agency Orientation Seminars

Is the agency licensed in this state and/or other states?

How many children were placed for specific programs?

What are the specific requirements for qualifying applicants?

Are there any restrictions that apply to applicants?

What is the typical total cost for adoptions?

What services are included in the fixed fees?

What fees are variable?

What is the fee schedule?

Is there a sliding fee scale for services based on income?

What is the waiting time to begin a home study?

What does the home study entail?

What is the average time from the application to placement?

What types of education programs are offered for pre-adoptive and adoptive families?

How does the referral or matching process work?

What kind of information does the agency provide regarding the health, development, and history of children and birth parents? When do they provide this?

What are the agency's guidelines for returning applicants' calls?

Can applicants talk with other families who have used the agency's services?

What happens if prospective parents decline a referral or placement opportunity?

What pre- and post-placement support services are available?

What are the post-placement supervision requirements?

provides a list of questions prospective adoptive parents can ask at orientation sessions). More importantly, these sessions afford prospective adoptive parents an opportunity to meet agency staff and listen to other pre-adoptive parents. The process of adoption can take several months to years, depending on the circumstances. Therefore, it is vital that prospective adoptive parents carefully select the professionals who will be helping them create a family.

Sometimes people feel uncomfortable about asking questions or raising issues at an orientation session. Prospective adoptive parents do not want to be perceived as being ignorant, insensitive, or even difficult. However, addressing concerns and questions as they arise allows prospective adoptive parents to avoid many problems and misunderstandings. Prospective adoptive parents should feel empowered and proactive throughout the adoption process. No question is wrong if the answer enhances a parent's confidence and supports the development of a strong family.

The Adoption Process

In order to ensure that children are placed in good families where they will be able to thrive, the adoption process is composed of several steps. The process begins with a detailed application process, followed by a home study that may take several months to complete as parents work to fulfill the requirements for themselves and their home. After the home study is completed and approved, prospective adoptive parents wait for a referral of a child from their agency or adoption professional. Once a referral has been made and accepted by the parents, the adoption process continues with the placement of the child in their home. While this might seem like the ultimate event of the adoption, it is really just the beginning of the post-placement period. The typical post-placement period is long enough to ensure that the adoption is going well, that parents and children are adapting to their new life as a family, and that they have been referred for any services they might require. Adoption finalization (i.e., legal recognition of the family's formation) is the last step in creating a permanent legal relationship between the child and his or her adoptive parents.

The Application Process

Adoption agencies ask prospective adoptive parents to complete and submit an application. Submission of an application demonstrates to the agency that a prospective adoptive parent is seriously interested in pursuing adoption. It allows the agency to gather basic information and begin the process. A fee is charged to process the application upon submission. There are no fees to adopt a waiting child from foster care through a state social services agency, and many private agencies waive or reduce fees for people who adopt a waiting child.

An adoption application generally requires autobiographical information, including:

- identifying information (name, address, contact information)
- date and place of birth
- citizenship status
- Social Security number
- marriage/divorce dates
- information about other children (living in and out of the home)
- education and work histories
- health and mental health histories
- financial history
- information about any other members of the household
- information about adoptive parents' preferences regarding children (number, age, gender, developmental abilities, medical needs)

Additional documents such as birth certificates, marriage certificates, divorce decrees, decrees of name change (if applicable), letters of employment, tax returns, a written statement from a physician regarding the health of each member of the household, a written statement from a mental health professional (where applicable), written references, and a request for criminal and child abuse clearance are required as well.

Some agencies may include additional questions on their applications regarding prospective adoptive parents' motivations for choosing to adopt, issues with infertility, connections to other families who have adopted or to people who were adopted, and available support networks. These questions help applicants prepare for the home study process, which delves into a variety of issues regarding adoption and parenting. Once the application package has been completed, the agency usually contacts the applicant within thirty days to begin the home study process.

The Home Study

A home study is an assessment of a prospective adoptive parent's living arrangements by a licensed social worker. Home studies are required for any form of adoption. The typical home study process takes three to six months to complete. In the best of circumstances, a home study can be an inspiring and educational process, but it can also cause anxiety and stress as prospective adoptive parents worry about being judged by adoption professionals. It is important to remember that social workers are not looking for superhuman or perfect parents. Prospective adoptive parents can sometimes choose the social worker who will conduct their home study and should interview him or her prior to making a commitment. Applicants need to feel comfortable with the social worker and should be sure to gauge their attitudes regarding specific issues that may be relevant in their case (e.g., single parenting, gay or lesbian parenting, parenting by cancer survivors).

There are three parts to the home study process. The first, mandated by the state, assesses basic suitability to parent and ensures that prospective adoptive parents can provide a safe and secure environment for a child. Home study providers are required to share their criteria for this assessment with prospective adoptive parents. Secondly, a home study should educate prospective adoptive parents about and prepare them for issues that may arise during the adoption process, as well as later during their life as an adoptive family. The third part allows the agency to get to know and understand who the applicant is and what type of family he or she hopes to have. This ensures a successful matching process with a birth mother considering an adoption plan, or a successful referral of a child in foster care who is awaiting adoption or of a child through intercountry adoption. Parent education programs may be offered or required along with or prior to the home study meetings.

While the home study process can vary by state or worker, some basic information is always collected first as part of the application process (see table 3 for a basic checklist of documents needed for the home study). In addition, there are several interviews with the social worker. This process allows the applicant to develop a relationship with the social worker. Understanding the family helps the worker offer them an appropriate adoption referral. The home study frequently involves at least four meetings, at least one of which is in the applicant's home. For couples, the home study also includes meetings with each individual. If additional family members or others (children, relatives, friends, etc.) live in the home, they also meet with the social worker either privately or together with the applicant.

During these interviews, some basic issues are discussed, including the applicant's background, upbringing, and relationships with parents and siblings; health status; income status; and criminal background. The worker explores how the applicant deals with stress and how he or she has coped with any past crises or losses. Couples are asked to discuss how they met, how they resolve differences, and how they envision their future roles as parents. Other issues include applicants' motivation for adopting; their views about accepting an adopted child, child rearing, and discipline; their understanding of and attitudes toward birth parents; and how they plan to incorporate acknowledgement of adoption into the lifelong parenting process. The home study also presents an opportunity for prospective adoptive parents to discuss the characteristics of children they would consider adopting, such as age, race, ethnicity, and the birth parent's and child's social, medical, and developmental issues.

The home study process includes a check of the safety and appropriateness of the home for a child. During home visits, workers assess the home to ensure that it meets state standards (e.g., that it has working smoke alarms and safe drinking water and adheres to lead paint regulations, and that

TABLE 3   Adoption Home Study: Basic Document Checklist

Required Documents
  Birth certificates
  Marriage license
  Divorce decree
  Change-of-name decrees
  Copies of driver's license

Health Information
  Medical forms/physician letters
  Mental health provider letter, if applicable
  Health insurance policy

Financial Information
  Tax returns
  Current asset statements
    Savings/checking/money market accounts
    Mutual funds/stocks/investments
  Debt statements
  Life insurance policies
  Letters of employment
  Proof of mortgage/rent payment

Safety Information
  Fire safety inspection certificate
  Water test certificate
  Lead paint inspection certificate
  Building code requirements documentation (local/state)

Background Checks
  Criminal background check report
  Fingerprinting clearance report
  Child abuse and neglect clearance from state Department of Social Services
  Child Support Enforcement Agency clearance
  Motor vehicle driving records

References
  Close friends
  Co-workers
  Faith leader

firearms are properly stored). The worker is not examining the applicants' housekeeping skills, but rather the family's ability to accommodate a new member. While a certain level of order is expected, workers are not looking for a perfect house; they are trying to imagine how a child will fit into the existing household living arrangements.

Most home study procedures require prospective adoptive parents to have a physical exam to assess their health, life expectancy, physical ability, and mental health. Prospective adoptive parents are required to submit a report about their physical health. In some cases in which agencies or countries only place infants with infertile couples, prospective adoptive parents may be required to have a physician confirm the infertility diagnosis. Most social workers just want assurance that prospective adoptive parents are basically healthy, have a typical life expectancy, and are physically and mentally capable of caring for a child. If an applicant has a medical condition that is under control, he or she may still be approved but should acquire up-to-date documentation from a physician to support claims regarding his or her current health status. Serious health problems that could affect life expectancy require further documentation from the applicant's doctor, usually in the form of a letter. The letter should describe the applicant's diagnosis and treatment, current medical status, prognosis for future medical risk, and life expectancy. It may also be necessary for the social worker to meet with a medical professional in order to fully understand the applicant's condition or situation.

In addition to verification of their health status, the home study process requires prospective adoptive parents to disclose and verify their income by providing income tax forms or paycheck stubs. Applicants are asked about their level of education, further plans for education, past and current employment, and plans for employment after the adoption. The social worker may also ask about savings, insurance policies (life and health), investments, and debt. These inquiries are meant to ensure that applicants are financially able to care for a child and that the child will have health insurance coverage. To adopt a child, prospective adoptive parents do not need to be wealthy, but they must show that they are responsible and able to manage their finances.

Finally, the social worker asks the applicant to write an autobiographical statement and provide personal references from non-relatives. The autobiographical statement is typically written in a life story format. Workers usually provide a set of questions to guide prospective adoptive parents through the writing process. While this exercise can be intimidating, it is important because it allows the social worker to better understand the applicant and prepare a fair and objective report about him or her. In addition, writing down a personal story helps applicants explore their feelings about becoming parents and preparing to adopt.

Individuals who are identified as personal references should be people who have known the applicant for several years and in many contexts (e.g., close friends, co-workers, faith leaders). An applicant's references may be interviewed, but more likely they will be asked to write a letter describing the prospective adoptive parent's character, ability to handle stressful situations, and interactions or involvement with children.

The social worker completes the home study by writing a report, which includes a summary of the home study findings and the worker's recommendations. It also indicates the age and number of children the prospective adoptive parents have requested or that the worker recommends. The summary report generally includes information about the prospective adoptive parents; for couples, the report includes information about their relationship. In addition, for all applicants, it includes information about family background, education and employment, daily life routines, parenting experiences and issues, and the role of religion in their lives; a description of the neighborhood; an assessment of their readiness to adopt; and the worker's approval or recommendations. Should the agency have concerns during the home study, these are addressed during the process. A home study cannot be approved until at least thirty days have elapsed from the date of the applicant's initial formal contact with the agency. Applicants are usually notified of the home study results within one month of their last session. Once the home study is approved, prospective adoptive parents are eligible to adopt.

Waiting

The time between being approved to adopt and receiving a referral for a child is often called the waiting period. At times, waiting for a referral can be difficult. People become frustrated by their lack of control over a process that is so important to them. There are numerous ways to cope with the uncertainty and the emotional stress of the waiting process. One way is to stay in communication with the agency or professional facilitating the process. Many agencies provide education and support groups with monthly or weekly meetings for waiting parents. Adoptive parents often find that one of the most useful aspects of these sessions is that they offer an opportunity to meet other pre-adoptive parents who are experiencing many of the same questions, concerns, joys, and stresses. Adoptive parent discussion groups cover a variety of topics such as loss and grief related to infertility and adoption, how to talk about adoption with extended family and birth parents, how to manage the wait and prepare for the placement, and what issues might arise in raising a child who was adopted. Prospective adoptive parents can also use this waiting period to read books on parenting and adoption and attend adoption- and parenting-related seminars.

Referral and Placement

In adoption, the first connection between pre-adoptive parents and a child or birth parent is called a referral, which happens differently depending on the approach chosen. Regardless of the kind of adoption, however, all referrals share some common characteristics. For example, at the time of the referral, prospective adoptive parents receive basic information that may include the race and national origin of the child and birth family, as well as background information such as family history and the psychological and medical status of the birth parents. If the child is not yet born, as is common in domestic infant adoptions, basic prenatal information is provided. For older children, more information is available regarding history, current care, and physical and mental health.

One difficult aspect of the adoption process is the limited nature of the quality and quantity of information available to pre-adoptive parents. Each adopting parent or couple has to decide what information they must have in order to accept the referral of a particular child. When significant medical or psychological risks are identified, potential parents are faced with difficult decisions. It is always advisable to seek competent professional advice and to discuss concerns with agency staff.

There may be specific concerns regarding the child's health or unresolved questions about the birth family's medical and psychological history at the time of the placement. In these situations, the agency will likely require the prospective adoptive parents to sign a statement acknowledging that they are accepting the placement with the understanding that there may be certain medical or psychological risks. Even when no specific health risks are known, many agencies ask parents to sign a statement acknowledging that the agency cannot be held responsible for the future physical or mental health of the child being placed.

If prospective adoptive parents accept the referral, the process moves forward. Plans are made for the adoptive parents to receive more detailed information regarding medical and mental health history and a statement of the child's legal status, as well as any other information relevant to the child's growth and development. Once the agency and the prospective adoptive parents reach an agreement about the referral, the agency develops plans to determine where and how the placement will take place. Adoption agencies usually charge an adoption placement fee when a child is placed. Since placement details differ among infant, waiting-child, and intercountry adoptions, please refer to chapters 3, 4, and 5 for more information.

Post-placement Period

After the placement of the child with the prospective adoptive parents, a certain amount of time must pass before parents may petition to finalize an adoption. This is called the post-placement period. Each state has mandated post-placement requirements. In many states it is typical that six months must pass from the date of placement before parents may petition legally to finalize an adoption. A few states require longer or shorter post-placement periods, while at least one state, Indiana, leaves the length of the post-placement period up to the discretion of the court hearing the adoption petition (see Appendix E). Some intercountry adoptions are finalized in the country of origin but may require readoption in the parents' state of residence (see chapter 5 for more details).

During the post-placement period, adoptive families have monthly contact with an adoption professional from the placement or supervising agency, during which they discuss family adjustment and the health and development of the child. At least two of these contacts take place in the adoptive parents' home. Other post-placement contact with adoptive families takes place through telephone conversations or meetings at the agency. Adoptive families and adoption professionals remain in contact until the adoption is finalized. Adoptive parents can use these conversations and meetings to obtain support, learn about ways to adjust to the new family arrangement, work through language barriers, ask and answer questions, identify resources, and explore adoption issues in general.

Finalization

Finalization is the last legal step in the process of adopting a child. This is the official event in court at which the adoptive parents are recognized as the child's legal parents. The agency or adoption attorney files a petition with the appropriate court of the adoptive parent's state of residence (see table 4 for a list of documents needed for the adoption petition). A date is set for the adoptive parents and child to appear before a judge for the signing of the adoption decree. For some intercountry adoptions, the adoption decree is signed in the child's birth country through an authorized agent. When this occurs, adoptive parents often choose to go through a readoption process, in which the state court recognizes the adoption and provides the child with a United States adoption decree. For more information on the readoption process, see chapter 5. Finalization is a memorable celebration. Photos or videos of the event make a great contribution to the family story and photo album or memory book. Having visual records of this event can also help children understand their adoption story.

TABLE 4   Documents to Support the Adoption Petition

Child's birth certificate or date and place of birth if the birth certificate is not available
Written statement of parent's desire to adopt and approval to adopt (an approved home study), including statement of financial ability
Written declaration that adoption is in the best interest of the child
Legal termination of birth parents' rights
Statement of adoptive parent's relationship to child (e.g., relative or non-relative)
Statement with date of custodial placement
Identification statement from the authority that awarded placement custody

Openness in Adoption

Adoption practices related to communication and contact between birth and adoptive families have been changing over the past several decades. In the past, it was common to see closed adoptions, in which little or no information and no contact was shared by birth and adoptive families. Originally, professionals involved in arranging adoptions believed that birth parents, adoptive parents, and children would experience less shame if information was kept confidential and contact between the parties was not permitted. This thinking stemmed from the belief that it was shameful and scandalous for unwed mothers to have children. However, over the last thirty years, stigmas associated with single parenting and having children outside of marriage have diminished. We have also learned that a closed, secretive approach to adoption can result in negative consequences for children, birth parents, and adoptive families. Secrecy and lack of information make it difficult for children to understand their history and identity and why they were placed for adoption. It also puts adoptive parents in the difficult position of not having access to information that could help them understand and meet the needs of their children. Lack of access to information also poses problems for birth mothers, who might be comforted by knowledge of their child's well-being. With information, birth parents are better able to manage their grief and are more confident with their decision to make an adoption placement. Increased communication and contact in adoption, referred to as "openness," has been a response to these findings.

"Openness" refers to a continuum of choices regarding the sharing of information and the amount of contact between the birth and adoptive families. For many adoptive parents, this may mean meeting the birth parents and periodically sending letters and pictures. This kind of openness is common in domestic infant adoptions and is often coordinated through the agency without the disclosure of information such as last names and addresses. Other kinds of openness include sharing identifying information and making plans to have contact during and after the adoption. Today, the majority of domestic adoptions in the United States are planned to include some level of information exchange.

The amount of openness in an adoption depends on the individuals involved. There is no prescribed amount of openness that fits all families. Whatever form adoption openness takes, it should be established and managed with the best interests of the child in mind. Conversations with agency staff and other adoption professionals can help adoptive parents and birth parents plan for the kind of openness that fits their adoption. Relationships take time to develop and can transform over time. Similarly, openness plans can evolve as the needs of children and adults change. It is important to note that adoption, whether more open or more closed, creates a connection or relationship between the birth family and adoptive family that lasts a lifetime.

An open adoption arrangement, also known as a cooperative adoption agreement, a communication agreement, and a post-adoption contact agreement, is usually considered a good-faith agreement. It is simply an agreement, either verbal or in writing, between the birth parents and adoptive parents that arranges for ongoing contact of some form. Contact may be face-to-face, or mediated by an attorney or employee of the adoption agency, and may or may not include the child's participation. Most often these agreements are mutually arranged without any formal compact between the parties involved. However, written agreements allow adoptive and birth parents to specify the type and frequency of open adoption contact (e.g., exchange of information, letters, photos, personal visits) that will take place between the child, adoptive parents, and birth parents so that there is no possibility of confusion or misinterpretation. Written contracts should be seen as legally binding even where there are no specific state laws that recognize these agreements (see Appendix F to determine which states legally enforce post-adoption contracts). However, failure to meet post-adoption agreements regarding contact cannot be used as grounds to revoke an adoption or force the relinquishment of parental rights.

When prospective adoptive parents first learn that it is the birth parents who choose a family for their child and that they often require some level of openness in the adoption, they may experience fear that contact with birth parents will interfere with the child's placement or that their roles as parents will be compromised because the child will be confused by the complexity of having two sets of parents (Grotevant & McRoy, 1998). As openness in adoption has become more prevalent, researchers have begun to focus on the outcomes of openness.

Research Spotlight: Open Adoption

Initially, participants in studies looking at the outcomes of open adoption were birth and adoptive parents. Over time, as children in open adoptions matured, they were also able to participate in studies. Studies on adoptions with varying degrees of contact and communication among triad members have examined outcomes for children adopted through domestic infant adoptions, older children adopted from foster care, adoptive parents, birth mothers, and birth families. Roby, Wyatt, and Pettys (2005) and Roby and Matsumura (2002) reported on openness in intercountry adoptions from the Marshall Islands. Other researchers have identified implications for adoption practice relative to what has been learned regarding these outcomes.

Outcomes in Infant Adoptions

Researchers examining outcomes for children who were adopted as infants have found no significant difference in self-esteem, curiosity, satisfaction, and socio-emotional adjustment among children who were adopted in more open and less open adoptions (Grotevant & McRoy, 1998). However, children who had more information about their adoptions were found to have a better grasp of the concept of adoption and higher levels of understanding of the meaning of adoption both in general and for themselves in particular (Grotevant & McRoy, 1998). It was also found that when siblings had different levels of openness in their adoptions, in an effort to maintain equity among the children, adoptive parents tended to restrict the amount of information about their birth families they were willing to share with their children according to the level of openness in the least open adoption (Wrobel, Ayers-Lopez, Grotevant, McRoy, & Friedrick, 1996).

In 2002, Kohler, Grotevant and McRoy reported on adopted adolescents' preoccupation with adoption and found a relationship between a child's gender and his or her level of preoccupation (i.e., girls were more preoccupied than boys). Kohler et al. (2002) also reported that higher levels of preoccupation related more to whether or not the adolescents felt alienated from their adoptive parents; the level of openness in the adoption did not seem to matter as much as whether or not the child felt trust for the adoptive parents.

Outcomes for Children Adopted from Public Foster Care

Many children who were adopted from public foster care reported that they were pleased to have been adopted and were satisfied with their relationships with their adoptive families (Logan & Smith, 2005). When children were able to maintain contact with birth relatives with whom they had previously experienced positive relationships, they were glad to visit with them (Fratter, 1996; Logan & Smith, 2005; MacAskill, 2002). Children who had experienced serious issues with members of their birth families reported that direct contact could be uncomfortable and distressing (Fratter, 1996; Neil, 1999). Fratter (1996) found that not all children continued contact, nor did all families find the contact to be helpful. Still, most of the children wanted to remain in contact with their birth families (MacAskill, 2002; Neil, 2003; Thomas, Beckford, Lowe, & Murch, 1999). Logan and Smith (2005) reported that of the children they studied, half of the children adopted from foster care wished for more contact, while the other half were satisfied with the level of contact they experienced.

Outcomes for Adoptive Parents

Adoptive mothers who experienced some degree of openness in their adoptions perceived their adopted children to be more competent, had a more positive parenting relationship with their child, and felt less threatened by their lack of knowledge about their child and his or her background than did those in traditional closed adoptions (Lee & Twaite, 1997; Neil, 2003). In addition, adoptive parents' satisfaction with birth family contact correlated more with their belief that it was the right thing to do than to the actual tenor of the visits (Grotevant & McRoy, 1998; Neil, 1999; Roby et al., 2005). Over time, the development of a trusting relationship with birth mothers helped adoptive parents perceive that contact could be safe (e.g., Grotevant & McRoy, 1998; Neil, 2003; Siegel, 2003). When adoptive parents possessed a strong ability to understand the perspective of others, they were more likely to view contact from a positive point of view and to maintain or increase such contact over time. These parents also demonstrated greater degrees of empathy and talked more openly about adoption with their children (Grotevant & McRoy, 1998; Neil, 2003). Openness has been found to benefit both parents and children; it helps adoptive parents answer their children's questions and provides them with better tools to parent. Adoptive parents in open adoptions have opportunities to access answers to their children's questions that they would not have had in closed adoptions (Siegel, 1993). In addition, openness gives the adoptive parents a sense of control, and both birth parents and adoptive parents have reported that they felt confident about their assessments of each another (McRoy, Grotevant, & Ayers-Lopez, 1994). Of all adoptive parents, those in fully disclosed adoptions who had ongoing contact with the birth mother reported the least amount of fear that she would return to claim the child (Fratter, 1996; McRoy et al., 1994; Siegel, 1993, 2003). Adoptive parents whose relationships with birth parents involved greater levels of openness reported that they perceived birth parents with compassion and had more respect for them (Lee & Twaite, 1997; Maynard, 2005; Siegel, 1993).

Openness may present some challenges for parents. In open adoptions, adoptive parents may be unable to distance themselves from their intimate knowledge of the birth parents. Adoptive parents have reported that knowing the birth mother sometimes impeded their ability to bond with the child (Siegel, 2003). Some adoptive parents who were initially willing to try to maintain contact with their children's birth mothers found that it was almost as if they were parenting a teen or young adult in addition to their child (Siegel, 1993). They regretted being unable to continue that relationship, and the birth mothers were also disappointed when it could not and did not continue.

In their study of open adoption relationships between U.S. adoptive parents and birth families from the Marshall Islands, Roby et al. (2005) found that the majority of the adoptive parents (forty-six out of fifty-one, or 87%) saw their agreements for openness with the Marshallese as morally binding. Parents felt that maintaining contact was something they ought to continue to do, even if the post-adoption contact agreements were not enforceable. While contact between the majority of the adoptive and birth families was not always maintained, Roby et al. report that some adoptive families still participate in informal networking with other families that adopted from the Marshall Islands and share information and continue contact, which often includes visits with birth families.

Outcomes for Birth Mothers

Research shows that women who chose open adoption acknowledged their pregnancies, sought prenatal care, and learned what to expect both during their pregnancies and from the adoption planning process. They felt that they made an informed decision to place their child and were able to create positive memories of the child (Lauderdale & Boyle, 1994). Regardless of the level of openness, birth mothers reported that children for whom they made an adoption plan are psychologically present to them during routine day-to-day life experiences, not just on special days, such as the child's birthday. This psychological presence is more positive in fully disclosed adoptions but is not markedly negative in less open and closed, or confidential, adoptions (Fravel, McRoy, & Grotevant, 2000).

Birth mothers appreciate receiving information through the agency about their children's health, character, skills, and interests (McRoy et al., 1994; Siegel, 1993). Birth mothers who experience contact with the adoptive family often see themselves as a friend or relative, not a mother (McRoy et al., 1994). Hughes (1995) observed that promises of direct contact may be a circuitous means to encourage birth parents to make adoption plans when they might not otherwise do so.

Outcomes for Birth Families

In a study of birth mothers and fathers whose children were adopted through the public foster care system, the majority of the birth parents expressed fear that their children would be angry that their birth parents did not try harder to keep them and would not understand why they voluntarily relinquished their rights (Maynard, 2005). All the birth parents who participated in Hughes's (1995) study wanted assurances that the child would be told about them and helped to understand that relinquishment did not equal rejection.

Some birth relatives find that contact helps them deal with their loss and enables them to feel more confident regarding the abilities of the adoptive parents to care for the child; thus, they are more supportive of the child's placement (Fratter, 1996; Neil, 2003). Birth parents and other members of birth families in both open and closed adoptions sometimes expect that children will return to them once they are old enough to search for information about their origins (Hughes, 1995; Logan & Smith, 2005; Roby &

Matsumura, 2002). In Hughes's (1995) study the birth parents had placed children several years earlier and were not looking for ongoing contact and communication, which they felt might be too painful for both themselves and the children. Still, those birth parents expressed the belief that after children turned eighteen they would make an effort to contact them. Logan and Smith (2005) talked with all members of the adoptive triad (i.e., birth parents, adoptive parents, and children) who were already in contact and learned that the birth parents did not feel that they had completely relinquished their children, and that they did hope that their children would come back to them when they could. In their study of birth mothers from the Marshall Islands, Roby and Matsumura (2002) describe the Marshallese view of adoption, according to which the child's placement with an adoptive family creates a kinship connection between the adoptive parents and the Marshallese birth family, who see children as family property that can be used as gifts to extend the boundaries of their family and build kinship connections that include "support and expanded rights" (Roby & Matsumura, 2002, p. 11). Walsh (1999) also points out that unlike the American idea of adoption, in which a child exchanges one set of parents for another, in Marshallese culture, children gain "additional sets of parents" (p. 9).

The majority of the birth parents surveyed felt that, in principle, they should have access to information about the adoptive parents and the child's development. At the very least, they supported some sort of mediated sharing of information that did not need to directly involve the child but would continue until the child became an adult. Several wanted to see this made a legal requirement of adoptions (Hughes, 1995).

Outcomes Affecting All Members of the Adoption Triad

Logan and Smith (2005) learned that adoptive parents in open adoptions realized that the agency did not prepare them to manage their feelings about birth relatives and contact. After the adoption, all members of the triad reported that they felt responsible for working out their own problems. While fully disclosed adoption works well for some families, it also presents challenges for members of the adoption triad, who must build a new network with new relatives (McRoy, Grotevant, & White, 1988). Also noteworthy is the fact that two-thirds of fully disclosed adoptions did not begin that way. Instead, over time, mediated or confidential adoptions evolved into fully disclosed adoptions based on trust and mutual respect. Variations in the amount and type of contact in open adoptions exist as a result of families' circumstances (McRoy et al., 1994). Openness allows birth parents and adoptive parents to focus on each other as individuals and to see the similarities in their goals and aspirations for the child. They realize that they all want what is best for the child (Maynard, 2005).

Implications for Practice

Because contact in open adoption has been defined to range from mediated information sharing to direct contact, professionals who help families arrange adoptions should not focus on promoting only one type or level
of openness. Fratter (1996) suggests an open-minded but cautious consideration of contact for children who are adopted. Since openness has not
been found to confuse children about adoption or lower their self-esteem
(Wrobel et al., 1996), professionals might initially encourage families to for-
mulate an arrangement that suits their unique needs. In addition, a plan to
renegotiate contact as the child grows up allows parties to the adoption to
feel comfortable as the child matures and the relationship between the families changes over time (Hughes, 1995; Siegel, 2003). Professionals may also
want to be able to share information on research outcomes regarding openness so that they can reassure adoptive parents, who may be concerned
about how openness will affect their role as parents.

Conclusion

Just as each individual is unique and every family is unique, so too will every
adoption be a unique interaction among the members of the adoption triad,
supported by the members of the adoption team. Research shows that in
many cases some level of openness is helpful for all members of the adoption triad for a variety of reasons. It can be useful for children to have access
to the answers to their questions about their birth families. It can also be
helpful for adoptive parents to have access to those answers, and to the answers to their own questions. Finally, having the ability to find out what has
happened in the life of the child for whom they made an adoption plan can
benefit the birth mother and birth family. It would seem that with flexibility,
sensitivity, and careful planning, some level of openness may benefit all
members of the adoption triad.

Chapter 2

Diversity and Adoption

American society and families have become much more diverse over the past twenty-five years. There are many ways to be a family, and more recognition is given to the different ways to be a family than ever before. There are two-parent and single-parent families, divorced families, stepparent and blended families, interracial families, families with gay and lesbian parents, and kinship families (i.e., families in which children are parented by grandparents or other relatives), as well as families formed through surrogacy and through a variety of assisted reproductive technologies. This variety makes it easier for adoptive parents to help their children understand that adoption is just another one of many normal ways in which families are formed.

Transracial Adoption

Among the many kinds of adoption are those in which parents and children are from different ethnic and racial backgrounds. These may be called transcultural adoptions or transracial, interracial, biracial, multicultural, or multiracial adoptions. In many families, children and parents do not look alike, but for families in which children and parents look ethnically or racially different, the fact that the child was adopted is more apparent to others. These families often report that strangers, people with whom they have professional relationships, and even friends and relatives can make insensitive and intrusive comments that can be very hurtful to the child as well as to the parent. Parents are more likely to have to address issues related to adoption with their children and others at unexpected times. Parents often must deal with issues of racism and intolerance that are entirely unfamiliar to them. They need to consider the impact on children as they encounter intolerance and ignorance from peers and adults.

Prejudice poses significant challenges to children and families. Children must acknowledge their ethnic and racial identities and deal with negative stereotypes in addition to dealing with their adoptive identity. Children may not know how to understand these situations or may not feel confident enough to raise their concerns with their parents. It is important for parents to take the initiative with these issues.

One of the most important issues for those who adopt multiculturally is not just whether parents can find ways to support their child's connection to his or her cultural heritage, but how parents can truly participate in the child's culture of origin. How can they make it part of daily family life? How can they express and share their commitment to confront whatever challenges related to race and ethnicity may arise? Parents need to understand important contemporary as well as historical aspects of racism. Parents should have, or seek to establish, relationships with adults of the same background as the child. Through these relationships, they can come to understand the issues their children may experience and be prepared to help them deal with today's social realities. These relationships may also provide role models for children. In addition, parents need to develop skills that will allow them to advocate the best interests of their children.

Life in a multicultural family created through adoption brings a unique mix of joy and responsibility. It is helpful to learn about the history of transracial adoption in the United States and also to consider its unique implications. Interracial adoptions began in the United States after World War II, when thousands of Japanese and Korean children were brought into this county to be adopted (Fenster, 2002). The Korean War also resulted in a large number of orphaned Korean children, many of whom were adopted into U.S. families (Hollingsworth, 2003). The next significant growth in numbers of transracial adoptions occurred during the late 1960s and the early 1970s, when there was a significant decline in the availability of white infants for adoption as a result of societal factors such as the legalization of abortion, the increased availability of birth control, and a decrease in the stigma associated with single motherhood. These factors, in combination with an increase in the number of infertile individuals who wanted to become parents (Fenster, 2002) and the civil rights movement, also played a role in increasing the number of transracial adoptions, as integration made the placement of minority children with white families more acceptable and commonplace (Fenster, 2002). Concurrently, an increase in the recognition and reporting of child abuse and neglect within families led to a surge in the number of out-of-home placements (Fenster, 2002).

A peak in the number of children of color placed with white families occurred in the early 1970s (Fenster, 2002). This led the National Association of Black Social Workers (NABSW) to take a strong stance against transracial adoption based on their belief that these adoptions would lead to black children growing up in predominantly white communities, which would deprive them of a sense of racial heritage and identity. Children would also be separated from their culture and absorbed into the dominant white culture, which would ultimately also be detrimental to the well-being of the black community (Fenster, 2002). The NABSW also voiced concern about the effect that transracial adoption might have on the socio-emotional health of children of color who were adopted into white families (Fenster, 2002). In 1973, the Child Welfare League of America instituted race-matching guidelines in adoption, which resulted in a dramatic decline in agency-arranged interracial adoptions. Consequently, there was a period of time during which very few transracial adoptions took place, as agencies perceived this practice to be forbidden (Fenster, 2002).

During the mid-1980s, challenges of and resistance to the NABSW's stance became more common in the literature as well as in the courts and media, and the number of transracial adoptions again began to rise. Since then, the NABSW has modified its position slightly, and its current policy is that transracial adoption can be considered an option for children of color, particularly when a child cannot be placed with a family of the same race (see National Association of Black Social Workers, 1994, 2003).

The National Association of Social Workers' adoption and foster care policy statement, published in *Social Work Speaks* (2003), is less clear on its views regarding transracial adoption but posits that placement agencies must "respect the integrity of each child's ethnicity and cultural heritage" (p. 147). However, it also advocates that ethnicity and cultural heritage must not act as barriers that prevent children from being placed in permanent homes.

Meanwhile, adoptions of children from Central and South America began to increase. Intercountry adoptions from Latin America represented only 8 percent of intercountry adoptions into U.S. families in 1973, but by 1993 that number had risen to 32 percent (Hollingsworth, 2003). Since then, noteworthy legislation has been passed regarding transracial adoption, including the Multiethnic Placement Act and an amendment to the act, the 1996 Interethnic Adoption Provision Act, both of which made placement preferences based solely on race-matching illegal except in cases in which it is justified by an individual child's needs (Fenster, 2002). However, the legislation does not specify how the child's needs should be assessed. This lack of clarity has since created new challenges for child welfare workers.

Another important piece of legislation that affects the domestic placement of children for foster care or adoption is the Indian Child Welfare Act of 1978, which allocates responsibility for Indian child custody proceedings to Indian tribes. Through the act, the United States Congress has indicated that it is a priority for Indian children to remain with their families. Child welfare workers must defer to tribal judgment on matters concerning the custody of Indian children, who must be placed in kinship care within their own families or Indian tribes if they are removed from their homes. State court proceedings that involve the custody of Indian children must follow strict guidelines. Any result in any individual case that is contrary to these preferences must be clearly justified. More information regarding foster and adoptive placement for Indian children can be found at the National Indian Child Welfare Association Web site (see Selected Resources). The National Indian Child Welfare Association is charged with keeping members informed on Indian child welfare practice issues, helping tribal communities proactively respond to Indian children's and families' needs, advocating adequate funding for tribal programs, and ensuring proper implementation of the Indian Child Welfare Act. The association's Web site also offers information regarding Indian tribes in the United States.

Recently, there has been an increase in adoptions of children from China (Hollingsworth, 2003). Between 2000 and 2005 China was the top sending country for intercountry adoptions (U.S. Department of State, 2008). These numbers likely reflect China's population policies and highlight the historical, social, and political implications and intricacies that have shaped and influenced the history of transracial adoption in the United States.

Unique Aspects and Issues concerning Transracial Adoption

Parents of transracially adopted children should strive to be aware and informed and should honestly challenge their own assumptions about race, culture, and ethnicity. It is of great value and benefit for adoptive parents to develop the capacity to acknowledge that asking for help is not a sign of weakness or defeat, but rather a sign of strength (Steinberg & Hall, 2000). With the help of professionals, prospective adoptive parents should explore the issues involved in multicultural adoption as they consider whether that approach to adopting is right for them. Families who have completed multicultural adoptions are excellent resources for information and support. Adoption agencies and professionals can connect prospective adoptive parents with multicultural families. Agencies and support organizations should also be able to help prospective adoptive parents identify knowledgeable professionals who can help them learn about these kinds of adoptive experiences.

The questions in table 5 are intended to help prospective adoptive parents increase their awareness of issues related to transracial adoption. These questions are not intended to encourage or, conversely, discourage one from seeking to adopt transracially, nor should these questions be considered a serious evaluation tool. They are simply meant to offer prospective adoptive parents and other readers a chance to become more self-aware and to consider some of the complex questions and issues related to this type of adoption.

Multicultural adoption is not for every family, just as adoption in general may not be right for every family. Prospective adoptive parents must assess their own values, biases, and attitudes. They should realistically evaluate the resources and limitations of their social support systems, community, and the schools in their community. They need to consider how they feel about interracial dating and marriage. Parents who choose to pursue multicultural adoption must remember that their family will be forever changed. While multicultural adoptions can be very successful, people who consider taking this approach to adoption need to know that they will become a multicultural family.

TABLE 5   Questions for Prospective Transracial Adoptive Parents

How important is it for you to adopt a child who looks like you?

How diverse is the community in which you live?

Is your community mostly or all one race or ethnicity, or is it racially diverse?

How many friends do you have who are of a different race or ethnic background than yourself?

How much have you traveled?

Have you traveled anywhere outside the United States?

Have you ever traveled to the countries from which you might be interested in adopting?

If you have a partner, are you of the same race?

What would your extended family members think if you adopted a child of a different race?

How many people do you personally know who have adopted or married outside their race?

Why are you interested in adopting a child of another race?

How would you feel about being married to a person of a different race?

How important do you think it is for children adopted transracially or trans-culturally to retain a part of their birth culture?

If more healthy children of your race were available for adoption in the United States, would you still consider adopting transracially?

How would you feel if people stared at your adoptive family and approached you to ask questions about adoption?

Why and how were you drawn to intercountry adoption?

How ready do you feel to take the next step in pursuing a transracial adoption?

If your child wants and needs cultural experiences and/or connections that are beyond your own experience, would you be willing to make lifestyle changes to meet these needs?

If a prospective adoptive parent is seriously considering transracial adoption, it is useful to think about issues related to personality, attitude, lifestyle, and awareness of race and culture. With respect to personality in particular, prospective adoptive parents should consider the fact that trans-racial adoption creates family differences that are readily visible to others. Parents should recognize the potential for difficulties if their instinct is to avoid seeking help from others or if they dislike contact with strangers. On the other hand, if they like the idea of being different and enjoy learning new ways to think about things, they might feel that they are able to meet the challenges of a transracial adoption. As for attitude, when the decision is made to form a family that is different from many other families, it becomes necessary for prospective adoptive parents to examine their own racial biases and attitudes, both subtle and overt. It is also important to understand that this is a lifelong process. Families considering transracial adoption need to make the time to explore certain issues in greater depth and with more personal honesty than is necessary for many other families.

Research Spotlight: Outcomes of Transracial Adoption

Two studies indicate that internationally adopted children adjust equally well regardless of whether they were adopted by single parents or by couples as long as they did not experience abuse or neglect and were not already past early childhood when they were adopted (Benson, Sharma, & Roehlkepartain, 1994; Kim, 1995). In the first study, Korean children adopted into white American families fared well and, in some cases, even fared better than did an American-born adopted sample (Kim, 1995). Contributing to this success may be parental characteristics such as family centeredness, racial tolerance, higher education and income levels (i.e., adoptive parents were often college educated and middle income), and multicultural orientation (Kim, 1995). High levels of secure attachment between adoptive mothers and internationally adopted infants were also found to predict better social and cognitive adjustment in middle childhood (Stams, Juffer, & van Ijzendoorn, 2002).

In a sixteen-year longitudinal study of domestic transracial adoptions, Vroegh (1997) researched fifty-two African American adolescents, thirty-four of whom were adopted into white families, and eighteen of whom were adopted into black families. Virtually all the adolescents were well adjusted. Of note, however, is that 33 percent of those adopted into white families self-identified as black, while 83 percent of those adopted into black families self-identified as black. These numbers serve as a reminder that there are unique and noteworthy variables that affect transracially and internationally adopted children's later adjustment, and it is of significant value for prospective adoptive parents and professionals to actively seek to expand their awareness of issues related to these types of adoption.

Stepparent Adoptions

The Child Welfare Information Gateway (2004a) indicates that stepparent adoptions are by far the most common form of child adoption. Through the adoption process, a stepparent who wants to share financial and legal responsibility for a child or children of his or her spouse works with the courts to release the noncustodial parent from his or her parental responsibilities. Because stepparent adoption is a relatively common event in the courts, states have instituted a streamlined process. For example, at the discretion of the judge conducting the hearing, a stepparent adoption may be the only type of adoption for which a home study may not be required, since the child is already in the home of the custodial parent. States typically have requirements regarding how long the stepparent must be married to the custodial parent before they will consider an application to adopt. States may also differ on their rules about relinquishment of parental rights and consents required for the adoption to take place. The most important point is that a person who is interested in conducting a stepparent adoption should become familiar with the laws in his or her state. It can also be practical to obtain the advice of a qualified adoption attorney who can help with any challenging aspects of the process. More information can be found on the Web site of the Child Welfare Information Gateway (see Child Welfare Information Gateway, 2004a).

Adoptions by Same-Sex Couples and Single Gay and Lesbian Individuals

Adoptions by same-sex couples and single gay and lesbian individuals have increased in recent years, and some states have enacted laws to support these families. The American Academy of Pediatrics Committee on Psychosocial Aspects of Child and Family Health (2002) has issued guidelines for these children and families and expressed support for families headed by gay or lesbian parents. Goldberg, Downing, Harp, and Sauck (2006) discuss a number of practices that adoption agencies and professionals can put into practice to demonstrate their support of same-sex couples and gay and lesbian individuals wishing to adopt. Agency personnel and adoption professionals should convey an attitude of acceptance and inclusion. People should not be treated differently because of their sexual orientation, and personnel should not make comparisons between same-sex couples and singles and their heterosexual counterparts. Adoption professionals must respect and acknowledge the unique aspects of the experience of adoption for lesbian and gay parents. It is the responsibility of professionals to suggest and support the search for useful resources and support groups. Professionals must be aware that sexual preference has not been found to correlate with the ability to parent effectively. They must also acknowledge that these parents' own experiences with discrimination may provide them with additional tools to help their children work through issues related to adoption stigma and discrimination.

Agencies and professionals can use their brochures, information sessions, and Web sites to indicate their openness to working with same-sex couples and gay and lesbian individuals. Materials that include visual representations of same-sex couples as clients instill confidence in gay and lesbian prospective adoptive parents seeking the services of adoption professionals. Applications and other forms that are designed for "adoptive parent 1" and "adoptive parent 2" as opposed to "adoptive mother" and "adoptive father" are respectful of nontraditional families. Professionals should be well versed in the laws that apply to adoption by gays and lesbians, such as the regulations of sending countries regarding intercountry adoptions. Prospective adoptive parents who are gay or lesbian may also have concerns regarding the home study process and questions about the requirements for co-parent and second-parent adoptions.

Goldberg et al. (2006) also identify steps that gay and lesbian prospective adoptive parents can take to empower themselves and avoid bias and discrimination as they navigate the adoption process. In addition to doing the research suggested for all prospective adoptive parents in the previous chapters, gay and lesbian prospective adoptive parents can assess agencies' and professionals' experience and openness to working with gay and lesbian clients by speaking with gay and lesbian parents who have adopted. It can be helpful to review Web sites and the print materials distributed by various agencies and professionals for images indicating openness to same-sex couples and gay and lesbian individuals. Likewise, it may be useful to take note of any religious affiliations or evidence of a liberal or conservative philosophy. Requesting references from previous clients who identified as gay or lesbian and permission to contact them regarding their experience with the adoption agency can also be of benefit.

Co-parent or Second-Parent Adoptions by Same-Sex Couples

In 2002, the American Academy of Pediatrics Committee on Psychosocial Aspects of Child and Family Health issued a policy statement advocating that "children who are born to or adopted by one member of a same-sex couple deserve the security of two legally recognized parents" (p. 339). Thus the American Academy of Pediatrics supports legislative and legal efforts to legalize the adoption of the child by the co-parent in these families. To protect children in families headed by same-sex couples, some states have enacted statutes or the appellate court has ruled that a nonmarital partner can be granted the rights and responsibilities of legal parenthood (see Appendix G). Typically in a co-parent adoption, one person is either the biological parent of the child or became the legal parent through adoption. The second parent petitions the court to adopt the child without terminating the other parent's rights.

In states in which second-parent adoptions are not legal, attorneys may still be able to draw up co-parenting or co-guardianship agreements or contracts authorizing the legally unrecognized co-parent to make decisions regarding the child's education and medical treatment. These documents create some legal protection for children in households headed by same-sex couples. However, these documents do not create a legally recognized permanent parental relationship and have limited effectiveness if the legal parent becomes incapacitated or if the parents separate.

Conclusion

Adoption is regulated by both law and culture and has changed a great deal over the last two centuries. Concerns may arise due to the diversity of American culture, as when children of color are adopted by white parents or when adoptive parents are single or are gay or lesbian individuals or couples. However, these are all aspects of the diversity that has become the norm in families in the United States today. It can be valuable for professionals to remember that clients who are members of the adoption triad may be members of diverse families, and that in today's world it is far more likely than it once was that every family will have some form of diversity. Awareness and understanding of the many different perspectives that families bring with them to the adoption planning process provide professionals with the ability to work with all families.

Legal Issues and Financial Aspects of Adoption

The adoption process consists of a series of services, most of which are governed by various aspects of the legal system and have concomitant fees associated with them. The financial and legal issues that parents and professionals may face include confidentiality and privacy, the interstate placement of children, the responsibilities of states regarding a child's health care, safe haven legislation, financial assistance and adoption subsidies, and unpaid leaves of absence for parents. It can be useful for professionals and parents to have knowledge of these issues and the options available to address them.

Confidentiality in the Adoption Process

Confidentiality would appear to be an easy concept to define—any professional involved in the adoption process is not allowed to provide specific information about a client in any form unless the client expressly gives his or her permission. However, confidentiality affects the rights of various parties to access records, and in actuality, it is almost impossible to ensure confidentiality all the time. The needs of the child, the birth parents, the adoptive parents, and various agency and government officials must be met. It is the responsibility of each professional to make sure that his or her client understands all aspects of the adoption process, including how everyone else is involved and what records and conversations may be kept confidential. The adoption process involves sharing information as well as keeping information confidential. It is unreasonable to obtain consent for every aspect of the process. However, it is equally improper for there to be only one blanket consent form that is valid for every aspect of the process. Thus, professionals must use their best judgment to determine what information will be shared with the various parties. Professionals may disclose confidential information only with the informed written consent of the client. They must do their best to ensure that the client understands the consequences that might result if confidential information is disclosed to others. If the client seems to fully understand the implications of disclosure and decides to consent, he or she signs a formal authorization form allowing specific information to be shared with designated others. Information is disclosed without informed written consent only as mandated by state law. In most states, this should only occur when it is necessary to protect against an imminent or likely risk of serious harm to someone, when there is a court order, or when there are suspicions of abuse of children or vulnerable adults. Current state and federal laws form an erratic, non-uniform conglomeration of protections regulating privacy and confidentiality. Some practices may be lawful in one state but not in another. Alternatively, some practices may be lawful under state law but illegal under a federal statute. Therefore, it is best to check with a competent attorney for the applicable laws.

All adoption professionals should take reasonable precautions to protect confidential information. For example, client records should be kept behind locked doors and separate from other records, and access should be limited to staff on a need-to-know basis. Adoption professionals should be trained to recognize and required to report any inappropriate inquiries, threats, or unauthorized demands. In order to respond to requests without unnecessary delay, it may be advisable for adoption professionals to research the adoption regulations and laws for their state and type of professional licensure before they are faced with a request for information.

The legal process requiring the production of records is ordinarily in the form of a subpoena *duces tecum* ("bring your records"), which requires the responsible person to attend court or to provide testimony at a deposition. It also may require him or her to bring along certain designated records. When adoption professionals are served a subpoena or other order for records, they should take the request to a supervisor and consult with the legal officer assigned to the agency to ascertain whether the order is in good form, and if there is a showing of good cause for its issuance. If the process, order, or subpoena is not in proper form or if good cause has not been shown, these defects should be fixed before any records are released.

Interstate Compact on the Placement of Children

The Interstate Compact on the Placement of Children (ICPC) ensures that children in need of out-of-home placement who move between states receive the same protections guaranteed to the children whose placement is within their own state. The compact, or law, provides states with uniform

---

Box 1   *ICPC in a Nutshell*

The Interstate Compact on the Placement of Children is a law in all fifty states that establishes uniform procedures for the interstate placement of children. The ICPC also places specific responsibilities on those involved in placing the children. The three principal goals of the ICPC are to:

- protect the children being placed
- ensure children receive the services they need
- facilitate permanent placements for those children who are in state custody

---

guidelines and procedures that have been established to promote the best interest of each child.

Why is a compact necessary? The need for a compact to regulate the interstate transfer of children was recognized in the early 1950s, when a small group of human service administrators joined informally to identify the problems of children who relocated to another state for foster care and adoption. They noted that states lacked uniform "import and export" statutes to provide professionals with the authority to ensure that these children were protected. Each state's jurisdiction ends at its borders, and it can only compel an out-of-state individual or agency to carry out its obligations to a child through a compact. Agency administrators were concerned that a state to which a child was sent was not required to provide supportive services, although it could agree to provide services on a voluntary basis. As a response to this and other problems of a similar nature, the ICPC was written.

The ICPC is a legally enforceable contract between all fifty states, the District of Columbia, and the U.S. Virgin Islands. It ensures that all parties involved in the interstate placement of children are held to uniform jurisdictional and administrative procedures. The ICPC also establishes uniform legal and administrative procedures governing the interstate placement of children. Children placed out of state are assured the same protection and support services that would be provided if they remained in their home state. They must also be assured of their right to return to their original jurisdiction should the placement prove not to be in their best interest or should the need for out-of-state services cease. The Association of Administrators of the Interstate Compact on the Placement of Children has authority under ICPC to promulgate rules and regulations to carry out the terms and provision of this compact.

The ICPC provides a mechanism for public and private child-placing agencies to obtain a home study of a proposed placement resource in another state prior to moving the child to the other state. It also provides for supervision of a home state court order over a child's placement in another state. The receiving state cannot legally supervise the court order from the sending state without an approved document that spells out the responsibilities of the receiving state.

Interstate Compact on Adoption and Medical Assistance

Most states participate in the Interstate Compact on Adoption and Medical Assistance (ICAMA). Only six states—Michigan, New Jersey, New York, Tennessee, Vermont, and Wyoming—do not currently participate in ICAMA. ICAMA regulates the payment of benefits to children with special needs when they are adopted from one state by a family in another state, or when the adoptive family moves from one state to another state. ICAMA was enacted in 1986 to resolve the differences in the processes first set up in 1980 by the Adoption Assistance and Child Welfare Act, which established the federal Adoption Assistance Program, and the Consolidated Omnibus Budget Reconciliation Act in 1985, which required states to grant Medicaid eligibility to children whose families signed an adoption assistance agreement with another state. ICAMA provides a structure with consistent policies and processes for special-needs children under these circumstances. It ensures that differences in state Medicaid programs do not have an adverse impact on children with special needs.

Box 2   ICAMA in a Nutshell

The ICAMA applies to children

- who move across state lines after their adoption is finalized
- who are initially placed out of state for adoption
- who are in residential treatment in a state other than the state providing the adoption assistance

The purpose of ICAMA is to ensure that a receiving state is not saddled with expenses for assistance negotiated in the sending state. Simultaneously, it ensures that children continue to receive assistance and benefits without having to submit expenses incurred to the sending state for reimbursement. In participating states, the sending state, or adoption assistance state (the state where the assistance was originally determined) makes arrangements to pay the receiving state (the state where the child is living) for benefits paid to the child. The receiving state may issue new Medicaid cards to children covered by Medicaid. Benefits coordinated under ICAMA include Medicaid and other federal government programs (Title IV-E and Title XX payments) and state subsidies.

The ICAMA administrators of the District of Columbia and the forty-four states that are part of the agreement united to form the Association of Administrators for the Interstate Compact on Adoption and Medical Assistance. This association provides adoption professionals with technical training, legal assistance, and information regarding issues related to the preparation of ICAMA adoption assistance agreements and the processing of ICAMA adoption agreement funds in both interstate and intrastate adoptions.

Infant Safe Haven Legislation

In 1999, in response to the abandonment of more than a dozen infants in the Houston area during a period of just ten months, Texas legislators enacted a law that allows mothers and fathers to safely and anonymously abandon their unharmed infants in a designated location (Child Welfare Information Gateway, 2004b). In the years since Texas passed the first safe haven law, all fifty states have enacted similar legislation. Only the District of Columbia has not enacted infant safe haven legislation. While the laws on infant abandonment in all states allow an individual to relinquish an unharmed infant at a specific location with some protection from prosecution and mandate that these locations must take steps to protect the infant, there remain considerable variations in the details of the legislation from state to state. For example, state laws vary on aspects ranging from the maximum age an infant may be at the time of relinquishment to the various rights of child and parent. One of the last two states to enact safe haven legislation in February 2008 (Alaska also enacted safe haven legislation in February 2008), Nebraska allows parents to drop off children of any age at a hospital without any fear of prosecution; the state then takes custody of the children. Generally, state legislation provides information about who can surrender an unharmed child to a safe haven; the maximum age a child may be at the time of relinquishment; safe haven locations and providers; requests for demographic information for the child that can be made of the person who surrenders the child at the safe haven; information that must be given to the person surrendering the child, such as post-abandonment time lines and procedures for parents to regain parental custody, if possible; public information campaigns; and evaluations of the effectiveness of the law (see appendices H and I for state-specific details).

The purpose of the law is to offer a solution to mothers in crisis after the birth of a child. The U.S. Department of Health and Human Services (2001) defines a child or infant who has been "abandoned" or "discarded" as a child twelve months of age or younger who was born alive and found either dead or alive (and, if dead, as a result of causes related to abandonment) in a public place or other inappropriate location, lacking care and supervision. In the United States, neonaticide and baby abandonment have been met with two main responses. The first is a "post-harm" legislative/judicial approach that imposes punitive consequences for parents who harm or unsafely abandon their children. All states have laws that prohibit parents from leaving a baby unsupervised and unprotected. The second response, infant safe haven legislation, is defined as a "pre-harm" approach that designates community-based "safe havens" where parents can safely leave their children. Safe haven legislation in some states also includes requirements that an advertising campaign be designed and implemented to attempt to lower teen pregnancy rates by offering young people information on ways to avoid pregnancy and by increasing awareness of adoption as an option in the event of an unexpected pregnancy.

Under infant safe haven legislation, the majority of the states require that the infant's mother or father be the person who surrenders the child;

however, sixteen states allow an agent of the parent to do so. There is a wide range among states in terms of the age a child may be at the time of surrender. While many states have legislated a maximum age of three days or seventy-two hours, in quite a few other states the maximum age for abandonment of a child at a safe haven ranges from one week to forty-five days old; however, North Dakota allows children to be up to one year, and Nebraska has defined no maximum age as long as the child is dropped off at a hospital. Safe haven providers generally include hospitals, emergency medical services, police stations, and fire stations. In some states, providers encourage the relinquisher to provide as much non-identifying information as they are willing and able to provide (e.g., regarding prenatal care, the mother's and father's physical and mental health, social and educational histories, and any history of parental substance abuse). Safe haven providers may also offer the person surrendering the child information about his or her rights, the safe haven law, and referral services. Because the law was designed to allow anonymous surrender without prosecution, the relinquisher is not required to provide or receive any information. Under the law, safe haven providers are required to obtain appropriate medical care for the infant but cannot be held liable for any harm the child suffers while he or she is in the care of the safe haven, unless there is evidence of major negligence. Of the fifty states with safe haven legislation, only twenty-nine specify provisions for court proceedings related to post-abandonment procedures; some have set time lines for resolution toward permanency. Moreover, several states do not require a search for the relinquishing parent, have eliminated the requirement to notify parents of the termination of their parental rights, or do not attempt to place the child with parents or relatives (Pollack & Hittle, 2003). Specifically,

- Five states stipulate that it is not necessary to notify parents of termination-of parental-rights hearings.
- Eight states have eliminated requirements to attempt to reunify the child and parents.
- Four states make clear that they are not required to search for or give preference to family members during permanency planning.
- A small number of states have legal requirements that a reasonable search must be conducted for the non-relinquishing parent—thirteen states mandate consideration of the non-relinquishing parent by requiring reasonable searches, which entail public notification and a search for relatives.

Many state courts have upheld fathers' rights and an "opportunity interest" in parenting. Thus, safe haven laws that do not establish minimum procedural due process standards for termination of parental rights, such as making diligent efforts to locate the father, may face constitutional challenges.

Finally, eighteen of the fifty states legislated that a public awareness campaign must accompany the enactment of the law. This element of the legislation is designed to make the public aware of the provisions of the state's safe haven legislation and how to locate legal safe haven providers. In an effort to measure the effectiveness of the legislation, twelve states also mandate that a report detailing whether or not any infants have been brought to safe havens and abandoned according to the provisions of the legislation be made to the state legislature.

Financial Aspects of Adoption

Adoption is really a series of services that lead to a child joining the family. Each of these services may have an associated fee. In some cases, such as adoption from public foster care through a state's social services agency, there are no fees or the fees are nominal. The state agency absorbs the costs. In the case of adoptions conducted by private agencies, each prospective adoptive family pays the fees associated with each step of the adoption process. Depending on the type of adoption, the fees for each part of the process vary greatly. Thus, there may be numerous fees associated with adoption. Differences in fees are related to the type of adoption and the agency or professional providing the adoption services. Some states' adoption regulations require that agencies make some accommodation for individuals and couples who cannot afford the agency's standard fees. Some agencies offer a sliding scale fee structure based on income. In addition, some state regulations require that agencies provide fee information to prospective applicants in writing at the time of their initial inquiry. Agencies may also be required to provide an itemized statement of expenses prior to the placement of a child. Prospective adoptive parents should check with their state's adoption licensing board to understand fee regulations for licensed adoption professionals prior to choosing an agency or professional to work with.

Component Fees for Domestic Infant and Intercountry Adoption

Component fees that may be incurred in a domestic infant adoption include fees for the application; home study; services related to placement; post-placement supervision and legal services; birth parent expenses; and, in the event of an interstate adoption, ICPC administrative fees. Out-of-state adoptions may also require fees for services provided by professionals in the other state. Table 6 presents the typical component fees for infant adoption as reported by Massachusetts-licensed adoption agencies. It shows both the mean and median fees for each component. It is important to keep in mind that fees are always subject to change.

TABLE 6   Fees for Domestic Infant Adoption

Component	Agency-identified adoption fee ranges	Parent-identified or agency-assisted adoption fee ranges
Application	Mean: $370 Median: $250	Mean: $298 Median: $250
Home study	Mean: $2,414 Median: $2,250	Mean: $2,297 Median: $2,250
Placement	Mean: $13,218 Median: $13,400	Mean: $6,536 Median: $5,000
Post-placement	Mean: $1,652 Median: $1,500	Mean: $1,343 Median: $1,200
Legal	Mean: $1,130 Median: $1,000	Mean: $1,211 Median: $1,050
Birth parent expenses	Mean: $2,160 Median: $2,150	Mean: $2,396 Median: $3,000
ICPC (sending state)	Mean: $766 Median: $750	Mean: $799 Median: $1,000
ICPC (receiving state)	Mean: $548 Median: $600	Mean: $684 Median: $1,000

Source: Center for Adoption Research. (2006). *Adoption in Massachusetts: Private and public agency placements and practices in 2004.* Worcester, MA: Author. Retrieved February 13, 2008, from http://www.umassmed.edu/uploadedFiles/2005AgencyReport(1).pdf

For intercountry adoption, typical expenses include fees for the application and home study, country-specific fees, post-placement fees, and legal fees. In addition to these fees, there are costs for travel; United States Citizenship and Immigration Services (USCIS) processing, including criminal checks and fingerprinting; and document translation and authentication or certification. Table 7 presents the fees for intercountry adoption services as reported by Massachusetts-licensed adoption agencies. Table 7 shows that two different fee structures are possible. This is because there are two ways a family can approach intercountry adoption. The first is through an agency's own program adoption, in which the prospective adoptive parents work with an agency that has its own adoption program with a specific country. In this case parents can have their home study and other local certifications completed by the same agency that works with them to find a child in their chosen country. On the other hand, prospective adoptive parents can choose to network with a second agency for an intercountry adoption. In that situation, prospective adoptive parents work with a local agency in their state to complete their home study and other state-required aspects of the adoption process. Then they work with an out-of-state agency that has a program with the country from which they have decided to seek a child to adopt.

TABLE 7   Fees for International Adoption

Component	Intercountry fee ranges (using agency's own program)	Intercountry fee ranges (networking with a second agency)
Application	Mean: $238 Median: $200	Mean: $329 Median: $250
Home study	Mean: $2,003 Median: $2,100	Mean: $2,057 Median: $2,000
Post-placement	Mean: $1,204 Median: $1,200	Mean: $1,268 Median: $1,200
Legal	Mean: $528 Median: $583	Mean: $813 Median: $500
In-country fees	Mean: $11,035 Median: $11,235	Mean: $8,808 Median: $7,425
Travel fees	Mean: $3,706 Median: $2,500	Mean: $1,750 Median: $1,500

Source: Center for Adoption Research. (2006). *Adoption in Massachusetts: Private and public agency placements and practices in 2004.* Worcester, MA: Author. Retrieved July 18, 2007, from http://www.umassmed.edu/uploadedFiles/2005AgencyReport(1).pdf

Costs for Waiting-Child Adoptions

The majority of state child welfare agencies do not charge fees for any part of their adoption process. Many private agencies reduce or waive fees for couples and individuals who adopt waiting children. In some situations, however, prospective adoptive parents using a private agency may have to pay application and home study fees and possibly hire an attorney. Other costs associated with waiting-child adoptions may include medical, counseling, and travel expenses. Depending on the special-needs status of the child, these may be reimbursable through an adoption subsidy.

Financial Assistance

The costs of adoption can be substantial. There are several resources for financial assistance for adoption expenses. Some banks offer special loan rates for adoption expenses. Loans and grants may also be available through the National Adoption Foundation, the Gift of Adoption Fund, and Shaohannah's Hope. Some companies offer adoption benefits such as reimbursement for costs, loans against retirement plans, paid or unpaid time off, and other support services.

Federal and state subsidy programs, often referred to as adoption assistance, are available to families adopting children with special needs. These funds are meant to help families provide the necessary services and the financial resources to meet the child's ongoing needs. Adoption subsidies may be available for children adopted both through the state agency responsible for placing waiting children for adoption and through private adoption agencies contracted by the state. For adoptive parents adopting from private agencies, however, it may be more difficult to have an application for subsidy approved. In either case, adoption subsidies are not designed to cover the full costs of adopting or supporting a child. Adoption subsidies must be negotiated before the adoption is finalized; once an adoption is finalized, the opportunity to negotiate is rarely available. Subsidies can be based on both current need and future anticipated needs even if there is no current need apparent. The benefits available through the adoption subsidy program are determined on a case-by-case basis. Benefits may include monthly cash payments, medical assistance through medical expense coverage (e.g., Medicaid), social services such as counseling, and nonrecurring adoption expenses.

Another form of financial assistance is the Title IV-E Adoption Assistance Program, established by Congress in 1980, which provides financial assistance to meet a range of needs for eligible children. While each state determines specific qualifications for children, the federal government mandates that children must meet the following requirements to receive a Title IV-E subsidy:

- The court has ordered that the dependent child cannot or should not be returned home to the birth parent.
- The child is considered a special-needs child, as defined by each state.
- The child could not be placed without a subsidy.
- Prior to adoption, the child was eligible for assistance under Aid to Families with Dependent Children or Supplemental Security Income.

Title IV-E Adoption assistance is based upon the needs of the child, not on the income of the adoptive parents.

The North American Council on Adoptable Children's Adoption Subsidy Resource Center can provide additional information on both state-specific and federal adoption subsidies (see Selected Resources).

Adoption Tax Credit

Adoptive families are afforded a very valuable benefit from the federal government, an adoption tax credit (Internal Revenue Service, 2008b). The tax exclusion for adoption benefits or adoption tax credit is an amount of money based on specific adoption-related expenses that is subtracted from the parents' total tax liability. As of 2006, the adoption tax credit was as much as $10,960 per finalized adoption. Qualifications for the tax credit are based on income and type of adoption. Families adopting children with special needs through the public child welfare system receive an automatic flat rate tax credit for the full amount and are not required to itemize expenses.

Qualifying adoption expenses reimbursed by an employer cannot be included in the calculation of the tax credit. However, certain qualifying adoption expenses that are reimbursed by an employer may be excluded from the family's gross income, which may affect a family's overall tax liability. The credit may be taken for the year in which the expenses were paid and the adoption finalized, or for the year following that during which the expenses were paid.

Qualifying expenses include reasonable and required adoption fees, attorney's fees, court costs, travel expenses for placement (including meals and lodging), and other expenses directly related to, and for which the primary purpose is, the legal adoption of a child. The credit and exclusion for qualifying adoption expenses are each subject to a dollar limit and an income limit. The income limit on the adoption credit or exclusion is based on the family's modified adjusted gross income. The amount of adoption credit or exclusion is limited to the dollar limit for that year for each effort to adopt a child. If an adoptive parent is eligible to take both a credit and the exclusion, this dollar amount applies separately to each.

In order to maximize the benefit, adoptive families must track and itemize all their adoption expenses and collect documentation throughout the adoption process. While it is not required, it may be helpful to engage a tax professional for advice about navigating the tax credit process and understanding eligibility requirements. A tax professional may also be able to determine how married couples should apply for the credit to receive maximum benefit.

More detailed information and the credit/exclusion form, Qualified Adoption Expenses (IRS form 8839), can be found at the Web site of the Internal Revenue Service.

Adoption Taxpayer Identification Number

If parents are in the process of adopting a child in a domestic adoption and the child is already living in their home, they may claim the child as a dependent and/or take a child care credit. In order to receive these benefits, the parents need to know the child's Social Security number. The Internal Revenue Service has a provision that allows parents who are not able to obtain the child's Social Security number to identify for tax purposes a child who is joining a family through domestic adoption. The Internal Revenue Service (2008a) issues an Adoption Taxpayer Identification Number (ATIN) as a temporary identification number for children whose adoptive parents do not know or have not been able to obtain the child's Social Security number. The ATIN is used by the adopting parents on their federal income tax return to identify the child while the adoption is pending. Parents should apply for an ATIN only if they are in the process of adopting a child and meet all the following requirements:

- It is a domestic adoption.
- The child is legally placed in the home for adoption by an authorized adoption agency or agent.
- The adoption is not yet final, and the parents are unable to obtain the child's existing Social Security number or are not able to apply for a new Social Security number for the child pending the finalization of the adoption.
- The adoptive parents qualify to claim the child as a dependent.

Instructions on IRS form 1040 explain how to determine whether adoptive parents qualify to claim the child as an exemption or to take the child care credit. To apply for an ATIN, adoptive parents can use IRS form W-7A, Application for a Taxpayer Identification Number for Pending U.S. Adoptions. Forms are available at any IRS location or can be downloaded from the IRS Web site.

If parents are adopting a child from a foreign country, they should simply apply for a Social Security number. The U.S. Citizenship and Immigration Services should supply enough documentation to satisfy the Social Security Administration's requirements for a Social Security number. If the Social Security Administration rejects the application because the documentation received from the USCIS did not satisfy their requirements for a Social Security number, the adoptive parents may then apply to the IRS for an Individual Taxpayer Identification Number.

Family Medical Leave Act of 1993

The Family Medical Leave Act of 1993 gives an employee the right to take an unpaid leave of absence for family or medical reasons. These include events such as the birth and care of a newborn child and the adoption or foster care placement of a son or daughter. The law requires employers with fifty or more employees to allow employees a total of twelve weeks of unpaid leave with continuation of benefits (not including accrual) and without jeopardizing employment during a twelve-month period. The law protects eligible employees from losing their benefits or job during the leave but does not require employers to provide any compensation to the employee. However, the law does allow employees to use their accrued earned paid leave such as vacation or sick leave. The law also requires employers to restore employees who take a leave of absence under the Family Medical Leave Act to the same or an equivalent position upon returning from leave. To be eligible, employees must have worked for their employer for at least twelve months (the twelve months do not have to be continuous or consecutive; all time worked for the employer is counted) and have worked for at least 1,250 hours over the previous twelve months.

Some companies and organizations provide other leave options for employees adopting, providing foster care, or giving birth. Employees can check their employers' human resources policies to understand their rights and responsibilities regarding a leave of absence. The Dave Thomas Foundation for Adoption offers a free Adoption-Friendly Workplace resource kit that has been designed to help employees approach their employers about adoption benefits. The kit includes free tools to help employers create adoption benefit programs, as well as a list of companies that offer adoption benefits (see Selected Resources).

Conclusion

As this chapter has demonstrated, there are several legal and financial aspects involved in adoption. Generally, adoption is regulated by state laws. However, federal policies dictate the governance of adoption across state lines and placement decisions based on a child's race. Since adoption laws differ for each state and at times federal laws may be in conflict with state laws, as in the case of confidentiality procedures, it is critical that professionals and parents understand the laws governing adoption in both their resident state and any other state in which they are working. Adoption attorneys and other trained professionals can be important resources to ensure a lawful adoption takes place.

While the focus of adoption is to provide a permanent family for a child in need, there are several professional services for which the prospective adoptive parents are charged fees. The cost of adopting a child can range from no or nominal fees for children adopted from the public foster care system to more than $20,000 for private domestic or intercountry adoption. There are several ways that people who are interested in adopting can finance the process. Adoptive parents and the professionals who work with them should be familiar with eligibility requirements for tax credits, employers' adoption benefits programs, and their right to and compensation for family medical leave.

Chapter 4

Public Adoption

Children who are available for adoption through the public foster care system, referred to as waiting children, range in age from infancy to adolescence. Children come into state custody for a variety of reasons, the most common being neglect resulting from parental substance abuse. The majority of children eventually return home, where they are either reunited with their birth parents or live with other birth relatives. However, throughout the country, more than 100,000 children need permanent families. They are free for adoption because the rights of their birth parents have been legally terminated. Once the birth parents' rights are terminated, it is critical that a child's well-being be ensured through placement with a permanent family through adoption.

To meet the needs of children waiting for permanent families, the social services agency responsible for foster care in each state has specific adoption programs for individuals and couples seeking to adopt children who are in the legal custody of the state. In addition, a number of private agencies have contracts to assist states to place waiting children. These agencies can coordinate the adoption process for people who are seeking to adopt a child who needs a family. Such private agencies may charge fees for their services, though many indicate that they will waive or reduce fees for people who adopt waiting children. The fees to adopt a waiting child are minimal. Parents can request that the state agency responsible for adoption of children from foster care reimburse them for fees paid to a private agency.

Many of the children available for adoption through foster care are considered to be children with special needs. Although the phrase "special needs" raises concerns, it is important to realize that there are many different kinds of special-needs adoptions. Each state has its own definition of special needs. Often, these are children for whom traditional efforts to find families have not been successful. They may be older, part of a sibling group that needs to be placed together, or of a particular ethnic group. They may have physical or mental disabilities, as well as medical, emotional, or psychological concerns. Children designated as having special needs are eligible for an adoption subsidy or financial aid (see chapter 3 for more information).

Some children from state foster care do not fall into this category but have a range of particular needs. These may include special education, counseling, or support needs. A child who has suffered from abuse or neglect, as well as from disruption of his or her birth family, and who has faced the fears of an uncertain future while in foster care may require a great deal of time, love, and understanding from an adoptive parent and family. Parenting such children can be challenging, but the rewards are great as a child learns to attach, trust, feel self-confidence, and accept and return expressions of love.

Information about adopting waiting children is available from state social services agencies responsible for foster care, private adoption agencies, and licensed social workers. Parents who have adopted from state foster care can share their experiences and identify helpful resources. Adoption professionals, organizations, books, magazines such as *Fostering Families Today*, and conferences related to adoption or offering information about the needs of children from foster care are important resources that can prepare and support parents. As with all adoptions, prospective adoptive parents should discuss their interest in adopting a waiting child with close friends and family to explore the degree of acceptance and level of understanding available from these members of their support system. As parents educate themselves, they may also need to educate members of their support network.

Children most often enter the care and custody of the state when they have been removed from their birth families as a result of neglect; physical, emotional, or sexual abuse; parental drug addiction; or family disintegration. At the time of an adoption placement, a child may be legally free, which means that birth parents' legal rights have been terminated by the court or have been voluntarily surrendered. Pre-adoptive placements in situations where the birth parents' rights have not yet been terminated or surrendered are called legal risk placements. In these cases the state agency may be engaged in concurrent planning, that is, working toward both family preservation and adoption as an alternative possibility for permanent placement for the child. In most cases, when the goal for a child in the care of the state is adoption, the state works to terminate the birth parents' parental rights through the court system. When possible, representatives of the state agency that is responsible for the child (e.g., social work adoption professionals) work with the birth parents to obtain a voluntary surrender of parental rights and determine the appropriate level of communication and contact between the parties involved.

The Application Process

The basic requirement to adopt a waiting child is that prospective adoptive parents must be able to provide a safe and healthy home environment. Each state has a minimum age requirement for adults to apply to become adoptive parents. Applicants can be single or married, and first-time or experienced parents. There are no minimum financial requirements for applicants, although their income must be stable and sufficient to support the needs of a family. Home ownership is not required, but living environments must meet basic safety and space requirements.

The first step in exploring the adoption of a waiting child is to call the local state agency to request information. The agency should answer any questions and complete an inquiry form during this initial call. Questions that prospective adoptive parents may ask include "What kind of information is provided to help parents decide if they are a good fit for a particular child?" "How are pre-placement meetings and visits with the child, foster parents, and birth parents conducted?" "What roles will the birth parents have in an adoption?" and "What post-placement services and resources are offered by the agency?" For those interested in moving forward, a registration or application packet and a form that permits the agency to conduct a criminal background check, the criminal offender record information form, should be completed and returned to the state agency. Once these checks have been completed, a social worker visits the home to conduct a safety check and to determine if the space is adequate for a child.

Pre-placement Training

An important and required step toward adopting a child from foster care is learning about the needs of the children who are waiting for families. Each state requires that parents receive a minimum number of hours of pre-adoptive training before a child can be placed in their home. There are several parent preparation programs throughout the United States. PRIDE (Parent Resources for Information, Development and Education) and MAPP (Model Approach to Partnership in Parenting) are the most common curricula used to prepare and train foster and adoptive parents. Generally these trainings provide prospective adoptive parents with an understanding of the foster care system, characteristics of children available for adoption, the impact of loss and of foster placements on children, the importance of planned and supported transitions, cultural diversity, and the legal aspects of public adoption. These trainings can provide opportunities for prospective adoptive parents to meet other families who have adopted from foster care. Self-exploration, conversation with other parents, and learning from professionals also help prepare prospective adoptive parents to care for a child who has experienced foster care. It is critical that people considering adoption from foster care have realistic expectations regarding parenting a child who may have a history of significant trauma or multiple foster care placements. In addition to the needs they may have as a result of complicated personal histories, most children need ample time to transition successfully to living with a new family with new rules, expectations, and ways of behaving. Parent preparation programs are an excellent opportunity for parents to learn about the children who are waiting for permanent homes and what pre- and post-placement services and supports are available. In addition, they provide parents with a chance to connect with other prospective families who could become part of their supportive social network during the waiting period and post-placement.

Once the training requirement is met, additional home visits have taken place, and the home study report describing family history, strengths, and limitations is completed, the management staff at the state agency determines whether or not to grant approval to continue the adoption process. After approval is granted, the wait for a referral or a match with a child begins.

While awaiting a match through the efforts of the state or a private agency, approved prospective adoptive parents can access additional resources to learn more about children awaiting placement throughout their state or the country. Interested prospective adoptive parents can register with adoption resource exchanges, which provide public service programs that help waiting parents learn about children who need adoptive homes (see Selected Resources for the Child Welfare Gateway's listing of adoption exchanges). Adoption resource exchanges, which are often viewable online, provide prospective adoptive parents with information about children waiting for a family. Adoption resource exchange photolisting books are also typically available at public libraries. The online photolisting of AdoptUsKids, a national directory of photos and biographies of hundreds of children awaiting parents, is a good resource as well (see Selected Resources). Adoption parties are a common recruitment approach; these events provide opportunities for children and prospective adoptive parents to get to know each other. These resources allow prospective adoptive parents to work proactively to find a child for their family. While waiting for a referral, parents can prepare by learning about post-placement resources, reading books on parenting and adoption and magazines such as *Adoptive Families* and *Adoption Today*, attending adoption- and parenting-related lectures, joining adoption and parenting support groups, and talking with other parents who have adopted waiting children.

The Referral or Match Process

During the referral or match process, approved families are presented with as much information as is known about a child. Information may include the child's age and gender; race and ethnicity; medical history; any mental health history (including psychological and developmental evaluations and any history of physical or emotional trauma); education; special talents and interests; social history; placement history; and the birth family's medical, mental health, and social histories. Information about the child's interactions with other children, adults, and caretakers; current living situation; and current legal status may also be included. Learning about the child from social workers and reading any written materials provided are the first steps for prospective adoptive parents to take to determine if they possess, or can acquire, the skills and resources necessary to accept the referral of a particular child. Questions prospective adoptive parents may wish to ask include

- Why did the child enter foster care?
- How many placements has the child had? If more than one, why was the child moved?
- What are the child's strengths and needs?
- What kind of attachment behavior has the child exhibited?
- What adjustment problems have been observed in prior placements?
- What are the details of the child's medical and psychological history?
- What information is available about the prenatal and early infancy period?
- Does the child have any specific education needs?
- Is this child legally free for adoption, or is he or she a legal risk placement?

In addition, depending on the circumstances and age of the child, during this process prospective adoptive parents should meet and have conversations with the child and his or her foster parents.

Placement Planning

The goal of the placement plan is to help the child make a successful transition from foster care to the adoptive home. The social workers assigned to the adoptive parents and to the child work to support everyone throughout the process. The placement plan may include a series of short visits with the child in his or her foster home or in the home of the adoptive family, as well as other activities. Often there is a progression to longer visits and overnight stays prior to the day the child is brought to the adoptive home to stay.

Children develop strong connections to their foster families, and it may be in their best interest to maintain contact with them. Foster parents can be an invaluable resource to help prospective adoptive parents learn about a child and help the child adjust to family life. The placement plan may include an agreement to continue contact with the foster family. Many children, when placed for adoption, already have connections to counselors and medical professionals that may be important to maintain. Understanding the significance of these connections and making plans to maintain or transition them is part of this process. Adoptive parents can also help children transition to their new family by collecting and preserving mementos of good memories, which can allow a child to appreciate his or her connections with the past while encouraging the child to also appreciate the ability to move toward the future.

Sometimes children being adopted through foster care reside in a different state than the prospective adoptive parents. The Interstate Compact for the Placement of Children, discussed in chapter 3, regulates the movement of children across state lines. Each state maintains an ICPC office (see Appendix J). ICPC administrators in both the sending state (the state in which the child is a legal resident) and the receiving state (the state in which the adoptive parents reside) are required to review each adoption to ensure that proper legal procedures have been followed. While agencies and ICPC administrators work closely to complete interstate approval as quickly as possible, it can take a considerable amount of time to complete the process.

The Post-placement Process

During this period, families may experience a roller coaster of feelings as they learn about and adjust to each other. Many children who have been through several foster placements may feel unsure about what is expected of them, may be nervous about meeting new people, and may doubt that they are truly in a permanent family. They may feel a sense of loss for their birth and foster parents and may try to test limits to see whether or not this will be their permanent home. Parents can expect to experience a range of feelings including frustration, confusion, exhaustion, and excitement. Flexibility and willingness to ask for help are necessary to address the challenges that may arise during this adjustment period. Pre-placement trainings should help parents understand what behaviors are typical or normal for children with histories of trauma and multiple placements. As soon as possible after a child has been identified, parents should seek support and resources from professionals who specialize in working with children who have experienced foster care. It is important for parents to remain physically and mentally healthy during the waiting and post-placement periods. Prospective adoptive parents can enhance their overall well-being by seeking professional help to reduce stress. In addition, maintaining a healthy diet and making a point to exercise are important objectives during the process. Learning from others who have had similar experiences can be significant and valuable. Participation in post-adoption support groups organized by community groups or agencies can be helpful for parents and children during this process.

During the post-placement period parents should expect, at a minimum, monthly visits from the social worker. Social workers can help parents understand the child's adjustment process and needs and also provide information about resources that might help them manage this time of transition. Specifically, they can identify and work with medical and mental health professionals as well as special education programs that provide services to help meet the needs of children adopted from foster care. Connecting with and using the services of specialists can be helpful to newly expanded families.

The ultimate step in the adoption is the finalization. As described in chapter 1, finalization is the legal transfer of parental rights. The fees associated with finalization are waived or reimbursed for adoptions of waiting children in state custody. For children adopted from public foster care, a recent trend is for finalizations to be scheduled for National Adoption Day, typically the Saturday (but sometimes the Friday) before Thanksgiving each November. Following a tradition begun in 2000, families, courts, members of the community, social service organizations, and social workers all unite on National Adoption Day to celebrate finalizations for children adopted from public foster care. In 2007, courts and communities in all fifty states, the District of Columbia, and Puerto Rico oversaw adoption finalizations for more than 3,000 waiting children. Families who adopt waiting children are celebrated on that day and during all of November, which is National Adoption Month. More information can be found at the National Adoption Day Web site (see Selected Resources).

Conclusion

While the process involved in adopting a child through the public foster care system can be involved and complex, it can also be rewarding. Parents and the professionals who help them complete the adoption can make an appreciable difference in the life of a child by giving him or her a safe, stable, and loving home. With additional support from professionals who provide educational, physical, and mental health services to children and parents, a family formed by adoption from foster care can thrive.

Chapter 5

Domestic Infant Adoption

Domestic infant adoption refers to the placement of newborns and infants with adoptive parents within the same country. In current practice in infant adoptions, parents whose children have already been born and expectant parents who are making an adoption plan for a pregnancy learn about and select the people they would like to parent their child.[1] Throughout this screening process it is critical that birth parents and prospective adoptive parents work with licensed adoption agencies and professionals to ensure that adoptions are legal. Both birth parents considering adoption and adoptive parents should be provided with clinical and counseling services regarding this decision and the emotional and social issues involved in making an adoption plan or adopting a child. In addition, legal services to ensure that appropriate procedures are followed should be made available as well. Making the decision to adopt or to make an adoption plan for a child requires information, careful thought, and time to understand the life-long impact of that decision. It is essential that birth parents who are considering adoption be offered an opportunity to explore their ability to parent their child in addition to information about adoption as an alternative to parenting. Birth parents should be encouraged to explore all the options available to them, including options related to kinship care placement for their child with parents, grandparents, or siblings. Birth parents should also be encouraged to seek independent legal counsel during the adoption planning and finalization process. While birth parents are usually not required to pay for any of the services they receive from licensed adoption agencies, it is important that they verify whether or not there will be charges for the adoption-related services they receive.

The direct exchange of money between adoptive parents and birth parents considering an adoption plan is illegal in many states and is not recommended in general, regardless of state law. Licensed professionals can guide all parties with respect to appropriate and allowable birth parent expenses—how or what type of financial support can legally be provided to the birth parent who is considering adoption, and at what stage of the pregnancy or post-partum these can be provided (see Appendix K for state-specific information)—and can act as a legal intermediary for the financial aspects of the adoption. In addition, professionals can familiarize adoptive parents and

[1] In this chapter, the term "birth parent" is used to refer to someone who is considering making an adoption plan for his or her child, regardless of whether or not the child has been born yet.

birth parents who are considering an adoption plan with the required time-frames for legal transfer of parental rights and post-placement assessments. It is possible for prospective adoptive parents to purchase an adoption insurance policy that will reimburse them for adoption expenses in the event that the birth parents choose not to make an adoption plan; adoptive parents may also want to discuss that option with an adoption professional.

Typically, a birth parent considering adoption as an option for his or her child begins the process by making contact with an agency that provides services to birth parents exploring the option of adoption. Agencies provide these parents with professional counseling to help them explore their ability and potential resources to parent their child, and to help them understand what adoption is about. If, after careful consideration, the birth parent decides that adoption is the best option, agency personnel work with him or her to develop an adoption plan. Birth parents are asked to provide information including their medical histories, information about the mother's health during the pregnancy (e.g., quality of prenatal care, physical and mental health, substance use, prescription and over-the-counter medications, exposure to toxins, results of pregnancy-related tests, confirmed sexually transmitted infections and treatment), educational status, and social histories, such as their religious affiliation, and details about interests or hobbies, social activities, and familial and community connections. It is in a child's best interest for the information collected from the birth parents to be as complete as possible. While this information can be important for prospective adoptive parents who are trying to determine whether they possess the ability and resources to accept a referral of a birth parent or infant, it is also critical to the child's health care planning.

In addition, if the mother has already given birth, it is quite important to collect the child's birth statistics along with records of any significant prenatal or birth-related circumstances. These may include the mother's labor experience and the child's method of birth (vaginal or cesarean delivery); birth-related complications or medical treatments for the child; the child's weight, length, and head circumference measurements; and the child's Apgar scores, which are an assessment of a newborn's heart rate, breathing, color, activity and muscle tone, and reflexes moments after birth. In some cases this information may not be easily accessible, but prospective adoptive parents can work with their agency or adoption professional to attempt to obtain this information in a timely manner. It is important to understand that some of this information may not be accessible after the finalization of the adoption unless some level of communication and contact is planned for the adoption.

When considering an adoption plan, birth parents need to decide on the level of communication and contact they would like to have with the child and the adoptive parents. In some cases, prospective adoptive parents are matched with an expectant mother and may help arrange the mother's prenatal care, support her during visits to the doctor, and be present for the birth. Both birth and adoptive parents should work with professionals to understand the responsibilities and rights of everyone involved if they decide to request that communication and contact be part of their adoption plan. Most states that allow agreements for continued contact in adoption mandate that those arrangements be made before the adoption is finalized. Identifying information, or information that would permit positive identification of the birth parents or other birth relatives, such as current name and some type of contact information, is only released with the consent of the birth parents.

Birth parents are also given an opportunity to consider what characteristics they would like to see in their child's adoptive parents. They may take an active role in selecting an adoptive family. This involves learning about interested families through letters and photo albums. Making an adoption plan requires much thought and is an emotional process that takes time. As a standard of professional practice, agencies should provide birth parents with information about all state laws regarding relinquishment of parental rights, what relinquishment means, when a parent can voluntarily terminate rights, and how long he or she may have to reverse that termination. In addition, agencies should provide them with information about clinical services available before and after the adoption. It is important to note that a birth parent can change his or her mind at any point in the process before signing an irrevocable consent to relinquish parental rights. Working with an adoption agency throughout a pregnancy does not mean that a person is legally, morally, or ethically required to place his or her child for adoption. Questions that both birth parents and prospective adoptive parents may wish to ask as they consider which agency to work with include

- Do birth parents usually choose adoptive parents?
- What is the process for selecting and referring adoptive parents to the birth parents for a potential match?
- Do adoptive parents usually meet the birth parents?
- What resources does the agency use to locate birth parents in need of services?
- What services does the agency offer to birth parents considering making an adoption plan?
- Does the agency provide prenatal support (e.g., transportation to medical care provider) to the birth mother?
- Does the agency assist the birth mother with non-medical issues (housing, food, or clothing)?
- Does the agency offer ongoing counseling or support for birth parents post-placement?
- What happens if birth parents considering adoption change their minds during the process?

- Will the social worker help resolve any conflicts that may arise around the openness agreement?
- What role will the social worker play in maintaining contact and communication between adoptive families and birth families in open adoptions?

The differences in approaches to domestic adoption relate primarily to the roles prospective adoptive parents and the agency or professionals play in identifying birth parents who are considering making an adoption plan. In an agency-identified adoption, the agency works with both prospective adoptive parents and birth parents who have contacted the agency seeking services. In an agency-assisted adoption, prospective adoptive parents work with their local agency to conduct the home study while using the services of another agency or facilitator (if allowed by state law) to locate a birth parent. In a parent-identified adoption, prospective adoptive parents identify a birth mother or parents considering making an adoption plan through networking, and they agree to work together to develop the adoption plan. The agency works with them to provide appropriate assessments, counseling, and legal services. It is highly recommended and, in fact, required by some states that a licensed agency or professional be used to coordinate the adoption process. Birth parents considering adoption and prospective adoptive parents should seek the help of licensed and trained professionals, since making an adoption plan for a child and adopting a child are both lifetime commitments.

Adoptions can be completed whether the adoptive parents and the birth parents reside in the same state or in different states. In the case of an interstate adoption, the agencies, attorneys, and professionals must work closely to ensure that the procedures of both states are followed, and that all legal issues are addressed appropriately. These kinds of adoptions are guided by the Interstate Compact on the Placement of Children, which provides states with uniform guidelines and procedures that promote the best interests of each child (see chapter 3 for more information). This ensures that children in need of out-of-home placements in and from other states receive the same protections guaranteed to children placed in care in their own state.

Parent Profiles

After their home study is approved, prospective adoptive parents are asked to create a parent profile to share with birth parents considering an adoption plan for their child. Parent profiles typically include a letter to the birth mother or parents and a photo album that provides a pictorial of the prospective adoptive parents to introduce them to the birth parents. Generally, the letter gives prospective adoptive parents the opportunity to share information that will allow the birth parents to connect with them. It is important that the letter provide an accurate and honest description of the prospective adoptive parents' personalities, daily routines, social involvement, desire to parent, and parenting philosophy.

Letters should be written in a positive tone and should not dwell on issues of loss related to infertility or other issues that may have prevented a prospective adoptive parent from having a child by birth. These types of losses are best presented in terms of lessons learned. There is no need for prospective adoptive parents to emphasize their financial well-being. Letters should be individual and personal and should avoid trying to present a portrait of perfection. The more honest and realistic the letter is, the more credible it will appear to a birth parent. Prospective adoptive parents' general interests should be highlighted, and photos should demonstrate how their life would connect with that of a child. It is equally important to include descriptions of siblings, extended family members, and friends who would be a part of the family's life. This allows birth parents considering an adoption plan for their child to envision how the child will fit into the adoptive family and the adoptive parents' social network. It is important for prospective adoptive parents to describe their experience with children, since this will give birth parents a sense of their interest in and commitment to children and may help birth parents feel more confident about placing their child with the adoptive family. Prospective adoptive parents should take time to thoughtfully structure and write the letter and then carefully review it to ensure that they have provided personal, accurate, honest, and thoughtful information to birth parents who are considering making an adoption plan for their child.

In addition to a letter, birth parents need to see pictures of the prospective adoptive parents. The photos that go in photo albums for parent profiles need not be professional but should be originals that are crisp and clear. Informal photos that portray the prospective adoptive parents as relaxed and real, rather than formal photos, which can appear staged, are preferred. Photos of celebrations and people who are important to the family are ideal, since they are often positive and provide birth parents with a glimpse of what the prospective adoptive parents deem to be important. Parent profiles help birth parents visualize what kind of parents the prospective adoptive parents will be. Several photos, including close-ups that depict a variety of situations and occasions, portray any other children or pets, and show the home and outdoor space, as well as how the family shares common activities, are essential.

Agency-Identified Adoption

In an agency-identified adoption, the agency works with prospective adoptive parents and birth parents who have independently contacted the agency seeking services related to adoption. Once the prospective adoptive parents' home study is approved and their portfolio is complete, the matching process between birth parents and prospective adoptive parents begins. The length of time for a match is unpredictable; the waiting time can vary. While it is rare for a post-placement revocation to happen or for birth parents to change their minds after the legal transfer of parental rights, sometimes birth parents who are considering adoption decide not to make an adoption plan. Prospective adoptive parents should be prepared for unpredictable wait times and the possibility that the birth parents may change their mind. Others who are also waiting for a match with a birth parent can be a good outlet to share frustrations and coping strategies. Many prospective adoptive parents join online groups in order to post questions and receive answers to questions or just to read about the thoughts, feelings, and experiences of others. This may help them feel less alone during the process of becoming a parent through adoption. This is also an excellent time for prospective adoptive parents to attend educational seminars and workshops on being an adoptive family and to read literature about adoption.

The matching process is an intense, emotional time. A match usually begins with a phone call from the agency telling the prospective adoptive parents that a woman considering an adoption plan who is either pregnant or has recently given birth is interested in working with them. The matching and placement phases follow different courses depending on the circumstances and preferences of the adoptive parents, the parents making the adoption plan for their child, and the agency's practices. Information received at the time of the match can include the birth parents' first names and ages, the status of the child or pregnancy, any prenatal background or descriptive information available, and any relevant legal information.

Meetings and phone calls between these two parties often take place during the matching process. While anticipation of the first contact can be exciting, it can also cause many worries and be a source of apprehensive feelings. If the adoption proceeds, this is the beginning of an important lifelong relationship between two families. Many adoptive parents who have this type of adoption experience feel fortunate to have had the opportunity to meet their child's birth parents.

Parent-Identified and Agency-Assisted Adoption

In an agency-assisted adoption, prospective adoptive parents work with their local agency to complete the home study while using the services of another agency, attorney, or facilitator to locate a potential birth parent. In a parent-identified adoption, prospective adoptive parents identify a birth mother or birth parents through networking, and the birth and adoptive parents agree to work together to make an adoption plan. An agency is used to conduct the home study and coordinate the process. As in the agency-identified adoption, prospective adoptive parents who use these approaches to domestic infant adoption should create parent profiles.

Some prospective adoptive parents choose to do the work to locate birth parents considering adoption themselves. They may network with friends and acquaintances and place various forms of advertisements to identify birth parents. Advertising is regulated by each state and is currently prohibited in at least twenty states. See Appendix D to determine whether or not advertising is allowed in a particular state. Prospective adoptive parents choosing either of these options to locate birth parents may use the services of an attorney, an out-of-state agency, or, if permitted, an adoption facilitator to network with birth parents considering adoption. When prospective adoptive parents choose to locate a birth parent in another state without the resources of a local agency or professional, it is important to select an out-of-state professional who is reputable. In both parent-identified and agency-assisted adoptions, it is likely that the services of out-of-state agencies, adoption professionals, and/or attorneys will be used to manage the adoption process. Prospective adoptive parents choosing this approach to locate birth parents should speak with their state's adoption regulatory authority to clarify the procedures for working with out-of-state networking resources.

Surrender or Termination of Parental Rights

Many individuals approaching the adoption process are concerned about legal issues, especially the surrender and termination of parental rights in domestic infant adoptions. Each state has its own statutes and regulations regarding when the surrender of parental rights may be finalized. Revocability of termination also varies from state to state. Prospective adoptive parents working toward a placement with birth parents from another state should be sure to have their agency or attorney explain the requirements for their particular situation. In certain states, once a surrender of parental rights is signed, it is considered irrevocable. However, this is not true in every state. Some states allow revocation within 30 to 90 days; Rhode Island allows up to 180 days. A situation in which only one or neither of the birth parents has signed a voluntary surrender at the time a child is placed is called a legal risk placement. Appendix L lists the timeframes for consent and revocation of parental rights by state.

Each state has different laws regarding the surrender of the birth father's rights, and some states require that a man register as a putative father in advance of the birth in order to preserve his right to participate in the development of any adoption plan established for a child he believes he may have fathered. The putative father registry allows men who think there is a possibility that they will be fathers to register to preserve their rights in the event they are identified as the birth parent of a child for whom an adoption plan is being considered. In these states, professionals and the courts are required to review the putative father registry as a means of locating a birth father (see Appendix M). In some situations, a birth father may choose not to surrender his parental rights or the agency may be unable to locate him. When this happens, agencies follow the procedures for the termination of parental rights through the state court system. In addition, an attorney representing the agency files a petition to terminate the rights of any named birth father. In most states, a legal notice must officially be made. If the birth father does not respond by contacting the court, the agency may return to court to have a termination order signed. In some states, an additional safeguard that terminates the rights of "all unknown and unnamed" birth fathers is required. This reduces the possibility of an unknown person coming forward at a later time to claim a child who was placed for adoption. To make use of this safeguard, agencies require a court termination process for most adoptions.

Prospective adoptive parents should consult with their agency during the adoption process to determine the legal status of the birth parents' rights and to ensure that they understand the plan for the surrender and termination of parental rights. Ideally, there should be a plan agreed upon by the agency, the adoptive parents, and the birth parents. A plan does not guarantee that things will not change. In fact, agency professionals should talk to prospective adoptive parents about the likelihood that the plan will need to be adjusted and the possibility that the birth parents may change their minds about the adoption plan.

It is worth noting that adopting parents using an agency may choose to hire an attorney to provide consultation and representation during the adoption process, but it is the agency's attorney, not that of the adoptive parents, who is typically responsible for processing the legal requirements of the adoption.

Research Spotlight: Birth Parents

Characteristics and Motivations of Birth Parents

Empirical studies conducted in North America have focused primarily on adolescent birth mothers. These studies compared mothers who made adoption plans for their children with mothers who chose to parent.

In all the studies reviewed, single white women of higher socioeconomic and educational attainment were the most likely to make an adoption plan, while single African American women were least likely to choose adoption for their child (Cocozzelli, 1989; Dworkin, Harding, & Schreiber, 1993; Warren & Johnson, 1989; Weinman, Robinson, Simmons, Schreiber, & Stafford, 1989; Wiley & Baden, 2005). Birth mothers who were younger (i.e., in their early to mid-teens) and of lower socioeconomic status tended to choose to parent their child. Birth mothers who were in their late teens and of higher socioeconomic status tended to make adoption plans. In addition, birth mothers who made an adoption plan had higher vocational aspirations and more specific goal-directed life plans than those who chose to parent (Cocozzelli, 1989; Dworkin et al., 1993; Low, Moely, & Willis, 1989; Warren & Johnson, 1989; Wiley & Baden, 2005).

Studies have shown that the mother of the birth mother has a strong influence on her decision whether or not to make an adoption plan. The strength of a birth mother's relationship with the birth father also has an impact on her decision (Chippindale-Bakker & Foster, 1996; Dworkin et al., 1993; Herr, 1989; Low et al., 1989; Wiley & Baden, 2005). Overall, the two most significant factors that motivate a birth mother to make an adoption plan for her child are her wish to offer the child a better life and her own future education plans (Chippindale-Bakker & Foster, 1996; Resnick, Blum, Bose, Smith, & Toogood, 1990).

Early Post-relinquishment

Empirical studies have explored the experiences of birth mothers during the first two years after they made an adoption plan. In these studies, birth parents were interviewed at various times during and after their pregnancies. Birth mothers indicated that the experience of making an adoption plan involves a powerful sense of loss and isolation. Those feelings occurred equally in open and closed adoptions (Brodzinsky, 1990; Wiley & Baden, 2005).

Researchers found that occasionally, birth mothers whose adoption plans were open became childlike in their dependence on the adoptive parents. They later reported feeling betrayed or discarded once they gave birth and the baby was placed with the adoptive parents. Birth mothers with closed adoption plan arrangements reported experiencing more traumatic dreams, sleep disruption, and the feeling that the whole experience was surreal. Birth parents in both open and closed arrangements reported feeling that they needed to get on with their lives (Brodzinsky, 1990; Sorosky, Baran, & Pannor, 1976; Wiley & Baden, 2005). Overall, the effect of making an adoption plan on the birth mother varied depending on her coping skills and support systems and the degree to which she was involved both in choosing to make the adoption plan and in the subsequent planning (Wiley & Baden, 2005).

Long-Term Post-relinquishment

Most of the information pertaining to the period of time two or more years after the birth parents placed a child for adoption was obtained from birth mothers who sought treatment through adoption support groups and organizations, or from birth mothers who volunteered to participate in response to advertisements in newspapers and adoption-related publications.

Clinical literature reports that some birth mothers experience ongoing symptoms of grief, isolation, post-traumatic stress, and the phenomenon of psychological presence, meaning that the birth mother experiences the adopted child's presence or frequently thinks about the child both on special occasions and during routine daily activities (Fravel et al., 2000; Jones, 2000; Robinson, 2000; Wiley & Baden, 2005).

Some studies found that making an adoption plan for a child has a negative effect on the birth mother's future relationships with spouses and children (Carr, 2000; Deykin, Campbell, & Patti, 1984; Simone, 1996; Wiley & Baden, 2005). The experience of an intense and prolonged grief response can be related to recurrent gynecologic infections, frequent or severe headaches, somatic symptoms, sexual difficulties, and an increase in the occurrence of secondary infertility (Askren & Bloom, 1999). Ironically, some literature suggests that birth mothers who report satisfaction with their decision to make an adoption plan, in spite of their feelings of grief and loss, have favorable sociodemographic and social psychological outcomes within four years after giving birth. For instance, birth mothers who reported lower grief levels also reported more personal achievements and greater satisfaction with their current marriage and the knowledge of their child's placement (Namerow, Kalmuss, & Cushman, 1997; Wiley & Baden, 2005).

Birth Fathers

Very few studies have researched how making an adoption plan affects birth fathers. The majority of birth fathers reported having minimal to almost no say about the adoption plan and reported that they felt disturbed that the adoption plan was being made without their input and agreement (Clapton, 2007). Birth fathers who reported that they felt coerced were five times more likely to oppose the adoption than those who reported either their lack of preparation or the feeling that this was what was best for the child as a reason to make an adoption plan (Cicchini, 1993; Clapton, 2007; Deykin, Patti, & Ryan, 1988; Wiley & Baden, 2005). Research indicates that some birth fathers do retain emotional and psychological feelings of responsibility for the child (Clapton, 2007; Wiley & Baden, 2005).

Conclusion

Domestic infant adoption creates a lifelong bond between two families—the child's family by birth and the child's family through adoption. Both family groups are people who care so much for the child that they thoughtfully considered the decisions that legally placed the child from one family into the other. When domestic infant adoptions are fully open, families must work to become comfortable with one another. When they are less open there may be less contact, but both parties still are very much aware of the other's existence. Domestic infant adoption requires open hearts and open minds in addition to careful planning by birth and adoptive parents, and adoption and legal professionals.

Chapter 6

Intercountry Adoption

During the past decade, the number of intercountry adoptions has increased dramatically from fewer than 10,000 per year to more than 20,000 per year. The U.S. Department of State (2008) reports that in 2006, Americans adopted 20,679 children from over thirty-five countries. The top four sending countries were Russia, China, South Korea, and Guatemala.

Hague Convention on Intercountry Adoption

Officially designated the Convention on Protection of Children and Cooperation in Respect of Intercountry Adoption, the Hague Convention is an international legal document created in May of 1993 through the Hague Conference on Private International Law, an intergovernmental organization that develops rules to promote mutual agreement and legal procedures among countries. The United States ratified the Hague Convention on Intercountry Adoption on December 12, 2007, and implemented the convention on April 1, 2008. This agreement is expected to streamline intercountry adoptions and reduce corruption and bureaucratic problems. The Hague Convention safeguards children's interests by ensuring that the best interests of the child are the priority in intercountry adoptions; that countries cooperate to protect children's interests by preventing child abductions and trafficking; and that adoption procedures adhere to basic standards, so that signatory countries recognize and support adoption procedures carried out in other participating countries. It also contains provisions regarding the matching of children with prospective adoptive parents, preparation of post-placement reports on the child and the adoptive parents, and post-placement services.

The Hague Convention also requires that a Central Authority be established to oversee the adoption process in each country; adoption and foster care providers must be certified by the Central Authority, or someone it delegates, in order to process intercountry adoptions with other countries that have ratified the Hague Convention. The Central Authority provides an authoritative point of contact for prospective adoptive parents to receive reliable and accurate information on the adoption process and is also responsible for addressing complaints involving violations of convention standards. The U.S. Department of State has been designated the Central Authority in the United States.

The convention only covers adoptions between nations that have agreed to abide by it, often called Hague countries. Adoptions between Hague and non-Hague countries are not prohibited by the convention, nor are they affected by it.

Considering Intercountry Adoption

People interested in intercountry adoption should consider how comfortable they would be incorporating the ethnic or cultural heritage of a child born in another country into their family. Adoption of a child from another country instantly creates a multicultural family. Prospective adoptive parents can learn what this means by talking to friends, relatives, and agency staff. In addition, reading and participating in programs for families raising children from different ethnic and cultural heritages is useful and important. Other families who have completed intercountry adoptions can be a great resource. They can provide information about the travel experience, the conditions in the country and its orphanages, and they can share how they experience being a multicultural family. Prospective adoptive parents should also understand what each country requires of adoptive parents. Some countries require parents to make more than one trip to the country before the child can be adopted. Some countries require an extended stay. It is reasonable to ask if an adoption agency can provide references, so that a family can talk with other families who have gone through the process with that agency. Prospective adoptive parents should feel comfortable with and confident in the services the agency will provide to them. Agencies and adoptive parent support groups can help put pre-adoptive families in touch with other parents. When used wisely, the Internet provides another way to learn about others' recent adoption experiences and obtain up-to-date information. Finally, one of the most important resources for prospective adoptive parents considering intercountry adoption is the U.S. Department of State, which can provide a wealth of general intercountry adoption information, in addition to country-specific information. The Intercountry Adoption Booklet available through the Department of State's Web site provides explicit information and guidelines for intercountry adoption on topics such as requirements for citizenship and immigration, visas, filing adoption petitions, and the various forms that are required (see Selected Resources).

The Application Process

Families choosing to pursue intercountry adoption must complete numerous forms, some of which may be repetitive. It is important to understand that the intercountry adoption process must meet the requirements of three entities—the agency, which should meet state adoption regulations; the U.S.

Department of State (i.e., the Central Authority of the United States); and the country of origin of the child. The documents collected for the foreign country are commonly referred to as the dossier. Items included in the dossier vary. In addition to an approved home study, most countries require notarized copies of the documents in the dossier. In general, an apostille seal is needed on these notarized documents. Recognized by all governments, an apostille seal, obtained in the United States through the State Department or through clerks of the judiciary, indicates that the documents have been certified as legal copies for international use under the terms of the 1961 Hague Convention (Hague Conference on Private International Law, 1961). In addition, most of these documents need to be translated by an officially recognized translator.

Some foreign governments require the U.S. Department of State to authenticate documents in order for them to be considered legal. In general, these are countries that are not part of the Hague Convention on Intercountry Adoption. This process is called authentication and is not the same as the apostille seal. The U.S. Department of State Authentications Office provides this service.

Intercountry adoption is a private legal matter between a United States citizen who wishes to adopt and a foreign country operating under country-specific laws and regulations. United States authorities do not have any ability to intervene on behalf of prospective adoptive parents in the courts in the child's country of origin and do not become directly involved in the adoption. The State Department cannot act as an adoptive parent's attorney or represent him or her in court. However, it can make inquiries of the U.S. consular section abroad regarding the status of a particular adoption case and clarify documentation issues and requirements. It can also make certain that United States citizens are not discriminated against by foreign authorities or courts in accordance with local adoption laws. In general, the U.S. State Department provides information about intercountry adoption globally and about U.S. visa requirements for intercountry adoption. The Office of Children's Issues in the Bureau of Consular Affairs provides brochures describing the adoption process in numerous countries. In addition, recorded information on intercountry adoption for several countries is always available at the Office of Overseas Citizens Services. Finally, there are certain U.S. requirements that both the prospective adoptive parents and the child being adopted must meet to qualify for a legal intercountry adoption.

To complete an intercountry adoption and bring a child to the United States, prospective adoptive parents must meet the requirements of the USCIS in the Department of Homeland Security, the child's country of origin, and the state in which the child and family will live. This process is designed to protect the child, the birth parents, and the adoptive parents. In addition it ensures the adoption is legal. The adoption agency and legal professionals work closely with prospective adoptive parents to file all the documents needed by USCIS. It is important to carefully follow the instructions provided by USCIS to ensure the proper and timely processing of the documents. It is recommended that several copies of the required documents be obtained to ensure a copy can be provided to all requesting parties (USCIS, the foreign country, and parental state of residence). In general, documentary proof of each of the following is required: United States citizenship, applicants' ages, marital status, health status, and financial stability; authorized fingerprint records; and satisfactory state and federal criminal records. In addition, the approved home study report is typically required by the foreign government and the USCIS. The government of the sending country and the adoption agency or attorney may require additional documents beyond those required by the federal government.

U.S. Immigration Requirements

Individuals and couples adopting a child from another country must comply with U.S. immigration procedures. Prospective adoptive parents must initiate a petition for an orphan visa through the USCIS to lawfully bring an adopted child to the United States. The orphan petition form has two parts: I-600 (specific child) and I-600A (unspecified child). An orphan cannot be brought to the United States without a visa, which is issued based upon a USCIS-approved petition. The USCIS office with jurisdiction in the prospective adoptive parents' state of residence can facilitate this process. At least one parent who is a minimum of twenty-five years old must be a U.S.-born or naturalized citizen to petition for a visa for an orphan child. A single U.S. citizen over twenty-five years of age may petition. In the case of married couples with U.S. citizenship, at least one member of the couple must be over twenty-five years of age to petition. The spouse of a married citizen need not be a U.S. citizen, but he or she must agree to the orphan adoption. People with legal immigrant status and long-term non-immigrant visa holders are not able to apply for visas for children to be adopted. A child adopted outside the United States by a non-citizen must first meet the two-year co-residence requirement. However, the Immigration and Nationality Act does not provide any way for the child to enter the United States to satisfy this requirement.

The I-600 form is filed in the United States prior to travel to the country where the child resides when the adoptive parents have identified an orphan child they wish to adopt. An I-600A form is filed if the prospective adoptive parents have not yet identified the orphan child they will adopt or if they plan to travel abroad to identify a child. Once the USCIS approves the application, they notify the adoptive parents, the adoption agency, and the appropriate U.S. consulate office in the identified country so that a file will be opened on behalf of the adoptive parents in preparation for the in-country parts of the adoption process. This is done through form I-171H, Notice of

Favorable Determination concerning Application for Advance Processing of an Orphan Petition. This notification must be sent by the USCIS to the U.S. consulate in the child's country of origin.

Approved I-600As are valid for eighteen months. However, fingerprint clearances obtained during the I-600A process are only valid for fifteen months. After a child is identified, the parents must file an I-600 petition with their local USCIS office or the USCIS or U.S. consular office in the sending country. If the I-600A expires before a child is identified, or before the filing of an I-600, then another I-600A must be filed and approved before the I-600 can be filed. Often the identification of a child occurs when one (or both) of the parents visits the country of origin. If a couple is adopting a child, at least one parent who is a U.S. citizen must be present to file the I-600 abroad. Under no circumstances can a third party sign for the adopting parent, even with a valid power of attorney. The completed I-600 must be signed by both parents in order to be properly executed. If the second parent is not present, then the traveling parent can use express mail to obtain the necessary signature. The following documents must be submitted with the I-600 petition:

- form I-600, Petition to Classify Orphan as an Immediate Relative
- a final decree of adoption if the orphan has been adopted abroad, or proof of legal custody for purposes of emigration and adoption
- the child's birth certificate
- proof of orphan status (e.g., evidence of abandonment, written relinquishment, parents' death certificates)
- proof that any pre-adoption requirements of the state of the orphan's proposed residence have been met if the orphan is to be adopted in the United States
- proof that the adopting parents have seen the child prior to or during the adoption proceedings

The USCIS adjudicates all aspects of the I-600 petition. This includes the determination of the suitability of the adoptive parents; compliance with any state pre-adoption requirements, if the child is to be adopted after entry into the United States; and the qualification of the child as an orphan according to section 101(b)(1)(F) of the Immigration and Nationality Act. Regardless of each sending country's definition of an orphan, the child must meet the orphan status as it is defined by the United States, which requires that the child's parents either have been declared deceased or have disappeared, that the child has been abandoned or deserted, or that the child is separated from or has lost both parents. The legal meaning of each of these terms is defined in section 204.3(b) of Title 8 of the U.S. Code of Federal Regulations. According to the U.S. definition of an orphan, in cases where the child has not lost both parents, the sole or surviving parent must be incapable of providing proper care and must, in writing, irrevocably release the child for emigration and adoption. When the petition has been approved, the USCIS notifies the U.S. embassy or consulate that processes visas for residents of the child's country.

An immigrant visa is required to bring a child legally to the United States. Prior to issuing the child's visa, the U.S. Department of State conducts the I-604 Orphan Investigation. This investigation ensures that the child is an orphan as defined by U.S. regulations and that the child does not have any medical condition that the adoptive parents are unwilling to accept. A visa to bring an adopted child into the United States is issued only upon the determination by the USCIS that all requirements have been met. There are two types of immigrant visas for children who are adopted from other countries: the IR-3 visa and the IR-4 visa. An IR-3 visa is for orphans who had a complete and finalized adoption in the country of origin with both adopting parents present, where both parents physically saw the child prior to or during local adoption proceedings, and where readoption in the United States is not required by the state in which the family will reside. An IR-4 visa is for orphans whose adopting parents have been granted legal custody or legal guardianship by the sending country for purposes of emigration and adoption and who have satisfied any applicable state pre-adoption requirements. As legal guardians, the adoptive parents can bring the child back to the United States with them, where the adoption may be completed and finalization can take place.

Two Basic Approaches to Intercountry Adoption

Prospective adoptive parents can use the services of agencies that have intercountry adoption programs with particular countries. These agencies coordinate all services needed for adoptions from those countries, including the home study, documentation preparation, dossier preparation, translation services, the orphan petition, travel, and escort arrangements. Agencies that do not have internal intercountry adoption programs can coordinate with other agencies, organizations, or facilitators (where allowable by law) throughout the United States and abroad that have programs in specific countries. Private agencies that use this model work with prospective adoptive parents to complete the requirements for adoption in the state of residence, while the other agency, organization, or facilitator works with the prospective adoptive parents to identify a child and coordinate the services necessary to complete the adoption in the country in which the child resides. Questions that prospective adoptive parents may wish to ask as they decide what agency to work with include

- With which countries does the agency work?
- Does the agency network with other programs throughout the country to locate placement resources?

- What is the average wait for referral of a child, from different countries, after the home study is approved?
- Does the agency provide education and support resources regarding the cultural issues involved in intercountry adoption?
- How does the adoption agency work with different governmental agencies to expedite adoption applications?
- What happens if a country's adoption program closes due to political or economic crises?

In situations in which more than one agency or organization is involved, it is important for prospective adoptive parents to have a clear understanding of who is responsible for particular services, the fees associated with the different services, and payment coordination. Appendix N shows the requirements of the fifteen most frequently used sending countries for intercountry adoption into the United States.

Procedures vary significantly from country to country; are often influenced by the social, economic, and political climate; and have the potential to change almost without notice throughout the process. As a result, there are variations in the length of time involved, age and marital status requirements for parents, and travel procedures. It is important for prospective adoptive parents to investigate thoroughly the adoption procedures for a particular country and program before proceeding. In addition to speaking with agencies about programs in particular countries, it is useful to read the Report on Foreign Adoption from the International Concerns Committee for Children and to review country-specific information and current country alerts distributed by the U.S. Department of State on their Web site (see Selected Resources). Prospective adoptive parents may also contact their USCIS field office to inquire about required forms, case status, and other concerns.

The Matching Process

The typical matching process in intercountry adoption, called the referral, is different from that in domestic adoption. International agencies, agents, or facilitators obtain information from parents about the characteristics they hope to find in the child they will adopt. They also inform parents about the children available through their particular program. Information provided by prospective adoptive parents about their preferences regarding a child's characteristics is included in the home study report. Whether parents can request the gender of the child depends on the agency program and sending country practice. Parents are unable to choose a child of a specific age but can request a child within a specified age range (e.g., newborn through twelve months old). Parents may be asked to complete a special-needs questionnaire regarding what physical and mental health issues they are willing to accept. This information and the dossier are used by agencies and the authorities in the foreign country to make decisions about which child will be matched with which prospective adoptive parents.

Once the referral is made, parents usually receive information about the child. This information may include pictures, videotapes, medical reports, reports on how the child came into care, the child's experiences in care, and, if available, information about the birth parents. Reports may be in the language of the country and may use terminology that, when translated, can be unclear and may not necessarily be accurate. In some situations, there may be little or no information about the birth parents. In addition, it may not be possible to verify the information that is available.

It is best if agency personnel, in addition to medical and mental health professionals with specific knowledge of the country, review reports with prospective adoptive parents to identify and address any concerns. Parents who have completed adoptions from the same country can also provide guidance about the reliability of the information received. If there are any concerns, prospective adoptive parents should ask the agency for more information. Sometimes it is possible to request additional information or to arrange for a child to receive additional medical evaluations.

After reviewing the available information about the child and raising any questions and concerns they may have, prospective adoptive parents need to decide if they want to commit to adopt the child. The timeframe for this decision varies from several days to several weeks. If the referral is accepted, then plans are made for travel and placement. If the prospective adoptive parents determine that they do not want to accept a particular referral, the agency or placement resource will ask them to provide the reasons for their decision in an effort to avoid repeating an unsuccessful process. Plans are then made to identify another child.

Processing the Adoption

Most intercountry adoptions are finalized in the foreign country. The legal process in some countries requires a waiting period between the filing of the legal documents in the country's court system and the day on which the adoption is finalized in court. Some countries require the adopting parents to be present when the adoption papers are filed in the country's court, while others allow an attorney or other representative to complete this step. In most situations, the final adoption decree is completed before the Department of State grants a visa to allow the child to enter the United States.

In intercountry adoption, at least one parent is usually required to travel to the sending country to complete the formal process and accept placement of the child. Procedures in each country determine the length of time a parent must reside in the country, as well as where adopting parents may need to travel within the country. Some agency programs organize escorted parent travel groups, while others send parents individually and make escorts available to them when they arrive in the country. In some situations, parents remain in the United States and an escort service accompanies the child to meet them in the United States.

Traveling to the child's birth country is valuable in that it allows parents to experience the culture firsthand. Photographs, stories, and mementos from the parents' trip to a child's birth country can offer the child more familiarity with and appreciation for his or her early life and country of origin. Experiences such as these, which can be shared with the child as he or she grows up, help show how the family came to be through stories about where they stayed, the people they met, and the places they visited. Visiting a child's birth country allows parents to reflect on and develop appreciation and understanding of the child's birth culture.

Adjusting to a New Life

Children coming to the United States from another country must go through a significant adjustment. They are leaving behind their life in one world with its known experiences and moving into an entirely new world filled with what may seem to the child to be overwhelming, unknown, and unanticipated experiences. There are new people, smells, sounds, tastes; a new language and climate; and so on. Parents must help their children make this adjustment. The time it takes for a child to adjust depends on the child and the number of transitions the child has already experienced or will be expected to make. Many agencies and adoption community organizations offer preadoptive educational programs for families adopting internationally to help parents prepare to help their children adjust. Referrals for medical assistance and developmental support such as early intervention (see chapter 8) are available through an assortment of service agencies to help parents meet their children's needs.

Readoption for Intercountry Adoption

To ensure the security of the adoption, families should consider readoption through their state court system. Readoption refers to the process by which an adoptive parent's state court reviews the international adoption paperwork and issues a new adoption decree independent of the foreign entity. To complete this process, families meet regularly with a social worker from the agency they are working with between the time of placement and the time when the adoption can be re-finalized. At the end of the post-placement process, the agency and its attorney help the family, and frequently the family's attorney, file the required documents in the appropriate local court. Some courts have intercountry adoption specialists who can provide helpful information on the post-placement process.

Readoption is only relevant in intercountry adoptions where adoptions are finalized in the country of origin. Readoption is not the same as an adoption finalization. Certain countries (e.g., Korea and India) do not finalize the adoption in the sending country but actually confer guardianship or a custodial relationship to the prospective adoptive parents. The adoption is then finalized in the United States according to laws of the adoptive parents' state of residence. Currently, twenty-nine states do not require readoption because they recognize foreign adoption decrees and automatically recognize the adoption. Readoption is required by statute in nine states. For information about a particular state, see Appendix O. Parents should work with an adoption agency or attorney to understand current procedures and requirements of readoption in their state.

Many adoptive parents choose to readopt even if it is not required by their state. There are several reasons for this. Courts in the United States are not required to recognize a foreign court decree, and readoption can protect the family from any post-adoption legal challenges a country might make that could retroactively affect the legal status of a foreign adoption. Once a readoption takes place, the United States adoption decree is recognized in every state and ensures that one need not rely solely on the legitimacy of a decree issued under foreign law. In addition, when a readoption takes place, the birth certificate and all adoption documentation are issued by the state government in English. These documents are generally less confusing than the foreign documents the adoptive parents received during the original adoption process, which may not be recognized or understood by people who are not familiar with them (e.g., school officials). Readoption also makes it easier for parents and the child to obtain duplicate copies of their official documents in the event the originals are lost or destroyed.

Each state has different requirements, paperwork, and procedures for readoption. In some states an attorney is required to process the readoption. Other states do not require an attorney, but the process can be arduous and time consuming for people unfamiliar with the legal requirements and procedures. Adoptive parents can choose to retain the services of an adoption agency or adoption attorney, who can explain state and local laws regarding readoption and can guide parents through the readoption process.

Children adopted from abroad now qualify for automatic citizenship under the Child Citizenship Act of 2000. This act automatically confers U.S. citizenship on adopted children born abroad who (1) were born on or after February 28, 1983, and are under eighteen years of age; (2) reside in the United States as lawful permanent residents; and (3) are in the legal and physical custody of at least one parent who is a U.S. citizen. Adoptive parents who wish to obtain legal proof of their child's U.S. citizenship are encouraged to apply for a U.S. passport on the child's behalf.

Conclusion

Here in the United States, intercountry adoption has been and continues to be a successful option for people who want to build families and bring children into their lives. However, as the implementation of the Hague Convention on Intercountry Adoption is realized, it is likely that there will be changes for parents who choose to form their families through intercountry adoption. It is important for parents who choose intercountry adoption to remember that such adoptions may be transracial, and that the children they adopt may have spent time in foster care or in the care of the social services organization of their country of origin. While children adopted through intercountry adoption may be of the same racial background as their adoptive parents, they are more likely to be from a different racial group, and from very different cultural and ethnic backgrounds. Prospective adoptive parents considering intercountry adoption should carefully research their options, consider all the information available to them, and seek the advice of adoption professionals to ensure that their decisions are appropriate for their families.

Chapter 7

Medical, Developmental, and Mental Health Considerations

Knowledge of the medical, developmental, and mental health issues that should be considered by individuals and couples planning the creation of a family through adoption is critical to informed decision making. These concerns are no more pertinent for children in adoptive families than they are for children in families formed by birth. This chapter covers a variety of issues related to the medical, developmental, and mental health considerations for parenting children who were adopted.

Adoption in Cases of Fetal Anomaly and Genetic Risks

Adoption is typically considered by expectant parents in cases of unplanned pregnancies and by individuals and couples who experience fertility issues. However, with ongoing advancements in prenatal technology and the recent completion of the Human Genome Project, it is becoming increasingly important that adoption be considered a viable option in additional situations.

Each year in the United States, approximately 3 percent of all pregnancies result in the birth of a child with significant birth defects (Centers for Disease Control and Prevention, 2007). Anomalies may result from prenatal substance abuse on the part of the mother, advanced maternal age at conception, and/or environmental or genetic causes. Most often, anomalies result from a combination of two or more of these factors.

Recent improvements in ultrasound technology and prenatal testing have made it possible to detect many of these abnormalities in the developing fetus. As a result, expectant parents and their health care providers are better equipped to prepare for the birth of children with special needs. However, this information also requires expectant parents to make a difficult decision regarding whether they should terminate the pregnancy, continue the pregnancy and parent the child, or continue the pregnancy and make an adoption plan. Individuals and couples who must make this decision may experience conflicting emotions not limited to grief, guilt, denial, detachment, and anger.

Because many pregnancies in which a fetal anomaly is detected are planned or accepted pregnancies, expectant parents may feel that termination is not an option for them. However, they may also feel overwhelmed and physically, emotionally, or financially unable to parent a child with a disability. It is important for expectant parents and health professionals to understand that there are families and individuals who are waiting to adopt infants and children with special needs. Prospective adoptive parents may choose to adopt a child with special needs for a variety of reasons. These individuals often have previous experience with certain disabilities and may feel better prepared to parent children with these conditions. Some individuals may have a wealth of knowledge regarding a particular disorder and may feel that they are in a position to care for a child affected by that disorder. Others may have personal experience, such as another child with a certain condition. Expectant parents should understand that while some families may be able to care for children with disabilities, other families may find this too difficult.

Genetic counselors and other health professionals such as obstetricians, midwives, and health center social workers are often the first resource that expectant parents encounter after a fetal diagnosis. The response of health care professionals can have a significant impact on parents' reactions and decisions. Because knowing one's options can diminish feelings of helplessness, health professionals can help minimize these feelings by offering unbiased information regarding options, support, and referrals. It is critical for health professionals faced with these situations to be familiar with adoption-sensitive language, as well as policies, laws, and resources. It is equally important that this information be conveyed in a non-directive manner in order to ensure that the most appropriate decision for the patient is reached.

Advancements in the identification of genes responsible for certain genetic conditions have resulted in increased pre-conception counseling and discussion of options. Genetic counselors and other health professionals are often faced with patients who either carry an identified genetic mutation or have a family history of a genetic condition. These patients may be interested in expanding their families but often do not want to risk passing the gene on to their children. In such cases, health professionals must be prepared with information regarding the options of domestic and intercountry adoption, as well as adoption from foster care.

Adopting a Child with a Developmental or Chronic Disability

It has been estimated that between 30 and 50 percent of children awaiting adoption have a developmental disability (Glidden, 2000). These disabilities may be emotional, mental, or physical disorders and vary in severity. Children may be afflicted with differing degrees of cerebral palsy or autism, physical malformations such as cleft lip and palate (which, in some cases, can be indicative of a larger disorder), genetic conditions such as cystic fibrosis, disorders resulting from prenatal maternal substance abuse (e.g., fetal alcohol syndrome), learning disabilities or mental retardation varying in basis, or genetic/environmental conditions such as epilepsy. One well-known disorder affecting multiple children awaiting adoption is Down syndrome. Down syndrome occurs in approximately one in eight hundred live births and is caused by the presence of an extra copy of chromosome 21 in the child's cells. As in other cases of genetic anomaly, individuals affected with Down syndrome exhibit varying levels of functionality. Some children born with Down syndrome have no sign of the disorder aside from some level of mental retardation and characteristic features such as upward slanting eyes and epicanthal folds (i.e., folds of skin at the inner corner of the eyes), a flattened nasal bridge, short broad hands, and a single deep crease in the palms. Others also possess heart abnormalities or vision and hearing impairments and may require extensive medical treatment throughout their lives. Ultrasound examination and maternal blood tests can indicate the risk of Down syndrome in the developing fetus; however, a definite prenatal diagnosis of this condition must be done through amniocentesis.

As with all children, those awaiting adoption may be afflicted with several other disabilities of varying natures. These conditions may have a genetic or non-genetic basis, and some may be identified through prenatal testing, while others may only manifest after birth. Cerebral palsy results when brain damage occurs, often as a result of the failure of oxygen to reach the brain near the time of birth. Muscle control is often difficult or unattainable for children with cerebral palsy. Cystic fibrosis, another chronic condition that may be present in children awaiting adoption, is a genetic condition that affects the lungs and digestive system. The body produces thick, sticky mucus that clogs the lungs and obstructs the pancreas, leading to lung infections and poor food absorption (Cystic Fibrosis Foundation, 2007). Some children in care may also show signs of autism, a developmental disorder affecting the areas of the brain responsible for abstract thought, language, and social skills. Children with autism can have both physical and behavioral disabilities. Epilepsy is another condition found in some children. This disorder is characterized by seizures and can result from genetic or environmental causes. Seizures can occur in the form of muscle convulsions, loss of consciousness, or other mental or physical anomalies. Spina bifida, a condition that may be present in some children and is often detected prenatally, is a birth disorder that affects the spinal cord. Vertebrae do not develop completely, which results in varying levels of difficulty with leg movement, sensation, and bowel/bladder control. The most common disorders affecting children awaiting adoption, however, are fetal alcohol syndrome and alcohol-related neurodevelopmental disorders. These conditions may be characterized by physical and/or mental challenges resulting from maternal usage of alcohol or other controlled substances during pregnancy. Possible manifestations of the disability include behavioral issues, characteristic facial features, and some level of mental retardation (Centers for Disease Control and Prevention, 2006).

Required medical services and other treatments are dependent upon each individual child's needs. Treatment may include physical, speech, and/or occupational therapy in addition to medical intervention. Prospective adoptive parents who wish to adopt a child with a disability must demonstrate the ability to care for a child with the disorder in question and should live near any required medical or related services.

Individuals and couples wishing to adopt a child with a disability may choose to contact their health provider for more information. Therefore, health professionals must be aware of adoption agencies that place children with disabilities and adoption-related resources that can support these individuals in making a decision. A variety of resources are available for birth parents and prospective adoptive parents of children with disabilities. Web sites focusing on children with specific special needs attempt to match waiting children with prospective adoptive parents through photolistings. In addition, organizations such as AKIDS Exchange, which matches children with Down syndrome to prospective adoptive parents, also work to recruit individuals and families willing to care for children with disabilities.

Adopting a Special-Needs or High-Risk Child through Domestic Adoption

Over the past several decades, the placement of special-needs and high-risk youngsters through domestic adoptions has increased. These tend to be older children with medical conditions, physical and developmental disabilities, and known emotional and behavioral problems, and those who have experienced significant abuse or neglect, or multiple placements. These children often have genetic predispositions to cognitive and learning problems, as well as to certain socio-emotional problems such as bipolar disorder, attention-deficit/hyperactivity disorder, and autism (Brodzinsky et al., 1998; Peters, Atkins, & McKay, 1999). The majority of these adoptions are successful (Rosenthal, 1993). However, these children can sometimes pose significant and often long-term challenges to caretakers. Parents and families need to carefully assess their ability to help these children deal with their medical, educational, and/or socio-emotional difficulties. Adoptive families that have successfully integrated children with more severe difficulties are generally cohesive, have experience raising children and realistic expectations of the child, exercise flexibility when making decisions, and are tolerant of differences between the child and other family members (Barth & Berry, 1988; Groze, 1994; Keck & Kupecky, 1995).

The types of behavioral health issues that can be seen in domestic adoptions range from relatively benign adjustment issues to more significant psychopathology such as bipolar disorder, attention-deficit/hyperactivity disorder, and post-traumatic stress disorder, as well as difficulties associated with cognitive and academic performance, such as various learning disabilities.

In general, none of these disorders are unique to children who were adopted, and there is very little evidence that suggests the majority of them appear more often in this population. However, possible exceptions do include several disorders whose development is heavily influenced by environmental events that may be part of the child's pre-adoption history, such as post-traumatic stress disorder resulting from physical and/or sexual abuse and reactive attachment disorder (RAD), which results from the disruption of early attachments to primary caregivers. A detailed discussion of specific mental health disorders is beyond the scope of this book; however, the Suggested Readings at the end of this book lists texts with more detailed descriptions of these problem areas.

If a child is having behavioral problems, discussion with a pediatrician who can make an appropriate referral for further assessment and possible intervention is important. Learning problems are generally assessed and remediated within educational settings. Behavioral and socio-emotional issues may be assessed by mental health professionals such as psychiatrists, psychiatric nurses, clinical psychologists, and clinical social workers, all of whom are trained to deal with these issues. Many adoption agencies offer post-adoption services or can make referrals to appropriate professionals; adoption support groups and associations are also good sources for referrals.

The first step should be a careful assessment of the child and the circumstances, including pre- and post-adoption history. This can be difficult if little is known about the child's early life. Exactly what is the concern? Whose concern is it? Is the concern one that is best construed as a normal developmental bump in the child's adjustment, or does it represent something more serious? Most professionals stress the importance of addressing these questions, as there is danger in overestimating difficulties, which can actually make matters worse (Nickman & Lewis, 1994). For example, children understand what it means to be adopted very differently at age seven than at age four. They may ask more questions about their biological heritage, which may reflect these changes in their level of understanding. This is not an indication of more significant psychological problems regarding their adopted status. Families, too, are subject to life cycle changes that may or may not be out of the ordinary as they face the challenges of dealing with adoption-related tasks (Brodzinsky, 1987). Attempts to help the child and family may not only prove futile but also frustrate them, adding stress to an already tense situation.

When an intervention seems necessary, the parents are often directly involved in treatment—this is generally true for child therapy. Treatment may take the form of parent management, education about the child's problems, or more structured family therapy sessions involving all family members. This is not necessarily an indication that the parents or family members have done something wrong but instead may reflect the belief held by many mental health professionals that children are very dependent on their parents and reactive to their environments, and that parents are usually the best source of help for their children. In addition to family counseling, treatment plans can also include individual counseling with the child. Use of medications has increased for a variety of child and adolescent problems ranging from attention-deficit/hyperactivity disorder to mood disorders. It is not uncommon for multiple interventions to be utilized.

In some instances, specialized treatments may be considered. For example, children who are suffering from a pervasive developmental disorder such as autism may profit from more intensive targeted interventions such as applied behavior analysis and sensory integration therapy (Bundy, Lane, Fisher, & Murray, 2002; Maurice, 1993). These therapies can be controversial, as professionals do not always agree upon their effectiveness. Researchers still are not able to predict which children will profit from which intervention. One of the more controversial treatments for children with severe attachment problems is holding therapy, which involves very lengthy and emotionally intense sessions with the child and the parents (Cline, 1990). Unfortunately, there is really no research evidence that it is effective, and it remains an experimental treatment.

Ancillary support services such as respite care can prove beneficial in helping families cope with difficult situations such as severe child behavior problems. Short-term hospital stays are mainly used to assess medication needs when this is not possible on an outpatient basis, and to stabilize behavior in acute crisis situations such as suicide attempts. Partial hospitalization programs and day treatment programs can offer a structured monitored environment on a short-term basis when needed. An alternative to these outpatient interventions is residential treatment, which can provide comprehensive educational and psychotherapeutic interventions for children who are unable to tolerate the intimacy of family life. The challenge in these cases is integrating the child back into the family once the child's individual issues are resolved.

General Guidelines for Working with Pediatricians

Prospective adoptive parents should screen potential pediatricians for their child. In addition to asking standard questions about their pediatric practice and philosophy, parents should ask pediatricians about their experience reviewing prenatal and birth histories for adoption-related cases to assess their understanding of health care considerations and practices for children who were adopted, and their willingness to learn about caring for children who were adopted. The American Academy of Pediatrics Committee on Early Childhood, Adoption and Dependent Care (1991) has issued recommended guidelines for pediatricians' practices around caring for children who were adopted and working with their families. Pediatricians should be able to provide comprehensive medical, developmental, and psychological evaluations of the child; help adoptive parents evaluate any information they have received about the birth parents and the birth history; evaluate any behavioral or emotional concerns and offer referrals to trained professionals; and distinguish between adoption-related issues and typical issues of development. In addition, they should understand the issues related to adoption that may arise and should have information about how to access professional and community resources for adoption-related issues, including information about parent support groups and mental health professionals. Finally, they should use appropriate language to describe adoption and related issues and demonstrate sensitivity regarding issues related to loss for all members of the adoption triad (children, birth parents, and adoptive parents).

Research Spotlight: Adoption and Overall Adjustment

Many questions have been raised by professionals over the past fifty years in regard to adjustment issues of adopted children relative to children who were not adopted. Studies have pointed out that children and adolescents who were adopted are overrepresented in both outpatient and inpatient mental health services (Brodzinsky, 1993; Wierzbicki, 1993). While this finding has been sustained over time, there is some controversy over what it means. Do children who were adopted indeed have more problems than those who were not, or are there alternative explanations for this phenomenon? For example, researchers have raised the possibility that this could be influenced by a differential referral bias for adoptive families. That is, families who adopt appear to be more sensitive and tuned in to their child's difficulties and are more apt to seek help for them, which may contribute to their greater presence in mental health services (Warren, 1992). However, studies of children in the general population have also found a modest but still significant presence of cognitive, behavioral, and emotional difficulties among adopted children in middle childhood and adolescence compared to children in the same age groups who were not adopted (Brodzinsky, 1993). Taken as a whole, the literature generally supports the idea that these youths are at an increased risk of developing various psychological, behavioral, and academic problems compared to non-adopted individuals.

However, research has also shown that the overwhelming majority of adopted youngsters are well within the normal range of adjustment, and adults who were adopted as children show no increased prevalence in receipt of mental health services (Bohman & Sigvardsson, 1990; Brodzinsky, Smith, & Brodzinsky, 1998). This research suggests that a developmental component may be involved. Furthermore, most studies that support the belief that children who were adopted are at increased risk for the development of problems do not differentiate the populations studied regarding what would appear to be important variables, such as type of adoption, age of the child at adoptive placement, reasons for placement, and pre-adoptive history (e.g., experiences of abuse and neglect, multiple placements). Some of these variables have been found to affect the risk that a child will develop problems in the adoptive placement, which makes it difficult to interpret the research findings. Finally, there is much evidence that a loving, supportive, and secure environment goes a long way toward alleviating the impact of adverse factors (Brodzinsky et al., 1998). The adoptive family's strengths have also been shown to have an effect on their potential for change when they are engaged in mental health treatment (Cohen, Coyne, & Duvall, 1993). Regardless of the risks, however, adoption remains the best alternative for children whose birth families are not able to care for them (Brodzinsky et al., 1998; Cohen et al., 1993).

Health Considerations for Children Adopted from Foster Care

People considering adoption of children from foster care are often concerned about the physical, emotional, and developmental consequences experienced by these children, who may have been abused or neglected prior to their foster placement. Children who have lived in foster care have a number of risk factors for poor health and disordered development. Prospective adoptive parents who are interested in adopting children from foster care should be aware of the health issues associated with the experience of foster care. Understanding the needs of these children can help parents address their needs promptly, provide them with stable and nurturing homes, and have a positive impact on their child's development. In addition to lack of access to appropriate medical care, issues that must be taken into consideration for children who have lived in foster care include their prenatal histories, chronic health problems, and various developmental and mental health issues.

Ideally, children's positive experiences in foster or adoptive care with secure and loving caregivers can counteract prior negative experiences and promote healing (Pearce & Pezzot-Pearce, 2001). Several studies have demonstrated the reversal of physical health conditions (e.g., elevated lead levels, growth delay) afflicting children in foster care once they are placed in a permanent and stable family (Chung, Webb, Clampet-Lundquist, & Campbell, 2001; Wyatt, Simms, & Horwitz, 1997). Other research has demonstrated that a child's foster care or subsequent adoptive experience itself can serve as a compensatory factor in developmental delays (Horwitz, Simms, & Farrington, 1994; Newton, Litrownik, & Landsverk, 2000). The hope and expectation is that once a child is placed in a loving and nurturing home, his or her health status will improve.

More than good intentions are usually needed to care for these children. Reports from health professionals who were involved in the foster care system during their youth suggest that health and child welfare professionals, while attempting to intervene to benefit the child, may actually unwittingly contribute to the trauma the child experiences (Cournos, 1999). Writing about her own perspective as a child placed into foster care after the death of her parents, Cournos described the experience as a series of inexplicable and mysterious events that made her feel threatened and humiliated. If foster or adoptive parents are poorly matched to the child or unprepared for the demands of the child's health issues, they may exacerbate the child's psychopathology. Adoptive and foster parents who must constantly deal with a child's difficult behavior and receive little support from agency or health professionals may become frustrated and unintentionally make the situation worse. Unfortunately, as a result, parents and other caretakers may personalize the child's behavior, blame the child, react in anger, or even further abuse the child. This can reinforce the child's perception of him- or herself as unlovable, and of others as dangerous and untrustworthy. In turn, these responses make future placements even more difficult. Well-trained professionals can help parents prepare to nurture a child who has experienced trauma and poor caregiving. Understanding common health problems and the consequences of different experiences increases the likelihood that parents will be able to help their children heal.

Health problems among children in foster care are the consequence of a number of factors. Inadequate prenatal care, along with prenatal exposure to drugs and alcohol, may lead to premature birth and/or low birth weight. Chronic maternal ill health and serious infections such as HIV and hepatitis C may affect the health of newborns. Poor nutrition, exposure to high levels of violence, chaotic and inconsistent parenting, parental unemployment and lack of education, mental illness, and homelessness are common factors that are detrimental to the early growth of children who enter foster care (Simms, Dubowitz, & Szilagyi, 2000). These children are more likely to have been exposed to toxins in the environment, particularly lead (Chung et al., 2001), and less likely to have received routine preventive health care prior to entering foster care (Combs-Orme, Chernoff, & Kager, 1991). They are less likely to have developed a consistent relationship with a health care provider. Instead, they are often brought to hospital-based clinics and emergency rooms, where record keeping and information sharing are inconsistent (Combes-Orme et al., 1991). To improve children's overall well-being, social workers and foster and adoptive parents should work together to ensure that children receive routine health care and have accurate medical records.

Obtaining Medical Information for Children in Foster Care

A number of best practices concerning health care for children who have been in foster care have been established. Adoptive parents should be aware of and understand the medical issues and barriers encountered by these children so that they can help them obtain the best health care.

Although acquiring medical information from scattered sources may be challenging, it is worth the time and energy to get a comprehensive picture of a child's health. The starting point for this undertaking is usually a discussion with the child's social worker. If the social worker has little health information about the child, he or she may be able to identify the child's most recent health care provider and help parents access the information that is available. The following medical information is very useful:

- health histories for birth parents, birth siblings, and birth relatives (as available), including diagnosed medical concerns, developmental or cognitive delays, mental health problems, smoking, alcohol and/or drug abuse, and genetic conditions, as well as medications prescribed and taken
- birth history, including problems with pregnancy, labor, or delivery; quality of prenatal care; gestational age (full term or premature birth); birth weight; information regarding issues such as withdrawal from opiates, infection, or jaundice; and any feeding difficulties
- past medical history, including hospitalizations, operations, immunizations, laboratory evaluations, and diagnoses of chronic illness
- records of developmental milestones and any treatment for developmental delays
- behavioral/mental health evaluations and treatment protocols prescribed
- allergies to medications and foods
- current medical problems
- current medications

When parents find a pediatrician to care for their child, they should request that their child's developmental assessment include the evaluation of gross and fine motor skills, cognition, speech and language function, self-help abilities, emotional well-being, coping skills, and relationships with others (American Academy of Pediatrics Committee on Early Childhood, Adoption and Dependent Care, 2000). It is important to identify a local pediatrician who is trained and willing to care for children who have lived in foster care. Parents should seek a primary health care provider who can give attention to the mental health needs of the child. When interviewing pediatricians, parents can ask a few specific questions:

- Have you ever cared for any children who have lived in foster care?
- Are you familiar with the American Academy of Pediatrics' guidelines for assessments of children who have lived in foster care?
- Can your office help me locate and acquire my child's health records?
- Do you perform developmental assessments at each visit and provide recommendations for follow-up?

- Are you familiar with the effects of trauma on child development?
- Will you make referrals to specialists who can address my child's physical, developmental, or mental health needs?

Developmental and Mental Health Considerations

It is critical for children in foster care to get routine developmental screenings and any necessary follow-up. Routine pediatric visits include developmental check-ups, but children may not be seen regularly by a pediatrician while living in foster care. A child's physical and mental functioning may improve if problems are recognized during routine developmental screenings and necessary treatment is provided.

Given that the life of a child in foster care is often filled with separation and loss, it is not surprising that behavioral and psychiatric issues are common in these children. While preschoolers in the general population are diagnosed with behavioral problems at a rate of 3–6 percent, 20–40 percent of young children in foster care have similar diagnoses (Hochstadt, Jaudes, Zimo, & Schachter, 1987; Leslie, Gordon, Lambros, Premji, Peoples, & Gist, 2005). Disproportionate rates of mental health problems persist for these children as they age. For instance, children in foster care are sixteen times more likely to receive psychiatric diagnoses and eight times more likely than their peers to take psychotropic medications (Racusin, Maerlender, Sengupta, Isquith, & Straus, 2005). Mental health issues for children in foster care can be exacerbated by lack of access to up-to-date screening and treatment methods. Professionals who work with this population can help children and caregivers understand the consequences of negative experiences on emotional and behavioral health.

Early interruption or poor quality of attachment often underlies many of the behavioral problems of children in foster care. Attachment is the ability of a child to form an emotional bond with a primary caregiver. Secure attachment allows children to explore their environment, develop relationships, and form a positive self-image. When this bond is disrupted or formed in a disordered way, a number of mental health problems result. Children with attachment disorders may show overly vigilant or overly compliant behaviors or display indiscriminate connections to every adult, or they may not demonstrate attachment to any adult. These disordered or disorganized attachments can lead to other adverse outcomes that, left untreated, can persist into adulthood (Harden, 2004; Leslie et al., 2005).

Attachment disorders can result from poor parenting; abuse; neglect; and insecure, interrupted, or poor foster placements. Maltreatment itself is associated with insecure attachment organization, poor emotional and behavioral self-regulation, and problems in development of the autonomous self and self-esteem. Toxic and traumatic events directly affect neural and brain development, as neuronal connections do not form well when stress hormone levels are high. These traumas also result in problems such as post-traumatic stress disorder (Leslie et al., 2005; Pearce & Pezzot-Pearce, 2001; Perry, 2001).

It is important to note that young children who are well attached to their birth parent or other caregiver in foster care go through significant stages of grieving when they are separated from these caregivers. Bowlby (1969) describes the stages of grieving as protest (crying and attempts to recover the attachment object), despair (appearing preoccupied and depressed, yet watchful), and, finally, emotional detachment with loss of interest in care-takers. It is important to recognize the difference between separation problems and attachment problems (Fahlberg, 1991). While they may lead to similar behaviors, treatment for separation issues may have a better prognosis than treatment for a true lack of attachment. Facilitation of the grieving process can help children become more open to the benefits of new attachments. To help a child through these issues, parents can seek assistance from professionals who specialize in treating children with traumatic histories. They can help parents understand the impact of these experiences on children's development and offer practical parenting strategies to foster healthy development for the child and family.

Beyond abuse and neglect, other conditions that result in foster placement present additional risk factors. Parental psychiatric illness has been documented in 46 percent of children in state custody; 60 percent of those birth parents were noted to be alcoholics, and 32–54 percent were reported to have problems with substance abuse (Pearce & Pezzot-Pearce, 2001). The effects of these problems include genetic predisposition to substance or alcohol abuse; prenatal exposure to teratogens; and especially dysfunctional parenting, including neglect and time spent living in impoverished environments. Poor supervision, inconsistent discipline, and lack of modeling or positive reinforcement have been found to be factors that contribute to developmental and emotional delays in children.

As children in foster care age, lack of recognition of the need for adequate mental health treatment may lead to further psychopathology. These disordered behaviors can be separated into two types: internalizing disorders (including depression and anxiety) and externalizing disorders, which result in aggressive, destructive, or antisocial behaviors. Children in foster care often receive diagnoses of both types of disorders. The most common problems identified include relational and coping difficulties and school failure. Of the emotional and behavioral disturbances that cause moderate to severe impairment of the child's ability to function and engage with others, most common are conduct disorders, attention disorders such as attention deficit disorder and attention-deficit/hyperactivity disorder, aggressive behavior, and depression (Leslie, Landsverk, Ezzet-Lofstrom, Tschann, Slymen, & Garland, 2000). Specifically, adoptive parents may encounter atypical eating behaviors such as food hoarding, rumination, swallowing problems, and failure to thrive. Children may also engage in primitive soothing behaviors such as rocking, head banging, scratching, and cutting. Inappropriate modeling or mimicking of adult behavior, even if it is abusive, is also common (Leslie et al., 2005; Perry, 2001).

It is essential that parents request assistance from professionals trained in the care of children who have experienced trauma. Children suffering from trauma do not ordinarily recover without treatment. One trauma specialist has pointed out that delaying treatment for trauma is the worst thing one can do, because over time the trauma becomes more deeply embedded in the psyche, and the person develops and employs less constructive defenses and coping strategies (Terr, 1991). According to Terr (1991), "If one could live a thousand years, one might completely work through a childhood trauma by playing out the terrifying scenario until it no longer terrified. The lifetime allotted to the ordinary person, however, does not appear to be enough" (p. 13). Therapy is vital if children are going to be able to live with foster families, be adopted, or be reunified with the birth parent. The impact of trauma evolves differently in each child. Child-specific diagnoses and treatments are critical. Adoptive parents can benefit from pre-placement preparation as well as post-placement support and training. By accessing resources from within the community, adoptive families can buttress their integration and strengthen their family development.

Fahlberg (1991) outlines strategies to support infants and young children in their transition from foster to adoptive homes. She notes that social workers and parents must pay close attention to the signals children send about their feelings. Initial contacts with adoptive families work well when they take place in the foster home, in the presence of foster parents, and when the pace is set by the child. It is also important that prior to placement, adoptive parents spend significant time visiting during different times of the day so they can become familiar with all aspects of the child's routines. Getting to know one another in the comfort of the child's current home setting can ease the process. Parents can provide children with a sense of history and belonging, which can help ease the transition to an adoptive home, by helping them create a life book, or memory book, a collection of photographs or mementos that document special memories, and by helping them maintain contact with siblings and peers.

Parenting Tools and Skills

Family stability is the first step toward developing the parenting tools and skills that help children who have experienced foster care learn to trust. These children need to reestablish their ability to trust nurturing adults. Trusting relationships help children achieve better self-control and cope with their many losses (Racusin et al., 2005). Family stability can be defined in many ways, but the family characteristics that most benefit children recovering from multiple losses include parental mental health, stable relationships between caregivers, and positive parenting (Harden, 2004). Parents and caregivers must be emotionally available. Home environments should be warm and stimulating, provide a sense of family cohesion, and be characterized by routine day-to-day activities. Caregivers primarily need to be constant and consistent and remain connected with the children (Harden, 2004; Leslie et al., 2005).

Once the child is in a stable situation, other ways to help include nurturing the child, trying to understand problematic behaviors before punishing, parenting based on the child's emotional age, being consistent and predictable, modeling and teaching appropriate social behaviors, relaxing and playing with the child, having realistic expectations of the child and of oneself, and caring for oneself and making wise use of support systems and resources.

Nurture the child. Children who have experienced foster care placement may not have previously had predictable, comforting, or loving relationships with adults. They may need to relearn what it means to be hugged, comforted, and touched in an appropriate way. Unfortunately, relearning love is much harder than learning it during infancy. Patience and persistence are required for children to develop healthy attachments.

Try to understand a problematic behavior before punishing. Understanding the consequences of attachment disorders allows parents and other caregivers to understand a child's behavior in context. A child who is hiding feces or hoarding food is displaying insecurity rather than being naughty. These disturbing behaviors are usually not improved by punishment but are indicators that parents must seek help from professionals to address the child's trauma.

Parent based on the child's emotional age. Children who have been maltreated have delayed coping skills. When stressed, angry, or fearful, they can regress further. While a child may be chronologically nine or ten years of age, emotionally he or she may only have the developmental skills of a two-year-old. If a child is behaving like a two-year-old (responding to stress with tantrums, crying, and demonstrating a loss of control), parents should treat him or her like a two-year-old during that episode. While verbal explanations are appropriate for children of that age in general, such advanced parenting strategies will not be helpful for a child who is not emotionally mature.

Be consistent and predictable. Neglected and maltreated children often have not had the security of routines and support during transitions. Children feel safe in a calm environment with scheduled routines. When presented with changes in routine or new settings (like a party or trip), children can become overwhelmed and may need extra support to help them cope with those changes.

Be consistent and predictable.   The fundamental problem with attachment disorders is that children do not learn how to interact appropriately with others. Experiencing consistency and love in daily life allows children to acquire the skills they need to behave appropriately. It helps for parents to identify their own behaviors, break those skills down into understandable components, and then explain them to the child. Physical contact can be challenging for children. Some may not know when to give a hug, how to break eye contact, or how close to stand to someone else. Others are indiscriminate with their affection and need to know where to set limits. The use of gentle modeling and redirection without embarrassing or drawing attention to the child can help him or her develop these skills.

Relax and play with the child.   Children may find it easier to relax and share their feelings during quiet and unstructured moments. During these times children should be helped to understand that all feelings are okay to feel, and that there are healthy ways to express their feelings. When the child is clearly happy, mad, or sad, ask how he or she feels and help him or her express those feelings in words.

Have realistic expectations of the child and of oneself.   Skills and abilities that are easily acquired soon after birth cannot be learned as easily when children are older. Progress is often slow, and parents have every reason to be frustrated by the task. Look for individual gains instead of comparing the child's progress with that of others. Rewarding small successes helps children develop confidence.

Care for oneself and make wise use of support systems and resources. No one can do this alone. It is important for adoptive parents to take care of themselves. If parents are stressed or frustrated, they will be unable to care adequately for their children. Professional resources can help and should be employed. Support groups for parents; respite care; and the cooperation of medical, psychological, and child welfare professionals are vital to successful parenting under special circumstances (Perry, 2001).

Finally, it is important to understand that separation and loss issues may continue to reappear throughout the child's lifetime. There are some predictable ages and stages of development during which the effects of earlier losses may resurface, leading to further grieving. More information on children's stages of development can be found in chapter 8. It is important to remember that early experiences, especially trauma, affect a person throughout his or her life span. Even adults may have feelings of separation and loss long after they have put those experiences behind them (for example, these feelings may surface when one's child reaches the age one was at the time the trauma or loss occurred).

Parenting children who have experienced foster care presents unique challenges and joys. Foster placement and adoption can be confusing, frightening, and traumatic on a number of levels. It is best if the transition in placement is well planned. It is critical that parents understand that the child's experience of neglect, violence, or loss prior to placement will affect how the child manages emotionally. Also, the emotional support offered to the child and family can have an impact on how he or she manages the experience (American Academy of Pediatrics Committee on Early Childhood, Adoption and Dependent Care, 2000, 2002; Simms et al., 2000). A child's successful transition from foster child to son or daughter through adoption requires the support of trained professionals, educators, and the community.

Recognizing the Medical Needs of Children in Foster Care

Finding the right doctor is critical for the adequate care of a child. There is ample evidence that even when children reach a medical professional, their needs are often under-recognized (O'Hara, Church, & Blatt, 1998). Formal medical and nursing education programs do not specifically address the medical needs of children in foster care, nor do ongoing educational opportunities provided to health care practitioners (Henry, Pollack, & Lazare, 2006; Simms et al., 2000). There is little communication among child welfare and health professionals, so information about a child's health is often not directed to the attention of those who can use or make sense of it. Despite the fact that children in foster care have significant unmet health care needs, untrained community providers are much less likely to refer young children entering foster care for evaluation and treatment of developmental and mental health problems than are foster care specialists.

The importance of communication and the need for the coordinated transfer of medical information among caregivers is vital. Foster and adoptive parents must be informed and involved in the evaluation of developmental and mental health problems. An accurate diagnosis is unlikely without their informed participation in the assessment, and treatment cannot be successful without their cooperation.

Research Spotlight: Physical, Developmental, and Mental Health Issues in Foster Care

Over 70 percent of children in state custody have a history of abuse and neglect (U.S. Department of Health and Human Services, 2003). As a result of circumstances surrounding their histories, these children are at risk for increased health problems that affect their overall well-being. The health problems of children in foster care exceed those of other high-risk groups, such as children living in poverty and children who are homeless. Multiple studies indicate that children in state care may experience growth delays, vision and hearing deficits, immunization deficiencies, dental caries, anemia, and obesity and may have communicable diseases (including sexually transmitted infections) and high lead levels. Developmental delays, as well as psychiatric and behavioral issues, are also more prevalent in this population.

Chernoff, Combs-Orme, Risley-Curtiss, and Heisler (1994) found that 92 percent of 1,407 children entering foster care in Baltimore, Maryland, over a two-year period had at least one problem noted on their physical exam. Ailments of the upper respiratory tract (66%), skin (61%), genitals (10%), eyes (8%), abdomen (7%), lungs (7%), and extremities (6%) were most common. In the same study, it was noted that one-quarter of these children failed the vision screen, while 15 percent failed the hearing screen. Growth delays and short stature were three times more prevalent for these children than for the general population. Half of the children had unmet dental needs.

Takayama, Wolfe, and Coulter (1998) found medical problems in 60 percent of 749 children entering foster care in San Francisco during a fifteen-month period. As was found in Baltimore, the most common problems experienced by the children were skin conditions and upper respiratory infections. In addition, one-third of the children had abnormal vision screens.

Flaherty and Weiss (1990) studied children in Chicago who were placed in protective custody during a twenty-two-month period. Nearly half had a health problem (44%), of which infections (otitis media, sexually transmitted infections) were the most common, followed by anemia and lead poisoning. It was particularly startling that seventeen of these children were found to have broken bones that had gone unnoticed.

Several studies indicate that there are health conditions that are ameliorated in foster care. Elevated lead levels in foster children in Philadelphia were found to drop significantly once the children were moved to a foster home (Chung et al., 2001). A Connecticut study found that children who were placed in foster care for the first time grew at an astonishing rate. Regardless of the child's height at the time of placement, nearly half of the preschool children studied experienced a large catch-up growth spurt during their first year in foster care (Wyatt et al., 1997).

Developmental delays are found in 30–60 percent of the foster care population, as opposed to only 4–10 percent in the general population. Specifically, problems that have been reported in this population include language delays (57%), cognitive problems (33%), gross motor delays (31%), and growth problems (10%) (Leslie et al., 2005).

Research Spotlight: Guidelines for and Barriers to Quality Health Care for Children in Foster Care

Guidelines that clarify what care is appropriate for this very special subset of children, in addition to routine well-child care, have been published based on what is known about the myriad health needs of children in foster care.

The Child Welfare League of America (1988) developed a template for child welfare agencies to organize health and mental health services for children in their care. Similarly, the American Academy of Pediatrics Committee on Early Childhood, Adoption and Dependent Care (1994, 2002) has laid out components of health care services that should be made standard for children in foster care.

Both organizations stress that care should be comprehensive and continuous. They recommend a health screening exam within seven days of placement to rule out signs of abuse or neglect and to determine if there is any evidence of infection or chronic illness, or a need for medication or immediate medical intervention. Within thirty days of placement, a comprehensive health assessment should be performed by a medical professional who is skilled in identifying abuse and neglect, and knowledgeable of the health needs of children in foster care. Developmental, educational, and mental health evaluations must be part of the evaluation. An enhanced well-child visit schedule is recommended after the assessment period to identify issues that may change with time.

The American Academy of Pediatrics' most recent recommendations stress the neurobiology of development. Traumatic events experienced in the first two or three years of life may have a long-lasting negative impact on a child's subsequent development. The American Academy of Pediatrics Committee on Early Childhood, Adoption and Dependent Care (2000) specifies how comprehensive evaluation, treatment, placement, and caregiving must be approached in order to ameliorate those effects. Assessments should include the evaluation of "gross and fine motor skills, cognition, speech and language function, self-help abilities, emotional well-being, coping skills, relationship to persons, [and] adequacy of caregiver's parenting skills and behaviors" (American Academy of Pediatrics Committee on Early Childhood, Adoption and Dependent Care, 2000, p. 1147). Treatment through the primary health care provider's office, with attention to the mental health needs of the child, is emphasized. Early interventions and immersion in stimulating environments are identified as the best ways to combat the effects of deprivation and trauma.

There are, however, barriers that prevent foster children from receiving comprehensive, high-quality medical care. A national study on health care policies for children in out-of-home care showed that almost all the participating child welfare agencies noted that they fell short of meeting the Child Welfare League of America's standards (Risley-Curtiss & Kronenfeld, 2001). One significant obstacle is the lack of medical information available for foster children. Obtaining this information has not traditionally been a priority in the often chaotic and unplanned placement of children into foster care. Given their adversarial relationship with the state agency that is removing the child from their care, birth parents are often hostile or may be missing or uninformed. Thus, little information about a child's health history and important health conditions is generally obtained at the time of removal. There may not be any place in child welfare records for medical information, and the transfer of medical information between foster agencies and foster homes is not well organized. It is not unusual for the new foster parent to receive no medical information for a medically complex foster child. Research has shown that the majority of foster parents do not have access to information on prior medical or mental health evaluations (Chernoff et al., 1994; Vig, Chinitz, & Shulman, 2005).

Other reasons for inadequate and inconsistent health care include lack of continuity of care because of foster home changes, limited access to health care providers, issues of consent and confidentiality, and poor communication about health care needs in a busy and overwhelmed child welfare system. In addition, a research study recently concluded that foster parents are not clear about what their role as a foster parent entails and do not receive either the quality or quantity of training, information, and support they need to address complex health issues (Pasztor, Hollinger, Inkelas, & Halfon, 2006). Poorly selected and multiple placements when a child is in care are also associated with poor health outcomes (Newton et al., 2000; Rubin, Alessandrini, Feudtner, Mandell, Localio, & Hadley, 2004). While foster parents are given the responsibility to see that the children in their homes receive physical and mental health care, they are rarely given any historical information, and they often cannot give legal consent for treatment. When anything beyond routine care is required, child welfare workers must find the birth parents to obtain their consent or obtain a court order for treatment. Separate consents may be required for developmental, educational, and mental health evaluations. At best, these requirements cause delays in care; at worst, they become insurmountable obstacles for a welfare system that is already stressed.

Though reimbursement issues are often cited to explain why children in foster care receive inadequate health care, most of these children are covered by Medicaid because they receive federal foster care or adoption assistance benefits or child welfare services (Centers for Medicare and Medicaid Services, 2008). Therefore they are eligible for the Early and Periodic Screening, Diagnosis, and Treatment Program, a federally mandated program developed to ensure that all children from birth to the age of twenty-one who are covered under Medicaid receive comprehensive well-child care, which includes the maintenance of health history records, physical examinations, developmental and mental health assessments, laboratory screenings, and immunizations. These standards are based on the American Academy of Pediatrics Committee on Psychosocial Aspects of Child and Family Health's (1997) Guidelines for Health Supervision II.

Most often, children in foster care do not receive these services. Most agencies responsible for foster children do not have formal policies or arrangements to provide health care. Foster parents rely on local or family physicians or clinics that accept Medicaid (Leslie, Hurlburt, Landsverk, Rolls, Wood, & Kelleher, 2003). They receive no training about accessing services for children with special needs. Social workers and case managers are similarly untrained regarding the medical services that foster children should receive and thus cannot effectively oversee their medical care needs. As a result, children with complex health needs are left in the hands of foster parents. Alone, the foster parent must navigate a complicated and confusing health system (Simms, Freundlich, Battistelli, & Kaufman, 1999).

Large caseloads and a high turnover rate among child welfare workers in many welfare agencies make it even less likely that children receive the health care services they need (Klee, Krondstadt, & Zlotnick, 1997). Assessment results may not be documented or communicated. As a result of overwhelming caseloads, a triage mentality is employed: only the most urgent cases receive attention. A U.S. General Accounting Office (2003) report outlining the state of U.S. child welfare agencies indicates that lack of staffing, high turnover among staff, and issues of worker safety have led to the assignment of much heavier caseloads than recommended. In addition, the report showed that services are often not provided in accord with best practice standards. A national survey of child welfare agencies revealed that fewer than 43 percent provide comprehensive physical, mental health, and developmental examinations for all children entering out-of-home care (Leslie et al., 2003).

Health Considerations for Intercountry Adoption

Adopting a child from a developing country can be a tremendously rewarding experience. Providing children who might otherwise grow up in poverty with a good home and a chance to maximize their potential can be a life-altering experience for the whole family. Since 1985, nearly a quarter of a million children have been adopted by families in America (U.S. Department of State, 2008). During the past ten years most of these children have come from China, Russia, South Korea, Ukraine, Kazakhstan, Romania, Vietnam, and Guatemala (U.S. Department of State, 2008). Children adopted from South Korea and Guatemala usually have been cared for in foster homes, where the risk of certain illnesses is lower. Children from China, Russia, Eastern Europe, and Southeast Asia are more likely to have been cared for in orphanages or baby homes, in which malnutrition, emotional and physical neglect, and infectious diseases are more common.

Choosing a Pediatrician

Individuals and couples interested in adopting a child from another country should identify a local pediatrician who can provide ongoing primary care for the child. Adoptive parents are encouraged to seek recommendations of pediatricians from other families that have adopted internationally. It is important to feel comfortable with the pediatrician one chooses, and to assess his or her experience with medical considerations related to intercountry adoption. Parents may opt to choose a pediatrician who has had little experience with children adopted from other countries but who is willing and eager to learn about the best practices for their care. The American Academy of Pediatrics has made recommendations about caring for children adopted internationally, and parents can direct interested pediatricians to the American Academy of Pediatrics for more information. During the interview process, parents should ask a series of questions to assess a health care provider's philosophy and experience with international adoption medicine. In addition to questions that are typically asked during the screening process, the following is a series of questions parents who are adopting internationally can ask while screening pediatricians.

Do you have any experience with children adopted from other countries? If so, from what countries?   It is helpful if a pediatrician has had experience caring for children from a country similar to that of the child. Different countries pose different health risks, and working with a provider who understands those risks is an additional benefit.

How many children in your practice were internationally adopted? Pediatricians who have other children in their practice who were internationally adopted are more likely to be aware of the common medical concerns for children who were adopted and are often familiar with the latest research and recommendations for their care.

Do you have experience reviewing pre-adoption medical records and videos of children? If so, from what countries have you reviewed records? Do you have any concerns about reviewing records?   When it is time to review the pre-adoption medical records during the child referral process, parents should use a health care professional who has extensive experience reading and understanding foreign medical records. Some foreign medical terms have no English translation. Practitioners who are familiar with country-specific records can determine the implications of certain findings. There are large research and university-based programs that specialize in reviewing pre-adoption records and can provide summaries and recommendations for a child's primary care physician since he or she will be responsible for providing ongoing primary care for the child. Similarly, prospective adoptive parents are advised to find a health care advisor who has experience reviewing videos of children. It is helpful for pediatricians to be aware of what the images of the child say about his or her state of health and development. Videos can help prospective adoptive parents and medical professionals assess a child's development, coordination, strength, and social interactions.

Do you make recommendations to parents about whether they should accept a child referral?   A pediatrician's role in reviewing medical records is to provide a current medical assessment of the child, and a prognosis for future care and development. Once parents have that information, they need to consider on their own whether they have the personal and financial resources to parent the child and meet his or her anticipated needs. A doctor cannot and should not make that decision for them.

Do you inform parents of their child's medical risk to the best of your professional abilities after reviewing the pre-adoption records?   Parents must be able to seek the expertise of a health professional to determine the immediate and future needs of the child and decide whether they have the resources to meet those needs.

Are you familiar with the American Academy of Pediatrics' recommendations for screening tests and assessment of immunization status for children adopted internationally?   Parents need a pediatrician who understands the immunization considerations for children adopted from other countries. Children are often under-immunized because of different practices or inefficient immunizations. It is important for children not to be over- or under-immunized. Parents should request blood tests to determine whether children exhibit the antigens for (i.e., protection from) specific diseases to determine which vaccines or immunizations they should receive and the appropriate schedule for those shots.

How soon after my child's arrival will you be able to see him or her?   It is recommended that a child be seen within two weeks of arriving in the United States unless the child is sick, in which case he or she should be seen as soon as possible after arrival. If the child is healthy, it is a good idea to wait a week or so before seeing a physician to ease the significant transition into a new family, surroundings, and culture.

How soon after my child's arrival can laboratory work be conducted?   It is recommended that children have a series of laboratory tests within a month of arrival. These tests can determine if your child needs additional immunizations or has any other medical issues that need attention.

Do you make referrals for vision, hearing, developmental, and mental health specialists?   It is important for any pediatrician to be able to make quality referrals for vision, hearing, speech or language, and developmental or mental health practitioners.

How often during the first year do you see a child who was adopted internationally?   Pediatricians should be willing to see the child as often as parents request. It is important during the first year after arrival that children be seen often enough to assess catch-up growth and to monitor any other developmental issues that may arise.

Do you have any information on resources for multicultural families? When adopting internationally, most families become multicultural. It is helpful if the child's primary care provider has information for families on multiculturalism as the child grows and experiences different social situations. Pediatricians often have information about community programs or support groups that families may find useful.

What is your opinion about late circumcisions? If for religious or other reasons parents would like to have their son circumcised, it is important to find a practitioner willing to perform the surgery after infancy.

At what age can a child no longer be seen by you? It is important for children to have continuity of care even as they age into adolescence and young adulthood. It is often important for children of college age to continue to be seen by the same pediatric practice that has been regularly caring for them, since health care can be fragmented without a primary provider. Once a child reaches adulthood, he or she can obtain an adult primary care physician.

Pre-adoption

Families planning to adopt a child from overseas should obtain as much information as possible about the adoption agency with which they plan to work. What kind of medical problems or developmental or behavioral issues have been reported in children adopted through the agency? Have the children usually been well cared for and well fed? Are any particular diseases common in the orphanages from which these children come? Adoption agencies provide families with medical information about the child to be adopted. Because many of these children have been abandoned at hospitals or orphanages, there is often little information about the ages and medical histories of the parents, problems during pregnancy, the child's birth history, or any medical issues the child experienced after birth. It is important for prospective adoptive parents to understand that there may have been problems during pregnancy, inadequate prenatal nutrition, or drug or alcohol use by the birth mother that might affect the child's later development. The child might have suffered emotional or physical abuse before being placed for adoption; such abuse could also affect later emotional development. Discussing these concerns with the agency is important.

Agencies provide a brief history and pictures or videos of the children to adoptive families. Videos can help prospective adoptive parents and medical professionals assess a child's development, coordination, strength, and social interactions. It is always reassuring to see a child who engages easily and smiles readily for visitors or for a caregiver. More consideration should be taken when children are indifferent to their surroundings. Pictures often show children bundled in several layers of clothes, propped in a seat or a walker, and may not provide extensive information about the child's overall condition. A series of pictures can provide useful information about a child's movements and interactions with his or her surroundings.

Based on these types of records, families are asked to make a decision as to whether or not they would like to adopt a particular child. Reviewing the information with a pediatrician or an adoption medicine specialist may help relieve concerns or raise questions. Careful examination of photographs may help rule out congenital malformations or problems such as fetal alcohol syndrome, limb anomalies, or cleft lip. If questions arise about the information provided in the referral, prospective adoptive parents should not hesitate to ask the agency for further information. Once the decision is made to adopt a particular child, the agency will provide periodic nutritional assessments, developmental assessments, and measurements of height, weight, and head circumferences for the adoptive family to review.

Russian medical records often contain dire-sounding terms such as "hypertension-hydrocephalic syndrome," "vegetovisceral dysfunction," and "perinatal encephalopathy." These terms do not have equivalents in Western medicine and do not necessarily mean that a child will have problems in the future. However, children who have a diagnosis of congenital syphilis or rickets should be carefully reevaluated once they arrive in the United States.

Travel Preparations

Traveling overseas increases the risk of medical problems such as malaria, hepatitis A, typhoid, and traveler's diarrhea. Families planning to travel overseas to adopt a child should discuss their upcoming trip with their primary care physician. They may also want to consult a travel medicine specialist to prepare for the trip and to decrease the risks of contracting travel-related illnesses. If young children will be accompanying the adoptive parents, they should be prepared for the trip as well; parents should make sure their routine immunizations are up to date and that any special medications or immunizations they need for the trip are provided in advance.

Before traveling, adoptive parents may want to meet with their chosen pediatrician to discuss how to manage possible illnesses while traveling with the child. It also would be beneficial to learn how to take temperatures. While orphanages usually have doctors who can help, and the U.S. embassy may be able to recommend local hospitals or doctors, once adoptive parents have embarked on the return trip to the United States, it may be helpful to have the pediatrician's phone number and/or an e-mail address.

During the past several years, several infectious diseases have complicated international adoptions. In 2003, outbreaks of SARS disrupted travel to China and Southeast Asia. In 2004, adoptions from China were temporarily halted because of measles outbreaks. No one knows how bird flu will progress and spread over the next few years, but it will be important for international travelers to be prepared to deal with outbreaks of infectious diseases and to know about current medical threats in countries or regions they are visiting. The Centers for Disease Control and Prevention provides current information about outbreaks of disease around the world on their Web site.

Some adoption agencies suggest taking an extensive list of medical supplies on the trip. Before spending a lot of money on antibiotics, creams, lotions, cold medicines, or remedies for head lice and scabies, prospective adoptive parents should discuss with the agency the kinds of medical problems families have encountered in the past. If they frequently see scabies or head lice in the children, it is worth taking a treatment such as Elimite Cream or Nix Shampoo. Antibiotics are usually not necessary. Diapers, antibacterial wipes, medication for fever such as acetaminophen or ibuprofen, soothing body lotions, and a digital thermometer are the most useful items to have. In addition, parents may wish to bring diaper rash ointments, a stroller, hydrocortisone 1%, diarrhea medication, insect repellants, sunscreen, bottles or sippy cups, a first aid kit, saline nasal drops, antihistamines, a medicine dropper, powdered formula, and powdered electrolytes, as well as prescription and over-the-counter medications for themselves. Again, parents should plan ahead, since due to airline restrictions, it may be necessary to pack these items rather than bringing them in carry-on baggage. It might also be quite practical to correspond with one's travel group, if there is one, to make a plan to share responsibility for bringing supplies.

The Trip Home

It is a difficult experience for a person of any age to be removed from the familiar environment of the only home he or she knows, and brought to a totally different place, perhaps halfway around the world. Remember, the child's regular schedule will be off. Sleep disturbances both during the trip and for the first few days or weeks after the arrival home are common. Parents can help relieve ear discomfort during an airline flight by giving the child food to chew or liquids to drink; acetaminophen or ibuprofen may also help. Children may have never traveled in a motorized vehicle and may suffer from motion sickness. Other suggestions for traveling with children can be found at the Flying with Kids Web site (see Selected Resources). Also, appetite may suffer from the impact of the time change; to encourage eating, parents should include some foods that the child is used to eating when packing for the trip home. Having an adequate supply of diapers and wipes may help because changes in diet may result in diarrhea. Crying is one natural response to separation and sadness a child may express. Hugging, caressing, and, if possible, a familiar object or two may provide comfort. Adoptive parents should try to keep as many of the child's original belongings, particularly clothing, as possible; the familiarity of their own clothes can help comfort a child during the initial transition. Some adoptive families take the time to learn a few words of the child's language so the child can hear some things he or she understands. Hearing the names of common foods, and the words for "milk," "sleep," and "I love you" may comfort a child. Self-stimulating behaviors such as rocking or head banging are common in children who have spent time in large institutions; these behaviors may resolve with time.

Arrival Home

Arranging for a complete medical checkup for the internationally adopted child shortly after arriving home is important. It may even be worthwhile for adoptive parents to schedule the appointment before leaving on the trip to pick up the child. At this first evaluation, the pediatrician will want to review all the medical information available about the child, including immunization records. Some adoption agencies provide translations of medical information; these are very helpful for the medical care provider. During the initial medical checkup, the pediatrician should conduct a physical exam, take body measurements, and make an effort to detect major problems or illnesses and to gain a general sense of the child's developmental status.

The physical exam is important to assess growth and nutritional status, to document birthmarks such as Mongolian spots, to detect the presence of any congenital anomalies or acute infections, and to document the child's level of development. Minor skin rashes, bald spots on the back of a child's head, thinning of the hair, and muscle weakness are not uncommon. Scars from illnesses such as chickenpox, from the BCG vaccine for tuberculosis, or from any surgeries should be noted. Occasionally children have scars that have no explanation. Congenital anomalies such as extra fingers or toes or skin tags should also be noted. Children should be carefully examined for features of fetal alcohol syndrome. Later, a more comprehensive evaluation should include immunization titers, screening tests, and remeasurement to assess catch-up growth. This should also be an opportunity for parents to ask questions regarding the child's health, well-being, behavior, diet and eating patterns, sleeping (both at night and at nap time), and defecation and urination, as well as any unusual behaviors parents have noticed or about which they might be concerned.

Many children who come from large orphanages or group homes in which they have had minimal amounts of exercise, stimulation, and nurturing experience delays in their growth and development. Many of their developmental and growth delays correct rapidly in a loving, nurturing environment where they are provided with adequate nutrition and stimulation. It is important for the adoptive parents and their medical care provider to enlist the help of early intervention services for the child. Early intervention staff can evaluate the child, offer suggestions on how to stimulate all aspects of development, and follow the child as long as he or she needs help.

Immunizing children against vaccine-preventable diseases is a key part of routine well-child visits. Thus, it is very important to review a child's immunization record at the first visit. Developing countries usually immunize children against tetanus, diphtheria, pertussis (whooping cough), polio, measles, and hepatitis B. But most developing countries do not immunize against Haemophilus influenzae or Streptococcus pneumoniae, bacteria that can cause meningitis, blood infections, and pneumonia. Many countries do not immunize against mumps, rubella, or chickenpox either. In some developing countries, vaccines may not be manufactured or handled as carefully as they are in the United States. In addition, they may be improperly stored or improperly administered, so they may be less effective than vaccines given in the United States. Many adoption medicine experts recommend reviewing a child's immunization record and documenting his or her response to previous immunizations by blood tests. These immunization titers either document a response to vaccines or demonstrate that certain vaccines may need to be given again. The pediatrician should discuss with the parents any catch-up immunization schedule that may be necessary.

Screening for infectious diseases is an important aspect of the initial medical evaluation. Many countries do not have accurate information on the frequency of certain infectious diseases within their borders. In a number of countries, diseases such as HIV, tuberculosis, and hepatitis C are actually underreported. Although some children have been tested for HIV, hepatitis B, or hepatitis C in their birth country, it is not possible in many cases to verify the accuracy of these tests. Most adoption medicine experts recommend that testing be done in the United States for HIV, hepatitis B, hepatitis C, syphilis, and tuberculosis. It is also important to send stool tests for intestinal parasites. Other important laboratory tests that should be scheduled by the child's pediatrician include a complete blood count; a lead level assessment; neonatal metabolic screens for thyroid, hemoglobin, and metabolic abnormalities; PKU/TSH tests for phenylketonuria and congenital hypothyroidism; thyroid function tests if growth or development is delayed; vision and hearing screens; a G6PD assay; and urinalysis and culture testing.

Tuberculosis is a lung infection caused by a bacterium called Mycobacterium tuberculosis. Adults with active TB can very easily spread the infection to children, and an adult with active TB working in a crowded orphanage could infect many children. Developing countries have a much higher incidence of TB than does the United States. All children adopted from a developing country should have a TB skin test shortly after arrival home.

Because of the high incidence of TB infection, many developing countries give a vaccine for TB, called BCG, to infants. This vaccine is given as an injection in the upper arm and usually leaves a small scar that looks like a pock mark. The vaccine is not very effective in preventing pulmonary tuberculosis, but many countries use it because it does decrease the chance that the child will develop TB meningitis. Because it is not very effective, we do not use the BCG vaccine routinely in the United States; in addition, it can cause some significant side effects, and it may interfere with the TB skin test. In some situations, the BCG vaccine may cause the TB skin test to be falsely positive. Until recently, there has been no way to differentiate a skin test that tests positive because of TB infection from a skin test that tests positive because of the BCG vaccination. The Centers for Disease Control and Prevention and the American Academy of Pediatrics recommend that positive skin tests be treated as indicating TB infection regardless of whether or not the child has received the BCG vaccine. A new blood test called Quantiferon Gold may help differentiate positive test results caused by presence of the disease from positive test results caused by the BCG vaccine. A child's health care provider can discuss this with parents. If a child's test is negative, it is a good idea to repeat the test in six to twelve months in case the child was exposed to TB shortly before his or her arrival in the United States. Some findings from the first medical exam after the child's arrival in the United States may indicate a need for concern, or that more testing is warranted. These more serious findings include indifference, asymmetrical movements, fetal alcohol syndrome stigmata (alcohol is a neurotoxin and is one of the most common teratogens), indications of mental retardation, poor pre- and postnatal growth, fine motor dysfunction, and irritability or hyperactive behavior. It is also important to determine whether bruises are indeed bruises, or if they may be mongolian spots, which are harmless skin discolorations often found in children with dark skin.

The newly arrived child not only needs to be evaluated physically but should be evaluated developmentally as well. This involves an assessment of the child's functioning within the cognitive, motor, socio-emotional, and behavioral domains. In most cases, a skilled pediatrician is sufficient for this purpose. However, in cases of questionable delays, a more detailed examination by a developmental and behavioral pediatrician may be warranted. This may also involve more formal testing by a developmental psychologist as well as other professionals. It is important to identify any difficulties as early as possible, as there are effective interventions to help children develop appropriate functioning. For infants and children under the age of three years old, early intervention programs that work with both the child and parent are helpful. Public school systems are important sources of both evaluation and intervention for developmental and learning problems among preschool and school-aged children. Local school systems are mandated by law to provide the services necessary to evaluate and meet the children's special needs in these areas when requested by a parent. Interventions may include academic support in cases of learning disabilities, speech therapy, occupational therapy, and modified academic instruction.

If a child exhibits more emotional or adjustment difficulties, a pediatrician may consider a referral to a child psychiatrist or other mental health professional such as a clinical psychologist or clinical social worker. Problems such as attachment difficulties, conduct problems, fears and worries, attention-deficit disorders, and peer problems, along with general behavior management concerns, are the types of issues that can be addressed by mental health professionals. Unfortunately, most mental health specialists have neither specific training nor extensive clinical experience in dealing with adoptive families. They may have problems assessing whether the issues families are experiencing are part of a normal adjustment process or if these need more intensive intervention. It is best to select a clinician who is familiar with these issues, especially if there is a large pool of professionals from which to choose. Seeking information about appropriate practitioners from adoptive support groups or other specialized services in the adoptive family's geographical area is a good starting strategy. Finding an appropriate mental health professional is especially critical for issues that are central to the adoption experience, for example, attachment difficulties.

Follow-Up

Children who have spent time in institutional settings are at risk for problems as they grow. Delays in development and socialization skills, in addition to slow growth, early puberty, dental problems, behavioral issues, and attachment disorders, may occur. Separation anxiety is normal at certain ages, as are temper tantrums, occasional stuttering, and picky eating. Thus, these may not actually indicate that a problem is developing.

The primary care provider should monitor the child carefully for these problems. It is important that parents recognize which of these problems are normal developmental issues and which are abnormal. Parents should be willing to share their concerns with health care providers and ask for help. It can also help to talk with other parents who have adopted children from overseas. Sometimes the necessary counseling or therapy may not be covered by insurance. While this is a potentially daunting aspect of caring for a child adopted internationally, at the same time, parents can take pride that the child has the opportunity for a new and better life than he or she might otherwise have had.

Behavioral Health Considerations

Intercountry adoptions, by definition, entail a cultural displacement that may have implications for the child's adjustment. This not only is true for the ultimate preservation of the child's native culture and heritage necessary for identification but is very obvious in simple day-to-day activities as the child transitions into the new household. For example, differences in language, routines, and customs associated with basic activities such as feeding and toilet training need to be addressed for the very young infant as well as for the older child. International adoptions may also involve multicultural considerations and require the adoptive family to deal with community values and prejudices.

Many other factors that are not unique to international adoption play a role in the child's ability to adjust. These include the child's age, biological makeup, temperament, cognitive ability, and pre-adoption experiences, as well as the adoptive family's characteristics. Some children adopted through international adoptions have special needs. Some children are in poor health or have neurological and developmental disabilities that may be initially unknown or undisclosed. Some children may have experienced the prolonged privation of institutional care or, in the case of older children, may have lived on the street and had to depend upon themselves for everyday survival. These factors can have profound long-term implications for the child's behavior, attachment, and overall functioning.

Behavioral health professionals have spent a good deal of time in the last ten years looking at adjustment issues in international adoptions. This research was prompted and made possible by the relatively large influx of children adopted from Romanian orphanages in the early 1990s (Wilson, 2003). Interest has focused on the institutional care that these children and other internationally adopted children experienced and its impact on their development. While the negative impact of institutional care and deprivation on young children has been well documented historically (Tizard & Rees, 1975), these more recent adoption studies have attempted to look at the long-term outcomes once the child has been removed from the orphanage and adopted into a family.

Researchers have found that institutionalized children have significant difficulties in various domains of functioning, including attachment, as well as cognitive, behavioral, and emotional problems (Johnson, 2000). For example, institutionalized children have been shown to exhibit difficulty establishing selective attachments with caregivers and show a range of negative affect from sadness to excessive worry, autistic-like features such as self-stimulatory behavior, cognitive delays, inattention and hyperactivity, peer difficulties, and conduct problems (Chisholm, 1998; Gunnar, Bruce, & Grotevant, 2000). However, the majority of these children showed significant improvement in these domains when reexamined two years post-adoption (Rutter, 1998). As would be expected, the persistence of these difficulties correlated positively with the amount of time that the child had spent in institutional care. Institutionalization remains a significant risk factor for the persistence of a variety of socio-emotional problems, despite the fact that the majority of these children ultimately achieve normal functioning.

It should be stressed that the above remarks pertain to internationally adopted children who had spent time in an institution. Indeed, recent studies demonstrate that overall, internationally adopted children do not present with more significant behavioral health problems than children who were adopted domestically. There is actually some evidence to suggest that these children may have fewer problems than those adopted domestically (Juffer

& van IJzendoorn, 2005). This evidence needs to be understood within the context of studies looking at the general population of adopted children here in the United States, which do point to the fact that adopted children are overrepresented in both outpatient and inpatient mental health settings (Brodzinsky, 1993). However, studies looking at the differential rate of learning and socio-emotional problems in community samples of adopted and non-adopted children show only modest increases for the adopted population, suggesting more of a differential referral pattern for adopted children to mental health services (Warren, 1992).

Families who are considering adopting children from other countries should plan and prepare to seek treatment for the potential cognitive and mental health issues these children may have. While love and caring alone may not be able to erase the influences of adverse genetics and experiences, they do enable adoptive parents to be sensitive to a child's needs and prompt them to seek realistic ways to help the child. The alternative, denial and minimization of problems at the outset, can lead to strained family relations and stress if the child's initial problems do not abate with time (Cohen, 2005). What at first might be tolerated may in time take a negative toll on the entire family.

For families thinking about an international adoption, an important place to start is to explore the various countries that are potential sources of children who are free for adoption and then to develop a working knowledge of the various situations that have made those infants and children potential candidates for adoption. Are these children usually available for adoption because they have been abandoned or their parents have died, or have they been abused or neglected? What are the customary ways that the culture deals with such children? Are these children usually cared for by relatives or forced to live on the streets, or are they placed in institutions? Are there particular institutions in which most children are placed? What are the conditions and practices in these places? What is known and shared with prospective adoptive parents about a particular child's background and experience? Answers to these questions can give adoptive parents a better understanding of the risk factors that a child and family may face.

Once a particular country is identified, becoming familiar with attitudes and customs regarding child rearing can help adoptive parents plan their child's transition from one culture to another. It can help to obtain information about the child's usual diet, feeding practices or meal time customs, behavior management, and toilet training practices. Once a child is selected for adoption, learning as much as possible about the child's most recent environment and experiences can be helpful for developing routines in the home that will support a smooth transition. For example, rocking the child as part of a bedtime routine may be important to incorporate into the new routine if this was an important part of the child's caretaking experience in the native country.

Intercountry Adoption Support Services and Resources

A number of organizations and resources offer information pertinent to health care issues that often arise in intercountry adoptions. The Immunization Action Coalition provides information on immunization issues specifically of interest to health care professionals working with families created through intercountry adoption. Another resource is Jane Aronson's Orphan Doctor Web site, which has helpful information about adoption and medical resources. Dr. Aronson is the director of International Pediatric Health Services and has helped thousands of parents with health evaluations of children adopted from abroad. ComeUnity's Web site on international adoption health and medicine provides information about the various ailments that may be found in children adopted from other countries, a directory of adoption medicine clinics, and information on health-related international travel issues. The Centers for Disease Control and Prevention is an excellent and reliable source of information on traveler's health issues that is particularly useful to parents planning a trip abroad to bring their child home. The American Academy of Pediatrics Section on Adoption and Foster Care is another useful Web site that provides information to improve the health outcomes of children who have been adopted and children in foster care. In addition to links to resources such as the American Academy of Pediatrics' recommendations for children's health care, it offers a directory of pediatricians who work with children in foster care, as well as a directory of pediatricians who work with children who were adopted. As its name suggests, Families with Children from China is a support network for families who have adopted children from China. Members share information they have learned on a variety of topics through efforts to strengthen their families. Their Web site provides links to information specifically about adoption from China, as well as some general adoption resources. Contact information for these organizations can be found in Selected Resources.

Conclusion

Adoption is a process, not an event. A family evolves and develops from the point of welcoming its newest member onward as the child matures into adulthood and independence. As children develop, their understanding of and feelings about their experiences change and evolve, becoming more complicated. What it might mean to be adopted at age three is different from it will be at age eight or thirteen or twenty. Family members' first impressions upon meeting and welcoming the child will surely evolve as they watch the child grow into adulthood. While problems can surely crop up at any point in this process, the joys are sure to be many and heartfelt. The reflections in the final chapter are intended as guidance throughout the entire journey, not just for the initial phase of adjustment.

Chapter 8

After Adoption

Parents can prepare for their child's homecoming and the post-adoption period by coordinating necessary paperwork and services and preparing the other members of the family for the arrival of their new relative. In domestic public and private adoptions, prior to the finalized adoption, adoptive parents should obtain the child's original birth certificate. This is important for passport applications and other documents. The child also needs a Social Security number, either new or with change of name. After the finalization process, a new birth certificate reflecting the child's new status is also issued.

Children who are adopted are automatically covered under their parents' health insurance. Group health insurance carriers are required by law to provide the child with insurance coverage under the parents' policy and cannot deny a child insurance coverage based on any preexisting conditions. Parents should contact the policy administrator within thirty days of placement to enroll the child and acquire an insurance identification number and card for the child. In addition, parents should identify any local services that will help them care for the child, such as day care, counseling, tutoring, and respite care. Parents may want to contact parent groups that can support their transition to being an adoptive family.

Preparing other family members for the arrival of a new child and allowing time for a transition period for everyone are essential steps for the new parents to take. Anytime someone new joins a family, regardless of whether it is through birth or adoption, there is an adjustment period for all members. Siblings of children being adopted need to understand how their roles may change when their new brother or sister arrives. Open acknowledgement of both their excitement and their anxiety can help prepare siblings for the arrival of the new family member. Children should be given basic information about adoption and how a new child in the family will affect their lives. Concrete examples of how life will be different with another child in the family can help children understand these changes. A child's understanding of events is contingent on his or her development; thus, the younger the child, the more basic the information that parents share should be. As children grow older and develop abstract thinking abilities, parents can provide more details about the adoption.

Being an Adoptive Family

Diverse families are more common in the United States today than ever before. Families are a result of relationships and can take many forms, some of which are legally sanctioned, while others are not. Adoptive families are unique in that they often represent multiple levels of diversity and can highlight the role of relationships versus biology, the normative developmental paths of children and families regardless of biological connections, and expanded definitions of what makes a family.

Families in which there are obvious indicators of nonbirth relationships may draw the attention of others. Families with children who appear racially different from their parents are usually assumed by outsiders to be adoptive families. Adoptive families need to be aware of this and prepare to talk about adoption with their children, including what information to share and when it is most appropriate to share specific details of their adoption story. Appreciating how children understand adoption throughout the stages of their development is critical when parents talk about adoption with their children (Brodzinsky, Singer, & Braff, 1984; Watkins & Fisher, 1993). This enables parents to honestly and appropriately incorporate adoption-relevant information into conversations. It also supports children's curiosity and desire for information about their adoption story, and it helps them understand the relevance of their adoption.

Children's Development and Understanding of Adoption

Children who were adopted go through the typical developmental trajectory experienced by any child. All children experience a variety of events as they develop. Therefore, there is no one developmental path for all children. However, the pre-placement experiences of children who were adopted, as well as their racial, ethnic, and cultural heritage, may add complexity to their lives. As is typical of all children's development, their interactions with family members, members of the community, and peers may also influence their development.

It is important to remember that there is room for tremendous variation in each individual's experience. Some children are powerfully affected by their adoption experience at different points of their lives, while others may seem unaffected. Moreover, each individual's adoption experience may pose different developmental challenges. For example, children adopted at older ages may face more issues related to attachment. Children from other countries may experience language-related delays. Children adopted transracially or transculturally may have more challenges related to identity development. As a result of earlier life experiences, many children who have experienced foster care have developmental lags. Because each of these experiences has a different impact on children depending on their chronological, physical, and emotional age, it can be helpful for parents to understand how adoption may affect their children's development, and how children may come to understand the meaning of adoption for their own lives.

Infancy to Four Years Old

Newborns' sensory, perceptual, social, emotional, and cognitive abilities, although initially limited, provide the primary seeds for the development of more complex skills, which are normally seen by the end of the first year of life. Even at birth, infants have patterns of behavior that allow them to respond to and engage with their environments in organized and useful ways. During infancy, emotional ties or attachments between infants and caregivers are formed (Bowlby, 1969). Relationships with caregivers and others develop during the first year and continue to evolve well beyond the toddler stage. Almost all infants develop an attachment; blind children, developmentally delayed children, physically disabled children, and even abused children become attached to a caregiver or set of caregivers (Cicchetti & Beeghly, 1990; Cicchetti, Toth, & Lynch, 1995; Sroufe, 1995). However, when there is no opportunity for enduring or ongoing interactions with a primary caregiver, there may be failure to form an attachment with others. This can be the situation for children who are institutionalized for extensive periods of time (Chisholm, 1998; Tizard & Rees, 1975).

While infants explore the world physically, toddlers become capable of exploring the world mentally. A toddler's rapid development of symbolic representation (ideas, images) leads to the development of language. Language is one of the most important accomplishments for children at this age, along with the ability to pretend, use gestures, and understand iconic symbols. Typically, infants and toddlers adopted internationally have experienced an entirely different language and culture in their country of origin. Initially, achieving social engagement with their new parents may be difficult because the child may need time to adjust to new and different sensory and social input. Frequently with intercountry adoption of older children, substantial time is needed to allow the child to learn a new language and cultural practices. This may result in delays in a child's language and social skills beyond the normative timetables. However, with the proper social support and guidance, most of these children eventually catch up to their peers (Glennen, 2002).

Following the toddler stage, preschool children between the ages of two-and-a-half and five years old have some cognitive limitations, such as difficulty integrating multiple pieces of information and distinguishing between appearance and reality. Children at this age are not able to understand the connection between birth and heredity (Johnson & Solomon, 1997). This is also a time during which children become increasingly aware of their own experiences versus those of others. Young children who were adopted often believe that all children were adopted. Many preschool children who were adopted share their story of adoption with others. Although they are quite adept at telling their story, children at this age really do not have a substantive understanding of what adoption really means (Brodzinsky et al., 1984).

Five to Seven Years Old

Around the age of five, children begin to develop the ability to recognize different perspectives, and they are able to understand that other people may have different points of view (Piaget, 1929/1990). During these years, children's self-esteem becomes more organized, and they develop a heightened self-awareness, which eventually leads to self-evaluation. Children become increasingly aware of others and often make comparisons between themselves and others. These comparisons influence their self-evaluation and, ultimately, their self-esteem. They also are able to distinguish traits they may share with biological parents (e.g., having green eyes) from those they share with adoptive parents (e.g., being funny) (Johnson & Solomon, 1997; Terwogt, Stegge, & Rieffe, 2003). Five- to seven-year-old children begin to have a broader range of social experience. They have multiple interactions with new peers. They may recognize that there are differences between their adoptive family and the birth families of their friends. Children in this age group may also begin to understand that in order for them to have been adopted, there had to be someone who could not parent them. They may perceive this as a loss.

Five- to seven-year-olds may also experience many different feelings and emotions about adoption and may be confused about these new feelings. They may need to be reassured that their feelings are normal. This is a good time for them to be able to meet and interact with other children who were also adopted through adoption support networks or other organizations. It is also important that children's school experiences reinforce positive feelings about how adoption fits into everyday life.

Eight to Eleven Years Old

At approximately eight years of age, children develop a concept of their overall worth as a person. Their self-image begins to solidify and they resist changes that may disturb their self-understanding (Harter, 2006). Cognitively, they have the ability to seek out common attributes and organize them into some type of classification system (Piaget, 1929/1990). This ability to classify enables children to begin to understand how they are like or unlike their peers. Beginning at this age, children become able to focus on several aspects of a problem at once and also are able to relate those aspects simultaneously. During these years, children seek peer acceptance and develop friendships based on mutual traits and interests (Hartup, 1992). Children also begin to comprehend how people are similar and different and are able to accept and reject differences.

By age eleven, children's friendships are becoming more stable. Friends are perceived as people who support one another, even when they have different points of view. Friendships are often based on trust and on how reliable the other individual is perceived to be. Cognitively, children at this age begin to move beyond concrete thinking (i.e., they develop the ability to go beyond what they can perceive just through their senses) to be able to think hypothetically, multidimensionally, and with an orientation toward the future (Piaget, 1929/1990).

Children in this age group have an increased capacity to conceptualize the events in their lives. Some children may begin to wonder if they have birth siblings. They may daydream or fantasize about their birth family. They also understand more clearly that they were either voluntarily placed by their birth parents or removed involuntarily from their parents' care. This is a time when children want very much to fit in and be just like everyone else. They do not want to be different in any way. For children who were adopted, and in particular those who were transracially or transculturally adopted, this can be a difficult time. Adoption can make them feel different, and feeling different may affect their behavior.

Adolescence

Adolescence is a time of rapid change for children, when major physical, cognitive, and socio-emotional changes occur. During this life stage, children must endure biological changes, attempt to grapple with and resolve identity issues, struggle with dependence versus independence, contemplate changes in parent-adolescent relationships, have an intense need for privacy, and often idealize others. Adolescence is a time for significant cognitive changes as well. The way that adolescents think about the world is qualitatively different from how children in middle childhood do so. For example, adolescents are able to engage in abstract thinking (e.g., employ propositional and relativistic thinking), emphasize and understand the possible versus the real, and make use of scientific reasoning when approaching conceptual problems.

Usually adolescence is a time for exploration. It can be a period during which children experiment with identity, sexuality, and alcohol and drug use, as well as a time to test the boundaries set by their parents. During these years, children may find heroes or other people to idealize. This may help them understand how to develop personal goals and recognize what the skills needed to achieve them are. It is also during these years that adolescents begin to date and experience and express feelings of intimacy, often leading to further exploration of sexuality and sexual behaviors.

Finally, a major challenge for adolescents is their need for emancipation from their families. At the same time, they also seek new ways to build connections with their families. Adolescents become increasingly dependent on their peers for social support and advice. It is usually peers who act as an adolescent's sounding board, helping him or her grapple with present and future identities.

All children go through enormous physical and emotional changes during adolescence. They may spend hours in front of the mirror trying to figure out who they are and who they look like. For teenagers who were adopted, this period of their lives can take on increased intensity. Do they identify with their adoptive parents, whom they know and love, but with whom they often struggle? Or do they identify with the birth parents they frequently do not know and with whom they may or may not have contact? How can they explore who they really are as they develop their identities? It can be a difficult time for both the child and the family as the child tries to understand who he or she is and struggles to develop a sense of mastery regarding his or her emergent identity. During adolescence, the issue of searching comes up for some people. It may not necessarily be a search for birth parents or birth family. It may be a search for information. Fundamentally, it is a search for oneself (Brodzinsky, Schechter, & Henig, 1992).

At times, adoption can seem like the most significant aspect of a child's existence. At other times, it may appear to fade into the background. It is always wise to sit back, particularly at times of crisis or upheaval, and be mindful that developmental issues affect all children. Some issues with which children struggle may relate to adoption, while others may not. Taking a broad view and examining all aspects of a child's life can usually shed some light on what appears to be but may not in actuality be a cloudy situation.

Searching

Children who were adopted ordinarily develop strong bonds with their adoptive parents, such that the parent is truly the child's psychological parent and there is no question in the child's mind that his or her adoptive parents truly care with no hesitations or reservations. Still, as children who were adopted mature, they may feel a need to search for connections with or information about their birth families. This is not a rejection of the adoptive family. It is far more likely an indication that the child is interested in finding out more about him- or herself. Because searching is such a common part of the adoption experience, it should not be a source of anxiety for members of the adoptive family. Likewise, it should not be a source of shame or anxiety for the child who was adopted. Many states and private organizations have created adoption registry or reunion registry lists for people who were adopted or who made adoption plans for a child or children. By enrolling in one or more adoption registries, the person who was adopted, the birth parents, or other members of the birth family can indicate an interest in making contact with birth family members. The information provided to the registry is then used to match people who were adopted with members of their birth families. One type of adoption registry is the active adoption registry, which does not require that both parties register and consent to contact. When one party registers, a registry administrator contacts the individual for whom the search is being conducted and requests his or her consent to release contact information. The passive adoption registry requires that both parties consent to the release of information by registering with the adoption registry. A registry administrator then attempts to match individuals and notifies parties if a match has been made. A quick search on the Internet reveals that there are many hundreds of adoption registries operating across the United States.

Talking to Children about Adoption

Open communication about adoption is essential in adoptive families. Discussing adoption as a way to create families, in addition to discussing the specifics about a child's own adoption experience, is very important. Even if children do not raise the topic, it is important for parents to discuss adoption. Children may construe a parent's failure to discuss adoption as disinterest, or as evidence that it is an unimportant topic or that there are feelings of shame related to their adoption—even if this is not true from the parent's perspective. In some instances, the discussion may arise as a result of a comment made by someone inside or outside the family, a school experience, or exposure to media outlets. The most effective way to discuss adoption with children depends on the child's developmental stage based on his or her experiences, not on his or her chronological age (Brodzinsky et al., 1984).

There are typical cognitive, emotional, and social stages of development. However, some children's experiences can result in development that does not follow a typical trajectory. Thus, when discussing adoption with a child, people should consider the child's cognitive limitations to determine what information and level of detail to share.

Those who adopt infants have an excellent opportunity to begin sharing their child's adoption story with them immediately. Beginning to tell the story early may help parents become more comfortable with the subject over time. Regardless of the age of a child at adoption, parents should begin to share their adoption story right away so they can incorporate it into an ongoing and developing narrative. Sharing the story with very young infants allows parents to become comfortable with the concepts of birth parents and adoption. In the process of sharing these stories, parents should reflect on their own feelings about the child's birth parents, their path to adoption, and their family. Genuine and open communication about adoption helps children constructively incorporate their adoption experience into their sense of self as they grow up.

Parents need not set aside specific times or occasions to talk to their children about adoption. As with other sensitive but important topics, parents should allow them to emerge naturally. Characters or themes in books, television, and movies and interactions with other people regarding adoption may all provide opportunities to talk about adoption in general or a child's adoption in more specific detail. Discussion can be casual and can vary in length; depending on the child's current level of interest and understanding, it may involve more in-depth or explicit explanations of circumstances. As a general guideline for talking about adoption with children, parents should begin by being open to exploring the topic as it arises, understanding the child's ability to comprehend aspects of the experience, reflecting on their own beliefs and feelings, and being honest about not knowing the answers to some questions. In situations where parents do not know how to respond to a child's question, they can suggest that the parents and child learn together. In some cases where children have difficult histories, it may be too complicated for the parent to respond appropriately. Learning from trained and experienced professionals, and speaking to other parents about strategies for answering difficult questions, is always recommended. Professionals who work with parents in these situations are wise to prepare to respond to parents' questions about how to talk with their children about adoption.

Developing an adoption memory book or life book to tell a family's adoption story, with details of the family's journey through their child's adoption process, can be a good way for parents to organize the story and have a guide to share with children. For older children and children adopted from other countries, memory books are a good way to capture images of their personal and family histories and provide a time line of the series of events that comprise their personal narratives. These can also be helpful as parents begin to add more details to the adoption story as the child grows older. For instance, very young children are not cognitively able to make the connection between reproduction and birth, so explaining an unplanned pregnancy or other details of their conception can be confusing and may lead to misunderstandings about birth and their biological connections to other people. Children's literature about adoption offers different perspectives for their readers' consideration. These books can become part of a child's book collection and can be read anytime the child chooses. They can be useful tools to convey positive messages about adoption as a way to be a family. Parents can share their child's stories and parts of their adoption by relating them to the experiences of the characters in the stories. Some popular children's books about adoption are

- *Zachary's New Home: A Story for Foster and Adopted Children* by Geraldine M. Blomquist and Paul B. Blomquist
- *Allison* by Allen Say
- *Over the Moon: An Adoption Tale* by Karen Katz
- *My Family Is Forever* by Nancy Carlson
- *Rosie's Family: An Adoption Story* by Lori Rosove
- *Tell Me Again about the Night I Was Born* by Jamie Lee Curtis
- *The Day We Met You* by Phoebe Koehler
- *Jin Woo* by Eve Bunting

Post-adoption Support and Services

While finalization is the end of the adoption process in terms of the legal sanction of a parent-child relationship, it is also the beginning of the rewards and challenges of being a family. Adoption affects a person and family for a lifetime. Families created through adoption may experience unique challenges and rewards specifically related to adoption. A child's genetic predisposition and prenatal and pre-adoption history can be relevant factors in his or her behavioral adjustment and socio-emotional and cognitive development (Stams, Juffer, Rispens, & Hoksbergen, 2000). Children who have experienced foster care, early deprivation, or multiple traumas may need ongoing services throughout their development. Post-adoption services provide families and children with periodic or ongoing support and are offered through private and public adoption agencies or organizations. Services such as support groups, search and reunion services, therapy, respite care, crisis intervention, camps for children with similar backgrounds, advocacy, birth land tours, emergency assistance, newsletters, educational programs, resource centers and libraries, and information and service referral are offered to birth families, adoptive parents, children, and siblings (Mack, 2006).

Children adopted from public foster care who are identified as having special needs often receive a subsidy to help their families care for them. In addition to financial aid, families should also have access to post-adoption support services. The need for post-adoption services may increase over time as the child and family experience developmental changes and challenges. Research suggests that post-adoption support is highly correlated with family health and stability (Avery, 2004; Groze, 1996). Services that help families develop skills and coping strategies can also help them understand the impact of certain experiences on children and family functioning and make families feel supported.

Post-adoption supports include an array of services designed to aid families throughout their development. Prior to adoptive placement, parents can identify local post-adoption services or referral programs. Families often find formal and informal contact with other adoptive families useful for learning about services that may be available in their area. Information about available services, supports, and resources; parent education tailored for the child's needs; respite care and babysitting; mental health specialists; educational and mental health advocacy; educational assessment and special education services; and multicultural forums may all be helpful to families with children who were adopted (Freundlich & Wright, 2003). The most common services available and accessed by families are support groups and counseling, which offer families an opportunity to meet others who share their experiences and to seek the assistance of experienced professionals (Mack, 2006).

Funding sources for post-adoption supports vary greatly and can affect a family's ability to access services (Avery, 2004). The types of services and financial assistance available to families also vary tremendously throughout the United States. Support groups and other meetings are usually free or require a minimal fee for adoptive parents. Mental health and other related services may be completely or partially covered by parents' private insurance plans or Medicaid. Private adoption agencies may offer services for a fee based on a family's income level. At the federal level, the Children's Bureau provides two major funding sources for post-adoption supports: Promoting Safe and Stable Families, which is part of Title IV-B of the Social Security Act, and Adoption Opportunity Grants. In addition, public and private agencies can obtain grants from foundations with a particular focus on post-adoption programs and other government funding, such as TANF, adoption incentive grants, Medicaid, and state mental health funding (Mack, 2006).

Working with Schools and Teachers

Teachers and parents are the most influential people in children's lives. They spend one-on-one time with children on a daily basis and lay the foundations for children's lives. It is essential that parents and teachers work together to ensure that children have a positive school experience. Acknowledgement of circumstances related to both adoption and foster care have a place in the classroom, and parents must make decisions about how to protect their child's privacy while sharing relevant information with teachers. Parents can be in an important position to model appropriate language, share relevant resources, and offer their personal perspectives on issues regarding their children. Parents can discuss which aspects of their child's adoption history or foster care experience they are willing to share with their child's teachers with the child present or in the child's absence.

Often teachers and other educators do not receive professional training around issues concerning adoption and foster care. School curricula and assignments that focus on families are generally designed to reflect traditional two-parent heterosexual families. Parents can talk with teachers to explore how acceptance of diversity is practiced in their classroom and curriculum. Visual displays, activities, assignments, and discussions should be representative and respectful of a variety of families, cultures, careers, leisure activities, and lifestyles. Parents can offer teachers suggestions of children's and young adult literature that portrays adoption in a positive light and as an acceptable way to create a family. Discussion of adoption in the classroom broadens children's definitions of family and challenges traditional conceptions of both what it means to be a family and how families can be formed. All children can benefit from teachers and schools having inclusive practices and curricula.

When a child begins school or transfers to a new school as the result of an adoption placement or grade change, parents should meet with teachers to share important information about their child's history or experience. Teachers should not expect parents to provide all the details of a child's experience, just those that will be relevant in the classroom. If a child has knowledge of his or her birth parents and openly shares that information with others, parents will want to make the teacher aware that this may happen. Parents should also be willing to share information about the type of connection the child has with the birth parents. Parents can share how they discuss adoption in their family as it relates to the child's birth parents. When children have been adopted from other countries, it is important that teachers understand what kind of knowledge the child has about the country so that he or she is not expected to be able to teach others about that country. Parents can ask children what information they would like teachers and others to know and then share their child's response with the teacher. Parents will want to help children respond appropriately to questions about their birth country in particular and adoption in general.

When parents meet with teachers to discuss classroom practices and curricula, they can explore how inclusive teachers are of all children in the class. First, parents can ask teachers about the typical assignments they require of children throughout the school year. They can find out what the intended goal of each assignment is and explore alternative ways to meet the goals if an assignment is not inclusive of children from different backgrounds or family structures. Teachers should reconsider assignments that require children to reveal private information about their family life or personal history.

Teachers should be willing to provide parents with a list of activities and assignments for the year, or they can offer to notify parents in advance of assignments related to personal information or family history. These practices give parents an opportunity to talk to their child about challenges that the assignment may present and then let teachers know that the assignment may present those challenges for their child. Teachers need to be aware that a child may act out, withdraw, become angry or upset, or otherwise react to the assignment during class or may avoid doing the assignment altogether. If a teacher is aware of how a particular assignment could affect a child, he or she can alter the assignment to allow all children to choose how to complete it. Teachers should not prepare special assignments for children with nontraditional families, since that causes children to feel singled out and different. Instead, teachers should offer assignments that have been designed to be expansive and inclusive of all children. Teachers can provide alternative assignments that all children can feel comfortable completing while still meeting the goals of the curriculum.

Families with children who were adopted or who care for children in foster care can work with teachers to help them create opportunities for choice in most assignments by becoming familiar with books and Web sites that are particularly helpful, sharing resource information with teachers who express interest in learning more, sharing a list of well-known people who were adopted or who experienced foster care with the child or the child's teacher, suggesting alternative assignments that still meet curriculum goals, identifying appropriate books to share with the child's classroom or school library, and offering teachers suggestions for classroom bulletin boards or community resources.

Adoptive families have identified several hot spots in school curricula that can be difficult for children from nontraditional families or with certain histories. These include baby picture activities; personal writing assignments; study of children's families (i.e., family tree exercises), immigration, and genetics; and sex education. All of these topics are important elements of a good education. However, there are alternatives to the way these topics are typically covered in American schools that can still meet the intended curriculum goals.

Baby Pictures

Baby picture activities allow children to observe change and guess which baby picture depicts which of their classmates. This activity can be a challenge for children who were adopted or who live in foster care. Some children from adoptive and foster families may not have pictures of themselves as babies. Often, older children who were adopted internationally do not have any traditional baby pictures because they have spent their early years in an orphanage or foster home. Sometimes children in foster care have moved several times since infancy and do not have any personal photographs.

As alternatives to the baby picture activity, teachers can have children collect pictures of baby animals and grown animals and create a collage of before-and-after images or introduce children to the metamorphosis cycle of caterpillars and butterflies. Children can also study the seasons to explore changes in weather, trees, and plants.

Personal Writing Assignments

Writing from personal experience is an important academic exercise. It allows students to develop important writing skills and offers an opportunity for self-reflection. However, some writing assignments can pose a challenge for children who were adopted or who live in foster care, especially autobiographies and those concerning the child's first memories. For these children such assignments may be quite difficult, and even distressing. Children who were adopted have varying degrees of information about their birth families. Even those children who have a good deal of information may still not be able to articulate the intense emotions related to that information and may not be willing or ready to share that information or their feelings with others. Therefore, assignments that require that children share this kind of information may cause distress for students and interfere with their learning. Children who experienced foster care also have histories that may not be easy to share with others. They have often had multiple caregivers during their placements and have various types of relationships with their birth families. Being asked to share that private information may be too stressful, complicated, and uncomfortable. In order to prevent discomfort, teachers can allow students to choose from a list of components to incorporate into their personal essays. For memory essays, children should be allowed to write about their happiest, funniest, or silliest memories, or their future goals and what they would like to be when they are adults. It can also be a good exercise for students to write a biography of someone they know or someone famous who has had a similar life experience.

Study of Family

The study of the family tree has a long history in American schools. This assignment, the goal of which is to trace one's heritage and family connections, can create uneasiness for children who have nontraditional family configurations. Children who were adopted may feel confused about how to incorporate their birth families and their adoptive families into one family tree. Children who have experienced foster care may feel defensive about their family and about tracing their family's history. Family-related assignments may make children who were adopted, or who have experienced foster care, feel markedly different from their classmates. Sharing their family differences with the class may create distress for these children. For these types of assignments, parents can suggest alternative ways for children to show the connections to important people in their lives, such as letting young elementary students choose how they would like to construct their family picture, and giving several options of how to depict family. For example, children might draw the traditional family tree with roots representing the birth family, or they may make adoption gardens with different flowers to represent the diversity in their family. Other possibilities include drawing a family forest, where each tree represents a different family member, or creating a diagram of the VIPs—very important people—in the child's life. Yet another option is for the student to trace the family tree of a celebrity or other well-known family.

Study of Immigration

Assignments related to the study of immigration can be a challenge for children who were adopted from another country. Many children adopted from other countries have limited information about, or firsthand experiences with, the cultural traditions in their country of origin. It can be tempting for a teacher to call on a child from another country to share information about that country with the class. Children who were adopted from another country may be sensitive about discussing immigration and the culture of their birth country, especially if they do not have a lot of information or know it well enough to share. They may feel pressured to know certain details about their country of origin. If they do not possess that information, the pressure may make them feel inadequate and affect their feelings of self-worth. It is a good idea for teachers to discuss how much a child knows about his or her birth country with the child's parents before asking him or her to share something about the country of origin. Taking a field trip to attend a naturalization ceremony can be a valuable and perhaps even more educational experience for students that can help them understand immigration to the United States. Having students study the history of Ellis Island and trace a family known to have gone through Ellis Island can be a meaningful way to study immigration as well.

Study of Genetics

Assignments that require children to trace a particular trait through their family may not respect the variety of ways families can be created. Children who were adopted have a difficult time tracing genetic links between themselves and their parents and grandparents. Children who have experienced foster care may not have any contact with their birth family and may feel uneasy or be unable to do so when asked to recall inherited family traits. When they are unable to trace genetic traits, they may feel singled out and different from their peers. These situations may prompt questions from others that children are not willing or prepared to answer.

Instead of requiring children to trace their own traits, teachers can have students study Mendel's work with pea plants and use Punnett squares of animal or plant traits to explain how genes and traits are passed down from parent to offspring (Dunn, 2003). Children can examine how animals from the same species are alike or different. In general, assignments concerning genetics should avoid requiring students to trace a personal characteristic or trait. Having students debate the social, legal, or ethical issues related to genetic engineering (e.g., plants, food) or cloning may be a good alternative as well. Older students can learn about the Human Genome Project and its implications for research and medicine.

Sex Education

Sex education is a part of all school curricula. While topics related to sexual reproduction and sexuality can make all children uncomfortable, this may be especially true for children who were adopted. These topics may cause these children to reflect on their own birth stories. It can also raise issues related to infertility, which may be a sensitive matter for children who were adopted, as their parents may have experienced it. Teachers and school personnel should be aware of the issues that sex education may raise for some students and be prepared to deal with the emotional response these students may experience. Parents should receive advanced notice of the general topic and specific information to be shared with students. This can help them support their children as they deal with any emotions that arise.

While there may be other curriculum areas that are difficult for children with traumatic histories and those from nontraditional families, parents can practice open communication with their child's teacher and school professionals. Checking in with teachers and children can help families work through uncomfortable school experiences. A partnership between parents and teachers is critical to a student's success and feelings of worth. The more respectful school curricula are of nontraditional and diverse families, the more children will flourish in school.

Multicultural Adoptive Families

Parents can support their children's adoptive and multicultural identities by being open to exploring cultural aspects of their identities with them, providing children with opportunities to experience other cultures by integrating traditions and other cultural activities into everyday routines, and not setting priorities or expectations around country-of-origin activities for children (e.g., it may not be advisable to insist that children attend culture camp every summer or that the family attend every festival related to the child's country of origin). Children should have opportunities to find out more about life in the country from which they were adopted when they feel ready, which often depends on their previous developmental experiences. Children may enjoy learning about a culture that is different from the one from which they were adopted. They may feel uncomfortable when they find themselves in a situation with older people of their ethnic background and cannot understand the language or do not react the way those adults, or even other children, expect them to. It is helpful for parents to begin by exploring their own cultural histories and their understanding of and feelings about other cultures. Then they should learn some basic information about their child's culture of origin and seek to expand their knowledge, along with that of their child. In the same way that children's understanding of adoption changes at different developmental stages, children have different conceptions of culture and its importance in their lives as they mature. Incorporating culture into family practice should be an ongoing process.

Connecting children with others who have also experienced adoption allows them to understand that many families are formed through adoption. Adoptive families can belong to groups composed of families with children adopted from a similar culture of origin. This has a twofold benefit: children have an opportunity to experience their birth culture with others who share it, and parents can connect with other parents who share similar experiences. These opportunities to interact with others allow children and families to develop social connections without feeling the need to explain their family or personal history.

Children in multicultural adoptive families have two components to their cultural identity: their birth culture and the adoptive family's cultures. Celebrating cultural holidays is one way to teach children about their birth heritage, but making the effort to weave parts of a child's culture of origin into everyday life through meals, books, fictional characters, toys, and games that reflect their cultural background is even more beneficial. Of course, parents should also celebrate traditions of their family's heritage, highlight cultural traditions in everyday routines, and encourage respect for different cultures. Children should be proud of who they are and all the components of their identity.

Parents can help children develop their identities by discussing ways to describe who they are and preparing them to respond to inappropriate or intrusive questions from others. Parents can help children respond to these questions by discussing their right to privacy and acknowledging that the child's experiences of adoption are not secrets or something to be ashamed of but are things that they have the option to share if they choose to. Talking about a family's diversity in addition to what unites them as a family can help children see that the basis for all families is love and commitment to care for and support each other. Children benefit from parents who model positive actions and language. Exposure to mature, honest, and carefully considered responses to criticism of their family, racism, prejudice, and the narrow-mindedness of others can help children grow up to be compassionate and considerate of family and individual differences. Parents cannot control the actions of others, but their own actions can speak powerfully as they both support their children and model appropriate behavior.

Some families celebrate both the child's birthday and the day the family was joined through adoption, which can be referred to by a name of the family's choosing, such as Adoption Day, Gotcha Day, Family Day, or Adoption Anniversary Day. Families have quite a few options regarding which event they choose to celebrate. It might be the first time they met their child, the day their child was placed with them, the day they all arrived home together, or the day the adoption was finalized in court. The main idea is to make a point of celebrating how their family came to be. This can provide children with a sense of pride about their family structure. Families can work to support each other by acknowledging that adoption is a normal and wonderful way to create or expand a family, and that multiple cultures are part of their identities. Birth children living in adoptive families should also be included in any discussions relating to adoption and their family. They too will be confronted by others who question their family and the connections among its members.

With or without warning, issues of adoption and culture can surface from time to time. At times, these issues may be at the forefront of the child's experiences and thus may be a major topic of family discussions, while at other times they will seem so minor that it may appear that they have been forgotten. Being willing to talk about adoption at home or to seek professional help if it is needed is never inappropriate. Appreciating the place of adoption in one's family is part of an overall healthy development.

Special Education Services: The Individuals with Disabilities Education Act

Regardless of whether they live with their birth parents or have been adopted, all children have unique developmental and educational needs. Children who were adopted sometimes have experienced challenges during their pre-adoptive histories that affect their developmental and educational needs and strengths. This means that children who were adopted often have greater developmental and educational needs and more need for support. It is important for parents to be aware of the variety of services and resources that are available for children and how to access those resources. In the United States, the Individuals with Disabilities Education Act (IDEA), which was most recently amended in 2004, protects children's rights to a free and appropriate public education in the least restrictive environment. Adoptive parents and their children are afforded all the rights and privileges identified in IDEA, regardless of how they were adopted. There are two sections of IDEA that are important for all parents to know about. Part C protects the rights of children from birth up to their third birthday, and Part B protects children's rights beginning at age three and remains in effect until they reach the age of twenty-one. Part C addresses early intervention, which is a federal entitlement implemented under the Individuals with Disabilities Education Act, according to which all children under the age of three are eligible for a free multidisciplinary assessment to determine eligibility for intervention services. Children who have experienced foster care or who were adopted domestically or internationally are eligible for and may benefit from assessment and intervention for developmental delays. Early intervention is a set of multi-disciplinary services provided to families of children from birth to the child's third birthday. Parents may request an assessment if they have any concerns or questions about their child's development, and a professional evaluation may provide reassurance to adoptive parents. Referrals for assessment and early intervention services may also be made by a physician, family friend, or professional (e.g., the child's preschool teacher). It is often difficult for parents to determine on their own if a child's physical, emotional, social, and cognitive development are within the lines of what is considered typical development. Babies develop at their own pace and according to their own individual temperament, so there is a broad range of competency within the spectrum of developmental norms, which makes a professional assessment extremely valuable. Assessments evaluate children's developmental abilities, determine whether children are eligible for particular early intervention services, identify children who need further and more specialized evaluation, and monitor children's progress. If a child is found eligible for early intervention services, an Individual Family Service Plan is developed. The Individual Family Service Plan identifies what services will be provided and with what frequency, the location and duration of sessions, and specific developmental goals and objectives that families can strive to achieve to optimize their child's development. Early intervention services are delivered by a multidisciplinary team of professionals who work in partnership with parents and families. These teams include speech and language pathologists, physical therapists, occupational therapists, educators, developmental specialists, social workers, and nurses. In keeping with IDEA's requirement to provide services to children in the least restrictive environment, early intervention services are delivered in natural environments for babies and toddlers such as at the child's home or preschool, a child care center, a library, a local park, or a favorite play space. The early years are critical to a young child's physical, cognitive, communicative, social, and emotional development. Early intervention can help young children with special needs develop to their fullest potential. It is important to remember that because young children spend the majority of their time with family members or other caregivers, interactions with people with whom the child is familiar and places in which he or she is comfortable provide many opportunities for learning and for support of a child's development.

Each state establishes its own eligibility criteria and its own definition of what constitutes a developmental delay. In some states, services are free. In others there are co-payments or participation fees. Generally the majority of the cost is covered by health insurance. In most states there are no service fees for children in foster care. Parents and professionals who have concerns about a child's development should contact the managing agency for early intervention in their state (see Appendix P) to find the appropriate early intervention program in the town or municipality where the child lives.

Part B of IDEA addresses the educational needs of children three to twenty-one years of age. Parents have the right to request an evaluation for special education or related services for their child at any point during their child's education. Such requests can be directed to the director of special education in the child's school system. For children who are enrolled in early intervention prior to their third birthday, a referral can be made to the lead education agency by early intervention staff if educational services are deemed necessary. The lead education agency is typically the local public school. Even if early intervention does not place a referral, a parent may request that a child be evaluated by the school. It is best to make requests for evaluation in writing so that there is a record of the date of the request, as schools are required to respond to the parent's request within a specified number of days. It is the school's responsibility to notify parents when it plans to evaluate a child or make any changes to a child's educational plan, or if it denies a parent's request for either an evaluation or a request for change of services. Parents must provide written informed consent for their child's educational evaluation or any programming decisions. The school is responsible for providing parents with written information regarding the evaluation schedule and the names of the personnel who will evaluate the child. If parents do not agree with the school's evaluation results, they have the right to obtain an independent educational evaluation, which can be conducted by qualified professionals who are not employed by the school system. Parents may request that the school system pay for the independent educational evaluation before it is conducted. Laws vary from state to state regarding reimbursement if a request is made after the independent educational evaluation is conducted. The education evaluation examines the child's current school performance and overall development, as well as how the child's disability affects his or her ability to learn. The school must reevaluate the child's educational needs at least once every three years, and the child's education programming must be reviewed at least once each calendar year. Children must be tested in the language they know best, and deaf children have the right to an interpreter during testing. It should be noted that children adopted through intercountry adoption, who may be most familiar with another language, are frequently evaluated in English if they will be participating in an English-language educational environment so that their educational needs in an English-language environment can be assessed. An Individualized Education Plan (IEP) must be prepared for any child who is identified as needing special educational services. The IEP provides a statement of the child's academic, social, behavioral, and physical status; expectations; and goals. In addition, the IEP explains what services will be provided for a child and identifies and determines modifications to, or exemptions from, state or district testing requirements. The IEP also details when services will begin, the location where services will be provided, how often the child will receive the services, how long each session will last, and the length of time for which services will be provided. Transitional services that will be necessary to prepare the child when he or she reaches the age at which he or she will transition to the next educational level are also outlined in the IEP. Parents have the right to and should actively participate in the development of and any necessary modifications to their child's IEP, and they are entitled to be kept informed of their child's progress. The school must make every effort to notify parents of meetings regarding the IEP; they should be scheduled at times that are convenient for parents. In addition, parents have the right to review all of their children's school records and to receive copies of the records for a reasonable clerical cost. If they find that the information in the record is misleading or inaccurate, parents may request a hearing to challenge the information or to file a complaint with the state education agency. It is advisable for parents to try to be positive when advocating for their child. Strength-based, positive communication between parents and school personnel can lead to a more effective IEP that fits the child's development and educational needs.

Conclusion

Adoption has been part of society for thousands of years. In the United States this practice began to receive legal recognition during the nineteenth century, and multidisciplinary teams and practices have evolved over time to support the children and parents involved. Adoption is a complex process that involves the coordination of professionals and lay people within the guidelines and procedures defined by state, federal, and international law.

The complexities of the process require that the members of the adoption team understand their roles and those of other team members. The best interests of the child should be the primary focus for all involved. It is critical that both the professionals involved in the adoption process and those who work with children and families understand the legal and historical aspects of adoption, as well as the importance of using appropriate language to describe the various characteristics of child adoption. Beyond this, having an understanding of the social, educational, physical, and mental health considerations that must be taken for those who are part of adoptive families enhances professional interactions. Children, parents, and families can benefit from working with informed professionals who are sensitive to the unique aspects of adoption and issues typical of child development. Parents who are well informed about the adoption process as well as the features common to adoptive families will have the knowledge to seek the most appropriate resources and properly educate those working with their children and families to garner the support necessary to be a successful family.

Appendix A

State Laws regarding Access to Original Birth Records

Alabama	An adult age nineteen or older who was adopted in Alabama and has a sealed original birth certificate on file at the Center for Health Statistics may obtain a non-certified copy of that certificate as well as the other documents maintained with the original record.
Alaska	Birth certificates are available to adopted individuals eighteen years old or older upon request.
Arizona	An adopted person must petition the court in which the adoption was finalized.
Arkansas	An adopted person must petition the court in which the adoption was finalized.
California	An adopted person must petition the court in which the adoption was finalized. An adopted person over the age of twenty-one may request a copy of his or her original birth certificate.
Colorado	• For adoptions finalized after September 1, 1999, an adopted person eighteen or older automatically has access to original birth records unless a birth parent files a confidentiality request within three years of relinquishment. • If an adopted person is part of an adopted sibling group, all members of the sibling group must be eighteen before records can be released. • If a confidentiality request is on file, the parties can still use a confidential intermediary process that allows the party seeking contact to request that a confidential intermediary contact the other party to ask if he or she will consider some sort of contact and/or release of the original birth records. • For adoptions finalized prior to September 1, 1999, birth parents and people who were adopted can have access to original birth records by mutual consent. Confidential intermediaries are able to secure the release of adoption records to mutually consenting parties. If a birth parent or child who is being sought is deceased, records are made available to the searching party.
Connecticut	An adopted person must petition the court in which the adoption was finalized.
Delaware	An adopted person age twenty-one or older can obtain his or her original birth certificate if, during the previous three years, the birth parents have not filed a written notarized statement with the Department of Health and Social Services Office of Vital Statistics forbidding the release of identifying information.
District of Columbia	An adopted person must petition the court in which the adoption was finalized.

Florida	An adopted person must petition the court in which the adoption was finalized.
Georgia	An adopted person must petition the court in which the adoption was finalized.
Hawaii	An adopted person must petition the court in which the adoption was finalized.
Idaho	An adopted person must petition the court in which the adoption was finalized. Birth parents and an adopted adult can request a copy after being reunited by the registry.
Illinois	An adopted person may receive his or her original birth certificate through the adoption registry or petition the court in which the adoption was finalized.
Indiana	An adopted person must petition the court in which the adoption was finalized.
Iowa	An adopted person must petition the court in which the adoption was finalized.
Kansas	The original birth certificate may be opened by the state registrar only upon the demand of the adopted adult or by a court order.
Kentucky	An adopted person must petition the court in which the adoption was finalized.
Louisiana	An adopted person must petition the court in which the adoption was finalized.
Maine	At present, an adopted person must petition the court in which the adoption was finalized. Commencing on January 1, 2009, anyone over age eighteen will have access to his or her original birth certificate. Birth parents may elect to request no contact.
Maryland	• An adopted person must petition the court in which the adoption was finalized if the adoption was finalized after July 1, 1947, and before January 1, 2000. • For adoptions finalized after January 1, 2000, adopted individuals age twenty-one or older can receive their original birth certificate and report of the decree or judgment of adoption. If the birth parents have filed a disclosure veto, all identifying information will be deleted. Birth parents of an adopted individual age twenty-one or older can receive a copy of the altered birth certificate and report of the decree or judgment of adoption. If the adopted adult files a disclosure veto, all identifying information is deleted. • For adoptions finalized before July 1, 1947, an adopted individual may receive the original birth certificate.
Massachusetts	• An adopted person eighteen years of age or older who was born in Massachusetts on or before July 17, 1974, or on or after January 1, 2008, can receive an uncertified copy of his or her birth record. However, these individuals must petition the courts for access to their original birth records. • An adoptive parent of an adopted person under eighteen years of age and born in Massachusetts on or after January 1, 2008, may obtain a copy (uncertified) of the adopted person's original birth record.

Michigan	• If parental rights were terminated prior to May 28, 1945, or after September 12, 1980, an adopted adult may receive a copy of the original birth certificate if there is no denial statement on file. • If parental rights were terminated between May 28, 1945, and September 12, 1980, an adopted adult must petition the court in which the adoption was finalized.
Minnesota	• An adopted adult can request a copy of the original birth certificate. Upon this request, the Commissioner of Human Services attempts to locate the birth parents to obtain consent to release the original birth certificate. If each birth parent is located and consents are given, the original birth certificate is released. • If there is no reply or contact with the birth parents, adopted adults adopted before August 1, 1977, must petition the court for release of the original birth certificate. • If the adoption was finalized on or after August 1, 1977, then the original birth certificate will be released to the adopted adult if the birth parents have not filed an access veto.
Mississippi	An adopted adult may receive the original birth certificate if the birth parents file an affidavit of consent.
Missouri	An adopted person must petition the court in which the adoption was finalized.
Montana	• For adoptions that took place on or before July 1, 1967, an adopted adult can receive a copy of the birth certificate by written request. • For adoptions that took place between July 1, 1967, and September 30, 1997, an adopted adult can receive a copy of the birth certificate upon a court order. • For adoptions that took place on or after October 1, 1997, an adopted adult can receive a copy of the birth certificate unless the birth parents have filed an access veto.
Nebraska	• Adults who were adopted on or after September 1, 1988, can receive a copy of the original birth certificate, medical records on file, and information about agency assistance in searching, unless a birth parent has filed a non-consent form. • Adults who were adopted before September 1, 1988, upon written request to the court, can receive identifying information and a copy of the original birth certificate if both birth parents have consented.
Nevada	An adopted person must petition the court in which the adoption was finalized.
New Hampshire	As of January 1, 2005, adopted individuals age eighteen and older who were born in New Hampshire have unrestricted access to their original birth certificates upon request from the Division of Vital Records Administration, Health & Welfare Building, 29 Hazen Drive, Concord, NH 03301. Individuals can call 603-271-4650 or 800-852-3345 ext. 4651 or go to the Web site of the New Hampshire Division of Vital Records Administration to request this information. There is a $12 application fee (which applies whether or not the birth certificate can be located).
New Jersey	An adopted person must petition the court in which the adoption was finalized.

New Mexico	An adopted person must petition the court in which the adoption was finalized.
New York	An adopted person must petition the court in which the adoption was finalized.
North Carolina	An adopted person must petition the court in which the adoption was finalized.
North Dakota	An adopted person must petition the court in which the adoption was finalized.
Ohio	• An adopted adult can receive his or her birth certificate through the Ohio Department of Health if the adoption was finalized before January 1, 1964. • Unless a photocopy of the vital records book is requested, the adopted adult receives only a computer-generated abstract of birth and death certificates as well as marriage and divorce documents. These computer-generated documents do not include all the information that the vital records book does. • Documents in the sealed adoption file usually include a copy of the original birth certificate and the adoption decree. • Adopted adults who wish to receive their birth certificate should file an Affidavit of Adoption, which can be downloaded or obtained from the Ohio Department of Health/Vital Statistics, and send $20 to the Ohio Department of Health/Vital Statistics, 35 East Chestnut Street, P.O. Box 15098, Columbus, OH 43215-0098, Attn: Special Registrations.
Oklahoma	An adopted person must petition the court in which the adoption was finalized.
Oregon	Adopted individuals age twenty-one and older have access to the original birth certificate. Birth parents may file a contact preference form.
Pennsylvania	Adopted adults can receive the information on the certificate if the birth parents file consent.
Rhode Island	An adopted person must petition the court in which the adoption was finalized.
South Carolina	An adopted person must petition the court in which the adoption was finalized.
South Dakota	An adopted person must petition the court in which the adoption was finalized.
Tennessee	• Adopted individuals age twenty-one or older, birth parents, adoptive parents, stepparents or legal parents, and birth siblings age twenty-one or older can receive a copy of the adoption records, which include the original birth certificate. • No contact shall be attempted in any manner with any of the individuals eligible to file a contact veto. The Contact Veto Registry was established by the Department of Children's Services for the purpose of permitting registration of individuals' willingness or unwillingness to be contacted by individuals who seek contact with them. All parties must go through this registry before contacting the subject of the search.
Texas	• To obtain a non-certified copy of the original birth certificate, an adopted person must provide the name of each parent listed on the original birth certificate, be at least eighteen years old, submit a copy of a valid photo ID issued by a government entity, and provide other legal documentation

(e.g., copies of official supplementary birth certificate based on the adoption, marriage certificate, divorce decree, or court-ordered name change if name has changed due to marriage or other legal reasons).
* Individuals should complete the Application for Non-certified Copy of Original Birth Certificate form and mail it and a $10 check or money order payable to DSHS to the Department of State Health Services Texas Vital Statistics, P.O. Box 12040, Austin, TX 78711-2040. Requests for non-certified copies of original birth certificates take six to eight weeks to process.

Utah	An adopted person must petition the court in which the adoption was finalized.
Vermont	The birth certificate can be obtained by an adopted adult if he or she has received identifying information through the registry.
Virginia	An adopted person must petition the court in which the adoption was finalized.
Washington	Birth parents can receive a photocopy of the original birth certificate for a fee of $15. An adopted individual age eighteen or older can receive the birth certificate if the adoption was finalized after October 1, 1993, and neither birth parent has filed an affidavit of non-disclosure.
West Virginia	An adopted person must petition the court in which the adoption was finalized.
Wisconsin	An adopted individual age twenty-one or older may receive the original birth certificate if the birth parents have filed consent.
Wyoming	An adopted person must petition the court in which the adoption was finalized.

Appendix B

State Agencies Responsible for Adoption from Foster Care

State	Agency
Alabama	Alabama Department of Human Resources Families 4 Alabama's Kids–Become a Foster/Adoptive Parent Phone: 866-425-5437 Web site: http://www.dhr.state.al.us/page.asp?pageid=308
Alaska	Alaska Office of Children's Services Northern region: 907-451-2650 Anchorage region: 907-269-3900 South Central region: 907-486-6174 Southeast region: 907-465-3235 Web site: http://www.hss.state.ak.us/OCS/Adoptions/default.htm
Arizona	Arizona Department of Economic Security Division of Children, Youth and Families–Foster Care & Adoption Phone: 877-KIDS-NEEDU Web site: http://www.azdes.gov/dcyf/adoption/
Arkansas	Arkansas Department of Health & Human Services Phone: 501-682-8462 or 888-736-2820 Web site: http://www.arkansas.gov/dhhs/sgChildren.html
California	California Department of Social Services Department of Child and Family Services Web site: http://www.dss.cahwnet.gov/cfsweb/CFSDAdopti_309.htm http://www.dss.cahwnet.gov/cdssweb/default.htm
Colorado	Colorado Department of Human Services Adoption recruitment line: 866-229-7605 http://www.cdhs.state.co.us/ http://www.changealifeforever.org/index.asp
Connecticut	Connecticut Department of Children and Families 505 Hudson Street Hartford, CT 06106 Phone: 860-550-6300 or 888-KID-HERO E-mail: KidHero@cafap.com Web site: http://www.ct.gov/dcf/site/default.asp
Delaware	Delaware Department of Services for Children, Youth and Their Families 1825 Faulkland Road Wilmington, DE 19805 Phone: 302-633-2655 E-mail: adoption.dscyf@state.de.us Web site: http://www.state.de.us/kids/information/adoption.shtml

District of Columbia	District of Columbia Child and Family Services Agency 400 Sixth Street, SW Washington, DC 20024 Phone: 202-442-6000 Web site: http://www.cfsa.dc.gov/cfsa/site/default.asp
Florida	Florida Department of Children and Families Phone: 800-96-ADOPT or 904-353-0679 (out of Florida) Web site: http://www.dcf.state.fl.us/adoption/
Georgia	Georgia Department of Human Resources, Division of Family & Children Services, Adoption Services Phone: 404-657-3550 Web site: http://tinyurl.com/qcz4y
Hawaii	Hawaii Department of Human Services Statewide adoption recruitment line: 808-441-0999 Intake phone: 808-441-1117 Main phone: 808-441-1115 or 888-879-8970 Fax: 808-441-1122 Web site: http://hawaii.gov/dhs/protection/social_services/child_welfare/Foster
Idaho	Idaho Department of Health and Welfare 450 West State Street, Fifth Floor P.O. Box 83720 Boise, ID 83720-0036 Phone: 800-926-2588 E-mail: careline@dhw.idaho.gov Web site: http://www.healthandwelfare.idaho.gov/site/3334/default.aspx
Illinois	Illinois Department of Children and Family Services Chicago Headquarters — 100 West Randolph Street 6-200 — Chicago, IL 60601 — Phone: 312-814-6800 — TTD: 312-814-8783 — Adoption hotline: 800-572-2390 Springfield Headquarters — 406 East Monroe — Springfield, IL 62701-1498 — Phone: 217-785-2509 — TTD: 217-785-6605 Web site: http://www.state.il.us/dcfs/adoption/index.shtml
Indiana	Indiana Department of Child Services Indiana Adoption Program, c/o IFCAA 509 East National Avenue, Suite A Indianapolis, IN 46227 Phone: 888-252-3678 E-mail: adoption@iquest.net Fax: 317-524-2609 Web site: http://www.ifcaa.org/ Web site: http://www.in.gov/dcs/adoption
Iowa	Iowa Department of Human Services Web site: http://tinyurl.com/25wrw5
Kansas	Kansas Department of Social and Rehabilitation Services Children and Family Services Phone: 877-530-5275 Web site: http://tinyurl.com/245my5

State	Agency
Kentucky	Kentucky Cabinet for Health and Family Services Division of Protection and Permanency/Adoption Services Branch 275 East Main Street, 3 E-A Frankfort, KY 40621 Phone: 502-564-6852 or 800-232-5437 Fax: 502-564-4653 Web site: http://chfs.ky.gov/dcbs/dpp/adoptionservices.htm
Louisiana	Louisiana Department of Social Services 627 North Fourth Street Baton Rouge, LA 70802 Phone: 225-342-0286 Fax: 225-342-8636 Web site: http://www.dss.state.la.us/departments/ocs/Adoption_Services.html Office of Community Services Regional Offices: http://www.dss.state.la.us/departments/ocs/OCS_Regions_Directory.html
Maine	Maine Department of Health and Human Services http://www.maine.gov/dhhs/children.shtml#adoption A Family for ME P.O. Box 754 Gardiner, ME 04345 Phone: 877-505-0545 Web site: http://www.afamilyforme.org/
Maryland	Maryland Department of Human Resources/Social Services Administration Phone: 800-39-ADOPT Web site: http://www.dhr.state.md.us/ssa/adoption/alladopt/adopt.htm
Massachusetts	Massachusetts Department of Social Services Attention: Adoption Support Services 24 Farnsworth Street Boston, MA 02210 Phone: 617-748-2000 or 800-548-4802 Adoption and foster care: 800-KIDS-508 or 800-543-7508 Web site: http://tinyurl.com/2nu9m5
Michigan	Michigan Department of Human Services Web site: http://www.michigan.gov/dhs/0,1607,7-124-5452_7116—,00.html
Minnesota	Minnesota Department of Human Services, Children's Services Human Services Building 444 Lafayette Road North St. Paul, MN 55155-3831 Phone: 651-296-3740 Adoption recruitment line: 866-665-4378 Fax: 651-297-1949 Web site: http://www.dhs.state.mn.us/childint/programs/Adoption/default.htm
Mississippi	Mississippi Department of Human Services Division of Family and Children's Services Mississippi Adoption Resource Exchange Phone: 800-821-9157 or 601-359-4989 Web site: http://www.mdhs.state.ms.us/fcs_adoptall.html

Missouri	Missouri Department of Social Services
	Division of Family Services
	Adoption Specialist
	P.O. Box 88
	Jefferson City, MO 65103
	Phone: 573-751-0311
	Adoption recruitment line: 800-554-2222
	Fax: 573-526-3971
	Web site: http://www.dss.mo.gov/cd/adopt.htm
Montana	Montana Department of Health and Human Services
	Child and Family Services Division
	Cogswell Building
	1400 Broadway
	P.O. Box 8005
	Helena, MT 59604-8005
	Phone: 406-444-5900
	Fax: 406-444-5956
	E-mail: Child&FamilyServicesDiv@mt.gov
	Web site: http://www.dphhs.mt.gov/cfsd/adoption/adoptioninmontana.shtml
Nebraska	Nebraska Department of Health and Human Services
	P.O. Box 95044
	Lincoln, NE 68509-5044
	Phone: 402-471-2306 or 800-772-7368
	Web site: http://www.hhs.state.ne.us/adoption
Nevada	Nevada Division of Child & Family Services
	4126 Technology Way, Third Floor
	Carson City, NV 89706
	Phone: 775-684-4400
	Fax: 775-684-4455
	Web site: http://www.dcfs.state.nv.us/DCFS_Adoption.htm
New Hampshire	New Hampshire Department of Health and Human Services
	Division for Children, Youth & Families
	Foster Care and Adoption Programs
	129 Pleasant Street
	Concord, NH 03301-3857
	Phone: 603-271-4711 or 800-852-3345
	Web site: http://www.dhhs.state.nh.us/DHHS/FCADOPTION/default.htm
New Jersey	State of New Jersey Department of Human Services
	Department of Children and Families
	Phone: 877-99-ADOPT
	Web site: http://www.state.nj.us/dcf/adoption/
New Mexico	New Mexico Children, Youth, & Families Department
	P.O. Drawer 5160
	1120 Paseo De Peralta, Room 226A
	Santa Fe, NM 87502-5160
	Web site: http://www.cyfd.org/adopt.htm

State	Agency
New York	Division of Development and Prevention Services Office of Children and Family Services New York State Adoption Service 52 Washington Street, Room 323 North Rensselaer, NY 12144 Phone: 518-474-9406 or 800-345-5437 Web site: http://www.ocfs.state.ny.us/adopt/
North Carolina	NC Department of Health and Human Services Division of Social Services Phone: 877-NCKIDS-1 Web site: http://www.dhhs.state.nc.us/dss/adopt/
North Dakota	North Dakota Department of Human Services 600 East Boulevard Avenue, Dept 325 Bismarck, ND 58505-0250 Phone: 701-328-2310 or 800-472-2622 TTY: 701-328-3480 Fax: 701-328-2359 E-mail: dhseo@nd.gov Web site: http://www.nd.gov/dhs/services/childfamily/adoption
Ohio	Ohio Department of Job and Family Services, Bureau of Family Services 255 East Main Street, Third Floor Columbus, OH 43215-5222 Phone: 614-466-9274 or 800-755-4769 Web site: http://jfs.ohio.gov/oapl/
Oklahoma	Oklahoma Department of Human Services, Children and Family Services Division: Adoption Services 6128 East Thirty-eighth Street, Suite 300 Tulsa, OK 74135-5814 Phone: 918-794-7544 or 918-794-7575 Foster care and adoption families recruiting hotline: 866-242-9088 Fax: 918-794-7582 or 918-794-7585 Web site: http://www.okdhs.org/programsandservices/adopt/
Oregon	Oregon Department of Human Services Adoption Assistance Unit 500 Summer Street NE E62 Salem, OR 97301-1067 Phone: 503-945-5651 TTY: 503-945-5896 Fax: 503-373-7032 E-mail: dhs.info@state.or.us Web site: http://www.oregon.gov/DHS/children/adoption/
Pennsylvania	Pennsylvania Department of Social Services Children's Services Statewide Adoption Network P.O. Box 2675 Harrisburg, PA 17105-2675 Phone: 800-585-SWAN Web site: http://www.dpw.state.pa.us/ServicesPrograms/ChildWelfare/003676622.htm

Rhode Island	Rhode Island Department of Children Youth and Families Adoption and Foster Care Preparation and Support 101 Friendship Street Providence, RI 02903 Web site: http://www.dcyf.state.ri.us/adoption.php
South Carolina	South Carolina Department of Social Services P.O. Box 1520 Columbia, SC 29202-1520 Phone: 803-898-7318 or 888-227-3487 Web site: http://www.state.sc.us/dss/adoption/index.html
South Dakota	South Dakota Department of Social Services Child Protection Services 700 Governors Drive Pierre, SD 57501 Phone: 605-773-3227 Sioux Falls area: 605-334-3431 Rapid City area: 605-343-2598 Fax: 605-773-6834 E-mail: CPS@state.sd.us Web site: http://dss.sd.gov/adoption
Tennessee	Tennessee Department of Children's Services Central Office Cordell Hull Building, Seventh Floor 436 Sixth Avenue North Nashville, TN 37243-1290 Phone: 877-327-5437 Web site: http://www.state.tn.us/youth/adoption.htm
Texas	Texas Department of Family and Protective Services 701 West Fifty-first Street Austin, TX 78751 Phone: 800-233-3405 Web site: http://www.dfps.state.tx.us/Child_Protection/services.asp
Utah	Utah Department of Human Services, Child and Family Services Adoption Program Utah's Adoption Connection Child & Family Services 302 West 5400 South, Suite 108 Murray, UT 84107 Phone: 801-265-0444 Web site: http://www.hsdcfs.utah.gov/adoption.htm
Vermont	Vermont Department for Children and Families Project Family 103 South Main Street Waterbury, VT 05671-2401 Phone: 802-241-2780 (in Waterbury) or 800-746-7000 Web site: http://www.projectfamilyvt.org
Virginia	Virginia Department of Social Services 7 North Eighth Street Richmond, VA 23219 Adoption hotline: 800-DO-ADOPT E-mail: dhscfs@state.nd.us Web site: http://www.dss.virginia.gov/family/ap/index.html

State	Agency
Washington	Washington State Department of Social & Health Services Children's Administration Foster Parent/Adoptive Parenting Information: 1-800-760-5340 Web site: http://www.dshs.wa.gov/ca/adopt/index.asp
West Virginia	West Virginia Department of Health and Human Resources Bureau for Children and Families 350 Capitol Street Charleston, WV 25301 Phone: 304-558-0628 Web site: http://www.wvdhhr.org/oss/adoption/
Wisconsin	Wisconsin Department of Health & Family Services 1 West Wilson Street Madison, WI 53703 Phone: 608-266-1865 TTY: 608-267-7371 E-mail: webmaildcfs@dhfs.state.wi.us Web site: http://dhfs.wisconsin.gov/children/adoption/
Wyoming	Wyoming Department of Family Services 130 Hobbs Avenue Cheyenne, WY 82009 Phone: 307-777-3570 Fax: 307-777-3693 Web site: http://dfsweb.state.wy.us/adoption.html

Appendix C

American Academy of Adoption Attorneys Code of Ethics

In order to further the cause of the ethical adoption, the members of the American Academy of Adoption Attorneys hereby make and establish this CODE OF ETHICS. Each member of the Academy agrees as follows:

1. A member shall be duly licensed to practice law in each state in which the member maintains a law office, shall fully comply with the Ethical Rules, Disciplinary Rules, Ethical Canons, or other Rules of Professional Conduct in effect in each state in which the member maintains an office, and shall maintain the highest standards of professional and ethical conduct. A member shall not engage in activities which bring discredit upon the Academy.

2. (a) A member shall assure that the member's clients are aware of their legal rights and obligations in the adoption, and that all parties to the adoption are aware of their right to separate legal counsel.

   (b) A member may inform a client as to the member's understanding of the laws of a jurisdiction in which the member is not licensed provided that the member discloses that the member is not licensed to practice in that jurisdiction.

3. A member shall not purport to represent both the prospective adopting parent(s) and one or both birth parents, where such representation is specifically prohibited. This rule shall not preclude a member from undertaking such representation of multiple parties if the member desires to challenge the statutes, court rules or case law of that jurisdiction, provided that the member has fully disclosed such intent and risks incident thereto in writing to each party to the adoption and has obtained the written consent of each party.

4. A member shall actively discourage adoption fraud or misrepresentation, and shall not engage in such conduct, and shall take all reasonable measures not inconsistent with the confidentiality of the attorney/client relationship, to prevent adoption fraud or misrepresentation, withdrawing from representation where necessary to avoid participation in any such conduct.

5. (a) A member shall assure that clients to an adoption are aware of any laws which govern permissible financial assistance to a birth parents.

   (b) A member shall not assist or cooperate in any adoption in which the member has reason to believe that the birth parent or parents are being paid, or given anything of value, in exchange for the placement for adoption, for the consent to an adoption, for a relinquishment for adoption, or for cooperation with the adoption of his or her child, without first making full disclosure to the appropriate court. This rule does not make it improper for a member to assist or cooperate with an adoption in which the birth parent or parents are reimbursed for reasonable and necessary pregnancy-related expenses actually incurred by the birth parent, or in which such expenses are paid directly on behalf of the birth parent, provided that such payment or reimbursement is allowed under the law of the affected jurisdiction.

   (c) A member shall comply with such standards regarding birth parent expenses as are, from time to time, established by the Academy or by its Board of Trustees.

6. A member shall assure that the member's fee arrangement with each client is carefully explained and fully understood by the client at the time the member accepts employment by an adoption client, and the fee agreement shall be in writing, wherever practicable.

7. A member shall not enter into an agreement for, charge, or collect an illegal or unconscionable fee. Advanced fees collected by a member shall be returned to the client if not commensurate with the services that have been provided by the member. A member shall not, directly or indirectly, charge a finder's fee for locating a birth parent. In determining whether a fee is unconscionable, the factors to be considered shall include, but not be limited to, the following:
   (a) The amount of the fee in proportion to the value of the services performed;
   (b) The novelty and difficulty of the questions involved and the skill requisite to perform the legal services properly;
   (c) The time limitations imposed by the client or by the circumstances;
   (d) The time and labor required; and
   (e) The experience, reputation and ability of the member performing the services.

8. A member shall not possess a financial stake in the success of any adoption in which the member is retained as counsel for any party. A member shall be considered to have a financial stake in an adoption if the member enters into a fee agreement by which the member is to receive a greater fee for a successful adoption than is warranted based upon the reasonable value of the services performed by the member; or if the member enters into a fee agreement in which the member is contractually entitled to a lesser fee than the reasonable value of the services performed by the member if the attempted adoption is unsuccessful.

9. A member shall disburse client trust funds only for those purposes specifically authorized by the client, and the member shall not exercise independent judgment or discretion over trust funds disbursements unless the client has specifically authorized the exercise and scope of such discretion. A member shall promptly account for all client funds held by the member, upon request by the client, and shall promptly reimburse to the client all client funds upon request by the client or upon completion of the case.

10. A member shall not make false or misleading claims in advertisements, nor shall a member include client testimonials in such advertising. A member shall not advertise in a manner which is unprofessional or which bring the adoption bar into disrepute. A member shall comply with those guidelines regarding advertising as, from time to time, may be established by the Academy or by its Board of Trustees.

11. (a) A member shall extend every possible professional courtesy to other members, and to the clients of other members. If a member is offered employment in an adoption where a birth parent has previously consulted with another member, the member shall forthwith contact the other member to confer regarding the matter. If a birth parent has previously consulted with another member, and has received financial assistance from the other member or clients represented by the other member, the member shall endeavor, if possible, to secure reimbursement of the financial assistance to the person(s) who provided same, from the prospective adopting parent(s) represented by the member, so long as the reimbursement represents legally permissible and reasonable expenses.
   (b) A member shall not induce or encourage a birth parent to change attorney representation unless the member is aware that the original attorney is not knowledgeable in the field of adoption law. A member shall not induce or encourage a birth parent to change selection of prospective adopting parents unless the member knows or has reason to believe that the proposed adopting parents can not obtain court approval of a placement with them.

12. A member shall not enter into any agreement with any person which would have the effect of restricting the member's ability to exercise independent professional judgment on behalf of the member's clients.

13. A member may, when appropriate and/or when requested by a client, refer parties to competent and professional medical providers, legal counsel, psychological counselors, or adoption agencies. A member shall avoid any appearance of impropriety and shall advise the parties of any family or professional relationship between the member and any other professional to whom the member may refer a party, including a doctor, hospital, counselor or birth coach. A member shall fully disclose to the parties any financial benefit received by the member from any professional or organization or counselor to whom a party may be referred by a member, or any financial benefit bestowed by the member upon any other person or entity for referring a party to the member.
14. A member shall be under a duty to investigate representations made to the member by prospective birth parents and prospective adopting parents if the member believes or has reason to believe that such representation is false. Under all other circumstances, a member may ethically rely upon representations made by the parties to an adoption.

Source: American Academy of Adoption Attorneys. (n.d.). *Code of ethics: American Academy of Adoption Attorneys.* Retrieved March 13, 2008, from http://www.adoptionattorneys.org/information/ethics_code.htm

Appendix D

State Laws for Advertising, Age of Adoptive Parents, and Use of Facilitators

State	Advertising by prospective adoptive parents for birth parents allowed	Minimum age of adoptive parents	Use of facilitators permitted
Alabama	No	Eighteen	Yes
Alaska	Not specified in statute	Eighteen	Yes
Arizona	Not specified in statute	Eighteen	Yes
Arkansas	Not specified in statute	Eighteen	Yes
California	No	Eighteen and at least ten years older than child to be adopted	Yes
Colorado	Not specified in statute	Twenty-one	Yes
Connecticut	Yes	Eighteen	Yes
Delaware	No	Twenty-one	No
District of Columbia	Not specified in statute	Unspecified	No
Florida	No	Eighteen	Yes
Georgia	No	Twenty-five and at least ten years older than child to be adopted	No
Hawaii	Not specified in statute	Eighteen	Yes
Idaho	No	Twenty-five or at least fifteen years older than child to be adopted	Yes
Illinois	Not specified in statute	Eighteen	Yes
Indiana	Not specified in statute	Unspecified	Yes
Iowa	Not specified in statute	Eighteen	Yes
Kansas	No	Eighteen	No
Kentucky	No	Eighteen	No
Louisiana	No	Eighteen	Yes
Maine	No	Unspecified	Yes
Maryland	Not specified in statute	Eighteen	Yes
Massachusetts	No	Eighteen	No
Michigan	Not specified in statute	Unspecified	Yes

Minnesota	Not specified in statute	Unspecified	No
Mississippi	Not specified in statute	Eighteen	Yes
Missouri	Not specified in statute	Unspecified	Yes
Montana	No	Eighteen	No
Nebraska	No	Eighteen	No
Nevada	No	Eighteen and at least ten years older than child to be adopted	No
New Hampshire	No	Eighteen	Yes
New Jersey	Not specified in statute	Eighteen and at least ten years older than child to be adopted	Yes
New Mexico	Not specified in statute	Unspecified	No
New York	Not specified in statute	Eighteen	No
North Carolina	Yes, with approved home study	Eighteen	Yes
North Dakota	No	Eighteen	Yes
Ohio	No	Eighteen	No
Oklahoma	Yes, with approved home study	Twenty-one	No
Oregon	Yes, with approved home study	Unspecified	No
Pennsylvania	Not specified in statute	Unspecified	Yes
Rhode Island	Not specified in statute	Eighteen	Yes
South Carolina	Not specified in statute	Unspecified	Yes
South Dakota	Not specified in statute	Eighteen and at least ten years older than child to be adopted	Yes
Tennessee	Not specified in statute	Eighteen	Yes
Texas	No	Eighteen	Yes
Utah	No	Eighteen and at least ten years older than child to be adopted	Yes
Vermont	Not specified in statute	Unspecified	Yes
Virginia	No	Unspecified	Yes
Washington	Yes, with approved home study	Eighteen	Yes
West Virginia	Not specified in statute	Unspecified	Yes
Wisconsin	Yes, with approved home study	Eighteen	Yes
Wyoming	Not specified in statute	Eighteen	Yes

Time from Placement to Finalization by State

State	Time from Placement to Finalization	State	Time from Placement to Finalization
Alabama	Sixty days	Kentucky	Child must be in home with adoptive parents for at least ninety days before finalization petition can be filed.
Alaska	At least six months		
Arizona	At least six months		
Arkansas	At least six months		
California	At least six months		
Colorado	At least six months	Louisiana	The child must have lived with the adoptive parents for at least one year, and at least six months must elapse after the court grants a temporary decree of adoption before the adoptive parents may petition for a final decree of private adoption.
Connecticut	At least six months		
Delaware	At least six months		
District of Columbia	Six months		
Florida	At least ninety days		
Georgia	Uncontested adoption petitions should be heard no later than 120 days after the date of filing.		
Hawaii	At least six months	Maine	No more than eighteen months
Idaho	Not addressed in statutes reviewed; an adoption cannot be overturned by any court after six months has passed from the date the order of adoption became final.	Maryland	Consent is irrevocable after thirty days. Finalization can occur anytime after that thirty days.
		Massachusetts	Six months
		Michigan	Six months
Illinois	At least six months	Minnesota	No less than three months residence with adoptive parents required.
Indiana	The length of the period of supervision is up to the discretion of the court hearing the petition for adoption.		
		Mississippi	At least six months
Iowa	At least 180 days	Missouri	Six months
Kansas	Not addressed in statutes reviewed	Montana	Six months
		Nebraska	Six months

Nevada	Six months	Pennsylvania	At least six months
New Hampshire	Six months	Rhode Island	Six months
New Jersey	Six months	South Carolina	At least ninety days
New Mexico	Petition for adoption must be filed within 60 days of placement in adoptive home if child is less than one year of age, and within 120 days if child is more than one year of age.	South Dakota	Six months
		Tennessee	Six months
		Texas	Six months
		Utah	Six months
		Vermont	180 days
		Virginia	Six months
		Washington	Post-placement report is due to court within sixty days after placement/adoption petition is filed.
New York	Three months		
North Carolina	Three months		
North Dakota	Six months		
Ohio	At least six months	Wisconsin	Six months
Oklahoma	Six months	Wyoming	Six months
Oregon	Six months	West Virginia	Six months

Appendix F

States in Which Post-adoption Contact Agreements Are Legally Enforceable

State	Post-adoption contact agreements legally enforceable	State	Post-adoption contact agreements legally enforceable
Alabama	No	Montana	Yes
Alaska	No	Nebraska	Yes
Arizona	Yes	Nevada	Yes
Arkansas	No	New Hampshire	Yes
California	Yes	New Jersey	No
Colorado	No	New Mexico	Yes
Connecticut	Yes	New York	Yes
Delaware	No	North Carolina	No
District of Columbia	Not mentioned in statute	North Dakota	No
Florida	Yes	Ohio	No
Georgia	No	Oklahoma	Yes
Hawaii	No	Oregon	Yes
Idaho	No	Pennsylvania	No
Illinois	No	Rhode Island	Yes
Indiana	Yes, for children over two years old	South Carolina	No
Iowa	No	South Dakota	No
Kansas	No	Tennessee	No
Kentucky	No	Texas	Yes
Louisiana	Yes	Utah	No
Maine	No	Vermont	Yes (in stepparent adoptions only)
Maryland	Yes	Virginia	No
Massachusetts	Yes	Washington	Yes
Michigan	No	West Virginia	Yes
Minnesota	Yes	Wisconsin	No
Mississippi	No	Wyoming	No
Missouri	No		

Legality of Adoption by Same-Sex Couples by State

State	Allows gay or lesbian individuals to adopt	Allows co- or second-parent adoptions
Alabama	Yes	Yes (case law)
Alaska	Yes	Yes (case law)
Arizona	Yes	No
Arkansas	Yes	No
California	Yes	Yes
Colorado	Yes	Yes
Connecticut	Yes	Yes
Delaware	Yes	Yes (case law)
District of Columbia	Yes	Yes
Florida	No	No
Georgia	Yes	No
Hawaii	Yes	Yes (case law)
Idaho	Yes	No
Illinois	Yes	Yes
Indiana	Yes	Yes
Iowa	Yes	Yes (case law)
Kansas	Yes	No
Kentucky	Yes	No
Louisiana	Yes	Yes (case law)
Maine	Yes	No
Maryland	Yes	Yes (case law)
Massachusetts	Yes	Yes
Michigan	Yes	Yes (case law)
Minnesota	Yes	Yes (case law)
Mississippi	Yes	No
Missouri	Yes	No
Montana	Yes	No
Nebraska	Yes	No
Nevada	Yes	Yes (case law)
New Hampshire	Yes	Yes (case law)
New Jersey	Yes	Yes

State	Allows gay or lesbian individuals to adopt	Allows co- or second-parent adoptions
New Mexico	Yes	Yes (case law)
New York	Yes	Yes
North Carolina	Yes	No
North Dakota	Yes	No
Ohio	Yes	No
Oklahoma	Yes	No
Oregon	Yes	Yes (case law)
Pennsylvania	Yes	Yes
Rhode Island	Yes	Yes (case law)
South Carolina	Yes	No
South Dakota	Yes	No
Tennessee	Yes	No
Texas	Yes	Yes (case law)
Utah	Yes	No (and unmarried cohabitating adults cannot adopt)
Vermont	Yes	Yes
Virginia	Yes	No
Washington	Yes	Yes (case law)
West Virginia	Yes	No
Wisconsin	Yes	No
Wyoming	Yes	No

Appendix H   State Infant Safe Haven Laws, Part I

State law	Maximum age of child	Who may leave a baby at a safe haven	Safe haven providers	Provider immune from liability	Responsibilities of safe haven providers
Alabama Safe Harbor Law (2000)	Seventy-two hours old	Parent	Emergency medical service providers in licensed hospitals	Yes	Perform any act necessary to protect the child's health Notify the Department of Human Resources Offer free medical assistance to mothers May request information about the child from the relinquisher
Alaska Safe Surrender of Infants Act (2008)	Twenty-one days old	Parent	Peace officers, physicians and hospital employees, and volunteers and employees of fire stations and emergency medical services	Yes	Provide appropriate care for the child Inform the parent that he or she may, but is not required to, answer questions regarding the name or identity of the child or the parents Ask the parent if he or she wishes to relinquish parental rights and release the infant for adoption (if the answer is affirmative, the safe haven must contact the Office of Child Care Services so that the parent can discuss that option with a social worker)
Arizona Safe Haven (2001)	Seventy-two hours old	Parent or agent of parent	On-duty firefighters, emergency medical technicians, staff at health care institutions and private child welfare agencies, licensed adoption agencies, and churches	Yes	Notify Division of Children, Youth and Families as soon as practicable Offer written information about referral organizations to person relinquishing child Request information about the child from relinquisher (a questionnaire may be filled out on a voluntary basis by the person relinquishing the child)
Arkansas Safe Haven Act (2001)	Thirty days old	Parent or person designated by parent	Medical providers and law enforcement agencies	Yes	Perform any act necessary to protect the child's health Upon receipt of the child, take a seventy-two-hour hold of the child Immediately notify the Division of Children and Family Services of the Department of Human Services

Appendix H   State Infant Safe Haven Laws, Part I—(*Continued*)

State law	Maximum age of child	Who may leave a baby at a safe haven	Safe haven providers	Provider immune from liability	Responsibilities of safe haven providers
California Safely Surrendered Baby Law (2001)	Seventy-two hours old	Parent or other person with lawful custody	Public and private hospitals and any location designated by the county board of supervisors	Yes	Provide medical care Provide the parent with a medical questionnaire Place a coded identification ankle bracelet on the child and offer a matching bracelet to the parent Notify Department of Child and Family Services within forty-eight hours Request information about the child from the relinquisher
Colorado Safe Haven for Newborns (2000)	Seventy-two hours old	Parent	Firefighters at fire stations and hospital staff at hospitals	Yes	Perform any act necessary to protect the child's health Notify law enforcement and the county office of the Colorado Department of Human Services within twenty-four hours
Connecticut Safe Havens for Newborns Act (2000)	Thirty days old	Parent or lawful agent of parent	Anyone on nursing staff at hospital emergency rooms	N/A	Take custody of the child Request medical history (relinquisher is not obligated to answer) Request the name of the parent and medical information Notify the Department of Children and Families within twenty-four hours Offer a numbered identification bracelet that links the parent to the child and an information packet about DCF and families' rights

	Age	Who may relinquish	Where		Requirements
Delaware Safe Arms for Newborns Act (2001)	Fourteen days old	Anyone who voluntarily delivers the child unharmed	Hospital emergency departments	Yes	Take emergency protective custody Make reasonable efforts to obtain medical history Notify the state police and the Department of Children, Youth and Their Families Attempt to give the child's ID number to the person leaving the child as well as information about the Safe Arms program, adoption, and counseling services Provide the relinquisher with a mail-back medical questionnaire, as well as information about the Safe Arms for Newborns law and a brochure with a list of telephone numbers for public and private agencies that provide counseling and adoption services Request information about the child from relinquisher
District of Columbia	N/A	N/A	N/A	N/A	N/A
Florida Safe Haven for Newborns (2000)	Three days old	Parent	Hospitals, emergency medical service stations, and fire stations	Yes	Provide any needed medical care Contact the Department of Children and Families, or make a report if abuse or neglect is suspected
Georgia Safe Place for Newborns Act (2002)	One week old	Parent	Employees, agents, and other staff of any medical facility, including hospitals, infirmaries, health centers, and birth centers (does not include the private offices of physicians or dentists)	Yes	Accept the child for inpatient admission Notify the Department of Human Resources Request ID and proof of address from the person relinquishing the child

Appendix H   State Infant Safe Haven Laws, Part I—(Continued)

State law	Maximum age of child	Who may leave a baby at a safe haven	Safe haven providers	Provider immune from liability	Responsibilities of safe haven providers
Hawaii Safe Place for Newborns (2007)	Seventy-two hours old	Anyone	Hospitals, fire stations, and police stations	Yes	Collect written information concerning any known family medical history, including major illnesses and diseases Ask the person leaving the newborn child for information about the child's parents Inform the person that the information will be kept confidential May provide the relinquisher with information about how to contact relevant social service agencies Notify appropriate law enforcement agencies Perform any act necessary to protect the health or safety of the child Inform the Department of Human Services within twenty-four hours but after the relinquisher has left the premises that a newborn has been left
Idaho Safe Haven Act (2001)	Thirty days old	Custodial parent	Hospital physicians, staff nurses, midwives, physician's assistants, and emergency medical technicians	Yes	Perform any act necessary to protect the health and safety of the child Notify a peace officer Take temporary custody of the child

Illinois Abandoned Newborn Protection Act (2001)	Seventy-two hours old	Birth parent expressing no intent to return for the child	Hospitals, police stations, fire stations, and emergency medical facilities	Yes	Provide any necessary emergency and medical care Determine whether the child has been abused or neglected Take temporary custody of the child until custody is discharged to a child-placing agency or the Department of Children and Family Services Arrange transportation of the child to the nearest hospital if the child is not relinquished at a hospital Make a report to child protective services if the child is not relinquished at a hospital and it is suspected that the child has been abused Inform parent of the location of the child if he or she returns for the child within seventy-two hours Inform the relinquishing parent that by relinquishing the child anonymously, he or she will have to petition the court to prevent the termination of parental rights and regain custody of the child Offer relinquishing parent an information packet containing all Illinois Adoption Registry and Medical Information Exchange application forms and questionnaire; the Web site and toll-free phone number of the registry; and a resource list of providers of counseling services, including grief counseling, pregnancy counseling, and counseling regarding adoption and other options for placement of the child May request information about the child from the relinquisher
Indiana Baby Safe Haven (2000)	Forty-five days old	Anyone	Emergency medical service providers	N/A	Take custody of the child Perform any act necessary to protect the health and safety of the child Notify the Department of Child Services

Appendix H State Infant Safe Haven Laws, Part I—(*Continued*)

State law	Maximum age of child	Who may leave a baby at a safe haven	Safe haven providers	Provider immune from liability	Responsibilities of safe haven providers
Iowa Safe Haven Act (2001)	Fourteen days old	Parent or person authorized by parent	Institutional health facilities	Yes	Take custody of the child Perform any act necessary to protect the health and safety of the child May request information about the child from the relinquisher Notify the Human Services Child Welfare Department May ask for parent's name or medical information
Kansas Newborn Infant Protection Act (2000)	Forty-five days old	Parent or person with legal custody of the child	Fire stations, city and county health departments, and medical care facilities	Yes	Take custody of the child Perform any act necessary to protect the health and safety of the child Notify local law enforcement
Kentucky Safe Haven Act (2002)	Seventy-two hours old	Anyone	Emergency medical service providers, police officers, and firefighters	Yes	Provide medical care Attempt to gather health and medical information about the child Notify the Division of Protection and Permanency
Louisiana Safe Haven Relinquishment (2000)	Thirty days old	Parent	Designated emergency care facilities, including hospitals, public health units, emergency medical service providers, medical clinics, police stations, fire stations, pregnancy crisis centers, and child advocacy centers	Yes	Provide the parents with a card with information on how to contact the department should the parent later have questions about the relinquishment or wish to disclose medical and genetic information Provide information regarding counseling and reclaiming parental rights Notify the Department of Social Services immediately See that the child receives medical examination and testing, and any other necessary medical care Request information about the child from the relinquisher

Maine Safe Haven (2002)	Thirty days old	Person who expresses no intent to return	Law enforcement officers, staff at medical emergency rooms, medical service providers, and hospital staff	Yes	May request information that may be helpful to the welfare of the child (date of birth of the child; any circumstances related to pregnancy and/or delivery; any known information about Native American heritage; any known medical and/or genetic information relating to baby, parents, or extended family; any history of substance use by either parent; social, familial, and cultural information; and any inclination on the part of the parents that they may want to seek contact with and/or custody of the child in the future) Notify the Department of Health and Human Services May request info about the child from the relinquisher
Maryland Safe Haven Act (2001)	Three days old	Mother or person who has the approval of the mother	Responsible adults and hospitals and other facilities designated by regulation	Yes	Take the child to a hospital, which must notify the local Department of Human Resources within twenty-four hours
Massachusetts: An Act relative to the Safe Placement of Newborn Infants (2004)	Seven days old	Parent	Hospitals, police departments, and manned fire stations	N/A	Immediately notify the Department of Social Services Make every effort to solicit the name of the child, the name and address of the parent placing the child, the child's birthplace, information relevant to the child's medical history, birth family's medical history, if available, and any other information that might assist DSS in determining the best interests of the child

Appendix H   State Infant Safe Haven Laws, Part I—(*Continued*)

State law	Maximum age of child	Who may leave a baby at a safe haven	Safe haven providers	Provider immune from liability	Responsibilities of safe haven providers
Michigan Safe Delivery (2000)	Seventy-two hours old	Parent	Fire departments, hospitals, and police stations	Yes	Take the child into temporary protective custody Provide the child with any necessary care, and transport the child to a hospital if necessary Inform the parent that by surrendering the child, he or she is relinquishing his or her rights to the child to a child-placing agency for adoption Provide written material that informs the parent of rights and available services Encourage the parent to provide family and medical information Notify a child-placing agency Make a child protection report if it is suspected that the child has been abused, or if the examining physician suspects that the child is not a newborn May request information about the child from the relinquisher
Minnesota Safe Place for Newborns (2000)	Seventy-two hours old	Mother or a person who has the mother's approval	Employees at licensed hospitals	Yes	May ask about medical history of the mother or the child May provide contact information for the Children's Services Department May request information about the child from the relinquisher Inform the local welfare agency within twenty-four hours

Mississippi: An Act to Require an Emergency Medical Services Provider to Take Possession of Certain Abandoned Children (2001)	Seventy-two hours old	Parent	Emergency medical service providers, including licensed hospitals that operate an emergency department, and licensed adoption agencies (does not include the offices of private physicians or dentists unless such an individual voluntarily assumes responsibility for the child)	Yes	Perform any act necessary to protect the health and safety of the child Notify the Department of Human Services
Missouri Safe Place for Newborns Act (2002)	Thirty days old	Birth parent or person acting on the parent's behalf	Hospital staff, firefighters, emergency medical technicians, and law enforcement officers	Yes	Take physical custody and transport the child to the nearest hospital Provide medical treatment as needed Notify the Division of Family Services and local juvenile officer
Montana Safe Haven Newborn Protection Act (2001)	Thirty days old	Anyone	Uniformed or otherwise identifiable employees of fire departments, hospitals, and law enforcement agencies when the individual is on duty inside the facility, and any law enforcement officer who is in uniform or is otherwise identifiable	Yes	Perform any act necessary to protect the child's health and safety, and transport the child to a hospital if needed Attempt to inform the relinquisher about the consequences of relinquishment and the availability of services Encourage the relinquisher to provide family and medical information If possible, determine whether the child has a tribal affiliation Notify the Department of Health and Human Services, Child and Family Services Division Make a protective services report if child abuse is suspected or if a physician suspects that the child is not a newborn Provide information pamphlet on consequences of relinquishment and availability of services May request information about the child from the relinquisher

Appendix H   State Infant Safe Haven Laws, Part I—*(Continued)*

State law	Maximum age of child	Who may leave a baby at a safe haven	Safe haven providers	Provider immune from liability	Responsibilities of safe haven providers
Nebraska: An Act relating to Children to Prohibit Prosecution for Leaving a Child at a Hospital (2008)	No maximum age stated	Anyone	A hospital licensed by the state of Nebraska	N/A	Within four hours, contact the appropriate authorities (law enforcement officer or Department of Health and Human Services) to take custody of the child Perform any act necessary to maintain the health and safety of the child
Nevada Newborn Baby Abandonment Law (2001)	Thirty days old	Parent	Hospitals, obstetric centers, emergency medical care centers, firefighting centers, and law enforcement agencies	Yes	Perform any act necessary to maintain the health and safety of the child Notify the Division of Child and Family Services within twenty-four hours May request information about the child from the relinquisher
New Hampshire Temporary Care and Control of Children at a Hospital or Safe Haven (2003)	Seven days old	Parent	Hospitals, churches where staff is present, police and fire stations, and 911 responders	Yes	Provide any medical services needed to protect the health and safety of the child Notify the Division for Children, Youth and Families and law enforcement officials within twenty-four hours
New Jersey Safe Haven Infant Protection Act (2000)	Thirty days old	Anyone	Police stations and emergency departments of licensed hospitals	Yes	If the child is relinquished at a police station, transport the child to the hospital, which shall take possession of the child without a court order, take any action or provide any needed treatment to protect the child's health and safety, and notify the Division of Youth and Family Services no later than the first business day after taking possession of the child

New Mexico Safe Haven for Infants Act (2001)	Ninety days old	Anyone	Staff of licensed hospitals and health care clinics	Yes	Provide any necessary medical care to the child and the person leaving the child Provide information about adoption services, including contact information for the Children Youth and Families Department, adoption services, information about the availability of confidential adoption services, brochures or telephone numbers for agencies that provide adoption or counseling services, and written information regarding whom to contact if the parent decides to seek reunification with the child Request the identity of the birth parents and medical information Notify the department within twenty-four hours May request information about the child from the relinquisher
New York Safe Haven (2001)	Five days old	Anyone	Any appropriate person (this is generally understood to be a hospital, police station, or fire station)	N/A	N/A
North Carolina Safe Haven Law (2000)	Six days old	Parent who indicates that he or she doesn't plan to return for child	Health care providers at hospitals, health departments, and community health centers; law enforcement officers; social services workers; emergency medical service workers; and any adult willing to take responsibility for the child	Yes	Take temporary custody of the child Perform any act necessary to protect the child's health and well-being May ask the parent for identification and medical history Immediately notify the Department of Health and Human Services or a law enforcement agency May request information about the child from the relinquisher

Appendix H   State Infant Safe Haven Laws, Part I—(*Continued*)

State law	Maximum age of child	Who may leave a baby at a safe haven	Safe haven providers	Provider immune from liability	Responsibilities of safe haven providers
North Dakota Safe Haven Law (2001)	One year old	Parent or agent of the parent	Licensed hospitals	Yes	Request information regarding the parents Provide the parent with information and a numbered identity bracelet for the child Notify the Department of Human Services within twenty-four hours, but not before the parent or agent of the parent leaves the hospital May provide the relinquisher with any relevant information, including information about the safe-place-for-abandoned-infant programs, adoption and counseling services, and whom to contact if reunification is sought Request information about the child from the relinquisher
Ohio Safe Haven Law (2000)	Seventy-two hours old	Parent	Emergency medical service workers, hospital employees, and peace officers	Yes	Perform any act necessary to protect the child's health and safety Attempt to provide the parent with forms to gather medical information and written materials that describe available services Notify the Bureau of Family Services. Ask relinquisher to fill out a voluntary medical form for the child with child and parent's information

Oklahoma Safe Haven Law (2001)	Seven days old	Parent	Medical service providers and child rescuers (i.e., any employee or designated person on duty at a police station, fire station, CPS agency, or hospital or other medical facility)	Yes	Perform any act necessary to protect the child's health Request information about the child Provide information about the parents' rights regarding reunification Notify the Department of Human Services, Children and Family Services Division. Offer parent information about sources of counseling May request information about the child but must respect the wishes of the parent if he or she desires to remain anonymous
Oregon: An Act relating to the Safe Surrender of Newborn Children (2001)	Thirty days old	Parent	Hospitals, birthing centers, physician's offices, sheriff's offices, police stations, and fire stations	Yes	Notify the State Office for Services to Children and Families within twenty-four hours Provide the State Office for Services to Children and Families with any available information about the child
Pennsylvania Safe Haven (2002)	Twenty-eight days old	Parent	Hospitals and health care providers	Yes	Take the child into protective custody Perform a medical evaluation Immediately notify the county children's services agency and law enforcement or the state police
Rhode Island Safe Haven for Infants (2003)	Thirty days old	Parent or person acting on the direction of the parent who indicates that he or she does not intend to return for the child	Hospitals, medical emergency facilities, fire stations, and police stations	Yes	Provide needed medical care to the child Offer information about the legal effect of relinquishment Notify the Department of Children, Youth and Families

Appendix H   State Infant Safe Haven Laws, Part I—*(Continued)*

State law	Maximum age of child	Who may leave a baby at a safe haven	Safe haven providers	Provider immune from liability	Responsibilities of safe haven providers
South Carolina Safe Haven for Abandoned Babies Act (Daniel's Law) (2000; amended 2006)	Thirty days old	Parent or person directed by parent	Hospitals and hospital outpatient facilities and, during hours when facilities are staffed, law enforcement agencies, fire stations, emergency medical service stations, and any house of worship	Yes	Provide needed medical care to protect the health and safety of the child Offer information to the relinquisher about the legal effect of relinquishment Attempt to obtain information about the child's medical history and background Notify the Department of Social Services no later than the close of the first business day after the child is relinquished Transport the child to a hospital or hospital outpatient facility within six hours Request information about the child
South Dakota Safe Havens (2001)	Sixty days old	Parent who does not express any intent to return for the child	Health care facilities and clinics, law enforcement officers, emergency medical technicians, firefighters, and child-placing agencies	Yes	Perform any act necessary to protect the child's health May ask the parent for medical information Notify the Department of Social Services May request information about the child

	Age	Who May Surrender	Locations		Required Acts
Tennessee Safe Haven (2001)	Seventy-two hours old	Mother who expresses no intent to return for the child	Hospitals, birthing centers, community health clinics, and outpatient walk-in clinics	Yes	Perform any act necessary to protect the child's health and safety May ask the mother for identification and health information May provide the mother with information about the legal effects of relinquishment and available social services Notify the Department of Children's Services within twenty-four hours, but not before the mother leaves the facility Provide contact information for relevant social service agencies and the name, address, and phone number of the department contact If possible, provide information concerning the requirements relating to recovery of the child both orally and in written format Inquire whenever possible about the medical history of the mother and newborn Whenever possible, seek the identity of the mother, the child, or the father
Texas Baby Moses Law (1999)	Sixty days old	Parent	Designated emergency infant care providers, including emergency medical service providers, hospitals, and child-placing agencies	Yes	Perform any act necessary to protect the child's health and safety Notify the Department of Family and Protective Services no later than the close of the first business day Offer the parent a form for voluntary disclosure of medical information
Utah Newborn Safe Haven (2001)	Seventy-two hours old	Parent or parent's designee	Hospital	Yes	Provide any necessary medical care May request identifying and medical information Notify the Department of Child and Family Services within twenty-four hours Prepare a birth certificate for the child, or a foundling birth certificate if the child's parentage is unknown May provide the person relinquishing the child with medical history forms and stamped envelopes addressed to the Department of Child and Family Services

Appendix H   State Infant Safe Haven Laws, Part I—(*Continued*)

State law	Maximum age of child	Who may leave a baby at a safe haven	Safe haven providers	Provider immune from liability	Responsibilities of safe haven providers
Vermont Baby Safe Haven Law (2006)	Thirty days old	Parent or person on behalf of parent	Employees, staff members, and volunteers at health care facilities; employees, staff members, and volunteers at fire stations, police stations, and places of worship; any entity that is licensed or authorized in the state to place minors for adoption; and 911 emergency responders at a location where the responder and the person have agreed to transfer the child	Yes	Take temporary custody of the child Provide any necessary medical care Provide notice to law enforcement that temporary custody of the child has been taken Provide notice to the Department for Children and Family Services, which must take custody of the child as soon as practicable May request information for the child
Virginia Safe Haven (2003)	Fourteen days old	Parent	Hospitals that provide twenty-four-hour emergency services and rescue squads that employ emergency medical technicians	Yes	Ensure the safety of the child Assess and treat any emergency medical conditions Obtain a medical history and other background information from the parent (parent should not be forced to give information or stay on the scene and should not be pursued) Notify the local Department of Social Services as soon as possible If possible, obtain a medical history and other background

Washington: An Act relating to the Safety of Newborn Children (2002)	Seventy-two hours old	Parent	Employees, volunteers, and medical staff at hospitals and firefighters, volunteers, and emergency medical technicians at fire stations	Yes	Provide referral information about adoption options, counseling, medical and emotional aftercare services, domestic violence, and the parent's legal rights Offer the parent an opportunity to provide medical information Notify Division of Children and Family Services within twenty-four hours Attempt to protect the anonymity of the parent Offer an opportunity for the parent to anonymously provide any information he or she has about the family medical history
West Virginia: Emergency Possession of Certain Abandoned Children (2000)	Thirty days old	Parent	Hospitals and health care facilities	N/A	Perform any act necessary to protect the child's health and safety May not require the parent to identify him- or herself Notify Bureau for Children and Families
Wisconsin Assembly Bill 54: Taking a Newborn Child into Custody (2001)	Seventy-two hours old	Parent	Law enforcement officers, emergency medical technicians, hospital staff, sheriff's offices, police stations, and fire stations	Yes	Take any action necessary to protect the child's health and safety Deliver the child to a Division of Children and Family Services intake worker within twenty-four hours Provide a toll-free number to the parent regarding health care services and providers File a birth certificate for the child within five days
Wyoming Safety for a Newborn Child (2003)	Fourteen days old	Parent or parent's designee	Fire stations, hospitals, police departments, sheriff's offices, and other places of shelter identified by the Department of Family Services	Yes	May not require the parent to provide medical or identifying information May provide any necessary medical care Notify the Department of Family Services no later than twenty-four hours after receiving the child If the child is relinquished somewhere other than a hospital, provide emergency medical care and deliver the child to the nearest hospital as soon as possible

Appendix I   State Infant Safe Haven Laws, Part II

State law	Post-abandonment time lines	Protections for the parents/effect on parental rights	Evaluation report to state government on outcomes required	Public information campaign
Alabama Safe Harbor Law (2000)	Waiting period or discovery period before the child will be adopted is not clearly defined.	Relinquishment to a safe haven is an affirmative defense to prosecution for nonsupport, abandonment, or endangering the welfare of a child. The department of child welfare/social services assumes control and custody of the child. When a parent relinquishes his or her child at a hospital, he or she is also releasing his or her parental rights.	N/A	N/A
Alaska Safe Surrender of Infants Act (2008)	N/A	N/A	N/A	N/A
Arizona Safe Haven (2001)	N/A	The parent may remain anonymous and is not required to answer any questions. A person is not guilty of abuse for leaving an infant with a safe haven provider.	Yes	Yes (provided by volunteer group)
Arkansas Safe Haven Act (2001)	N/A	Voluntary relinquishment by a parent is an affirmative defense to prosecution for endangering the welfare of a minor but does not provide a defense for any abuse or neglect that occurred prior to the relinquishment of the child. Division of Children and Family Services of the Department of Human Services initiates a dependency action to place the child in a permanent home. The missing child registry must be searched to ensure that the child has not been reported missing or kidnapped.	N/A	N/A
California Safely Surrendered Baby Law (2001)	The Department of Child and Family Services files a dependency petition, and the parent has fourteen days to reclaim custody by means of a coded identification ankle bracelet.	No person leaving an infant with a safe haven provider may be prosecuted for abandonment, failure to provide, or desertion.	Yes	Yes

Colorado Safe Haven for Newborns (2000)	N/A	The names of parents who safely relinquish a child are not added to the state central child protection registry. Relinquishment to a safe haven is an affirmative defense to prosecution for placing a child in a threatening situation. The Department of Human Services places the child in an adoptive home and proceeds to terminate the parent's rights as soon as is lawfully possible.	Yes	April 4, 2007, was proclaimed Safe Haven for Newborns Day to promote awareness of law.
Connecticut Safe Havens for Newborns Act (2000)	Within twenty-four hours, the Department of Children and Families takes custody of the child and begins to develop a plan for permanent care. The court schedules a hearing within thirty days of DCF's application, and parental rights can be terminated at the first hearing.	Information about the parent is kept confidential. Leaving an infant with a safe haven provider is not a violation of the law of child abandonment. The Department of Children and Families is required by law to notify both parents of its intent to keep custody of the infant and to seek termination of parental rights. If the relinquishing parent gives his or her name and address or the name and address of the other parent, a court officer notifies the relinquishing parent or the other parent of the court action and the first hearing date. If names and/or addresses of the parents are not known, DCF may publish notice in the local newspaper; that will be the only notice the parents receive. The department assumes custody of the child and takes any action needed to achieve safety and permanency for the child. The parent or an agent of the parent may submit a request for reunification. Such a request should be made to DCF as soon as possible. The parent should also apply to the court for an attorney. This is very important because the court can terminate parental rights at the first hearing.	N/A	Yes (voluntarily implemented by DCF)

Appendix I   State Infant Safe Haven Laws, Part II—*(Continued)*

State law	Post-abandonment time lines	Protections for the parents/effect on parental rights	Evaluation report to state government on outcomes required	Public information campaign
Delaware Safe Arms for Newborns Act (2001)	If reunification is not sought within thirty days of surrender, the baby is considered abandoned, and the Department of Services for Children, Youth and Their Families proceeds with the termination of parental rights.	The relinquishing parent may remain anonymous. If the parent chooses to remain anonymous, no investigation is initiated unless there is evidence of abuse or neglect of the child. Any information gathered is kept confidential. Relinquishment to a designated provider is a defense from prosecution for abandoning or endangering the welfare of the child. The surrendering person irrevocably consents to termination of parental rights. The surrendering person also irrevocably waives any right of notice unless he or she manifests intent to exercise parental rights within thirty days. DNA testing is required for reunification.	N/A	Yes
District of Columbia	N/A	N/A	N/A	N/A
Florida Safe Haven for Newborns (2000)	N/A	The parent has an absolute right to remain anonymous. The parent is not subject to a child protective report or a criminal investigation unless there is actual or suspected child abuse. The parent is provided immunity from prosecution for abandonment if there is no abuse or neglect. It is presumed that the parent has consented to termination of parental rights. The parent may reclaim the child anytime prior to termination of rights. The parent is given the opportunity to claim or reclaim his or her child up until the court enters a judgment terminating his or her parental rights. DNA testing is required for reunification. The Department of Children and Families must search the missing child registry to ensure that the child has not been reported missing or kidnapped.	N/A	Yes (funded through an independent foundation)

Georgia Safe Place for Newborns Act (2002)	The Division of Children and Family Services takes physical custody of the child within six hours.	Relinquishing mothers are not prosecuted for cruelty to a child, contributing to the deprivation of a child, or abandonment. The Division of Children and Family Services brings the child before the juvenile court to determine placement.	Yes	N/A
Hawaii Safe Place for Newborns (2007)	N/A	The department may search for relatives of the child as a placement or permanency option or implement other placement requirements that give preference to relatives, provided that the department has information as to the identity of the child, the child's mother, or the child's father.	N/A	N/A
Idaho Safe Haven Act (2001)	A petition for termination of parental rights is filed after thirty days.	A relinquishing parent is not required to reveal his or her identity and is immune from prosecution for abandonment and neglect. Any information provided by the parent is kept confidential. The Department of Health and Welfare must check the parental rights claim registry before parental rights are terminated. The Bureau of Vital Statistics maintains a registry of people who claim parental rights of abandoned children. The child is placed in a prospective adoptive home as soon as possible. Prior to an order terminating parental rights, the parent may file a claim of parental rights to the child. The process for terminating parental rights has been streamlined for children left at a safe haven. Social workers are not expected to work for reunification; deliverance of the child to a safe haven is handled like a request to place a child for adoption. DNA testing is required for reunification. The missing child registry must be searched to ensure that the child has not been reported missing or kidnapped.	N/A	N/A

Appendix I   State Infant Safe Haven Laws, Part II—*(Continued)*

State law	Post-abandonment time lines	Protections for the parents/effect on parental rights	Evaluation report to state government on outcomes required	Public information campaign
Illinois Abandoned Newborn Protection Act (2001)	If the parent returns to reclaim the child within seventy-two hours after relinquishment, the facility must inform the parent of the name and location of the hospital to which the child was transported. Proceedings to terminate parental rights are initiated no sooner than sixty days after relinquishment. Within three business days after assuming physical custody of the infant, the child-placing agency files a petition in the division of the circuit court in which petitions for adoption are normally heard. The petition alleges that the newborn infant has been relinquished in accordance with this act and states that the child-placing agency intends to place the child in an adoptive home. No action to void or revoke a termination of parental rights may commence after twelve months from the date of the relinquishment.	If there is no evidence of abuse, the parent may remain anonymous. Neither a child protective investigation nor a criminal investigation may be initiated solely because the child has been relinquished. The act of relinquishment is not by itself considered abandonment or endangerment of the life or health of a child. Department of Children and Family Services must search the putative father registry. The relinquishing individual remains anonymous if he or she completes a Denial of Information Exchange. While the law does not require the relinquishing person to provide his or her identity or complete an application form, he or she can do so. The Illinois Adoption Registry and Medical Information Exchange can request that the hospital, police station, fire station, or emergency medical facility submit the forms to them. There is a presumption that the child's parent consents to termination of parental rights. The parent may petition for the return of custody of the child prior to termination. Failure of the parent to file a claim before the termination of rights bars the parent from any future action. DNA testing is required for reunification. The missing child registry must be searched to ensure that the child has not been reported missing or kidnapped.	Yes	Yes
Indiana Baby Safe Haven (2000)	The attorney for the Department of Child Services, without unnecessary delay, asks the juvenile court to authorize the filing of a petition alleging that the child is in need of services, hold an initial hearing no later than the business day after the child is taken into custody, and appoint a guardian ad litem or a court-appointed special advocate for the child.	A person who voluntarily leaves a child is not required to disclose his or her name or the parent's name. Relinquishment according to the law is a defense to prosecution for abandonment or neglect of a dependent. The local child protection services agency assumes care, control, and custody of the child. Efforts to locate the child's parents or reunite the child's family are not necessary. The missing child registry must be searched within forty-eight hours to ensure the child has not been reported missing or kidnapped.	N/A	N/A

Iowa Safe Haven Act (2001)	A petition to terminate parental rights is filed as soon as possible, and the hearing to terminate parental rights is held within thirty days of filing. Requests to appeal the termination order must be made within thirty days of issuance of the termination order. The period for request for vacation or appeal by a parent whose rights have been terminated cannot be waived or extended, and vacations and appeals are not granted for requests made after the expiration of this period.	Relinquishing parents are not required to give names or medical information. Identifying information is kept confidential, and immunity from criminal prosecution or civil liability is provided. Either parent may request custody of the child before termination. The putative father registry must be searched before parental rights can be terminated and the child placed for adoption.	N/A	Yes
Kansas Newborn Infant Protection Act (2000)	N/A	A person leaving a baby with a safe haven is not prosecuted for abandonment if the baby has suffered no harm. The Newborn Protection Act does not guarantee anonymity to the parent who leaves a newborn at the health department, fire station, or medical facility. Other child welfare laws say the state must attempt to identify the parents and grandparents of an abandoned infant. The parents' right to a relationship with their child cannot be terminated by the state without due process, which includes identification of the child's parents and notification of both parents of the intent to place the child for adoption. A petition for termination of parental rights that includes a request that the court find that reunification is not a viable option is filed, and an expedited hearing is held on the petition. Relinquishing a child at a licensed child-placing agency allows the parents to remain anonymous. In addition, the agency assists the mother with providing the child's medical history so that the child's medical history will be available to potential adoptive parents.	N/A	N/A

Appendix I　State Infant Safe Haven Laws, Part II—(*Continued*)

State law	Post-abandonment time lines	Protections for the parents/effect on parental rights	Evaluation report to state government on outcomes required	Public information campaign
Kentucky Safe Haven Act (2002)	If the court places temporary custody with the Cabinet for Health and Family Services, the custody order remains in effect for a minimum of thirty days. If a claim of parental rights is made at anytime prior to the court order, the circuit court may hold the action for involuntary termination of parental rights in abeyance for no more than ninety days and immediately remand the case to district court. If a case is remanded to district court, an adjudicatory hearing is conducted within ten days of the assertion of parental rights.	The relinquishing parent's identity remains confidential; he or she retains the right to anonymity. No investigation for abandonment is conducted against parents. The child is placed with a foster family. The Cabinet for Health and Family Services provides concurrent placement services to assist the foster family in working for reunification of the child with the birth family, or to adopt the child if reunification is not achieved. After thirty days, a petition for termination of parental rights is filed. A parent may file a claim of parental rights before termination is finalized. DNA testing is required for reunification. The missing child registry must be searched by Cabinet staff to ensure that the child has not been reported missing or kidnapped.	N/A	N/A
Louisiana Safe Haven Relinquishment (2000)	The Department of Social Services takes physical custody of the child within twelve hours of the child's discharge from the hospital. The child is placed in a foster or adoptive home. The child's status as a child in need of care in state custody continues, and the procedure for termination of parental rights begins immediately. A parent who has relinquished the child may file to reclaim parental rights within thirty days after relinquishment. If the relinquishing parent does not make a timely claim to the child, and no timely claim is made by a non-relinquishing parent, a petition for termination of parental rights is filed within forty-five days of relinquishment. Once ninety days after the judgment or a decree for adoption have passed (whichever is earlier), no action to annul a judgment of termination of parental rights can be brought.	Relinquishment in accordance with this law is not a criminal act of neglect, abandonment, cruelty, or crime against the child. The missing child registry must be searched to ensure that the child has not been reported missing or kidnapped.	N/A	Yes

Maine Safe Haven (2002)	N/A	Relinquishment of a child in accordance with the law is an affirmative defense to prosecution for abandonment. All personal information about the parent is kept confidential.	N/A	N/A
Maryland Safe Haven Act (2001)	N/A	Relinquishing parents are immune from civil liability or criminal prosecution. A birth parent who has relinquished a child may revoke the intent to relinquish the child by filing a petition to establish parental rights before parental rights are terminated.	N/A	Yes
Massachusetts: An Act relative to the Safe Placement of Newborn Infants (2004)		Voluntary relinquishment by itself does not constitute either a finding of abuse or neglect or a violation of the criminal statute for child abuse, neglect, or abandonment, nor does it constitute an automatic termination of parental rights. The parent is not required to supply any information. The Department of Social Services accepts the child for placement in foster care and initiates all actions authorized by law to achieve the safety and permanent placement of the child in a manner consistent with the best interests of the child. DSS also initiates a petition to terminate parental rights.	Yes	Yes
Michigan Safe Delivery (2000)	The parent has twenty-eight days to petition the court to regain custody of the child. If a custody petition is not filed, the child-placing agency files a petition to terminate parental rights. After twenty-eight days, there is a hearing to terminate parental rights. No notice of the hearing is given to the parent.	None of the information provided by the parent is made public. Relinquishment to a safe haven is an affirmative defense to prosecution for injury or abandonment. The parent has twenty-eight days to petition the court to regain custody of the child. If a custody petition is not filed, the child-placing agency files a petition to terminate parental rights.	N/A	Yes
Minnesota Safe Place for Newborns (2000)	N/A	Relinquishing parents are not required to provide any information and are not prosecuted for relinquishing a child. The local children's services agency takes custody of the child and is not required to attempt to reunite the child with the parents.	N/A	N/A

Appendix I   State Infant Safe Haven Laws, Part II—*(Continued)*

State law	Post-abandonment time lines	Protections for the parents/effect on parental rights	Evaluation report to state government on outcomes required	Public information campaign
Mississippi: An Act to Require an Emergency Medical Services Provider to Take Possession of Certain Abandoned Children (2001)	N/A	Relinquishment to a safe haven is an affirmative defense to prosecution for abandonment, neglect, or exposure of the child. The Department of Human Services assumes control and custody of the child.	N/A	N/A
Missouri Safe Place for Newborns Act (2002)	A non-relinquishing parent wishing to establish paternity or maternity has thirty days to identify him- or herself to the court and to state his or her intentions regarding the child.	A parent is not prosecuted if the child is five days old or younger. Relinquishment in accordance with the law is an affirmative defense to charges of child endangerment if the child is no less than six days old, but no more than thirty days old. The Department of Social Services must check the putative father registry. The child becomes a ward of the court. The parent's relinquishment of the child constitutes an implied consent to voluntary relinquishment of parental rights.	N/A	N/A
Montana Safe Haven Newborn Protection Act (2001)	A parent has sixty days after surrendering the child to petition the court to regain custody of the child.	Information provided by the parent is not made public. A criminal investigation or prosecution for abandonment may not be initiated based solely on relinquishment. By the act of relinquishment, the parent releases the child for adoption. Putative father registry must be searched by a representative of the Child and Family Services Division. The parent may not receive personal notice of any proceedings. Any Indian heritage brings the child under the jurisdiction of the Indian Child Welfare Act.	N/A	Yes

Nebraska: An Act relating to Children to Prohibit Prosecution for Leaving a Child at a Hospital (2008)	N/A	N/A	Yes	N/A
Nevada Newborn Baby Abandonment Law (2001)	N/A	Relinquishing parents are not required to provide identifying or medical information, and relinquishment to a safe haven is not considered a violation of the laws against abandonment, abuse, neglect, or child endangerment. The parent is presumed to have intended to consent to termination of parental rights to the child. Newspaper advertising to parents regarding their rights to the child is required.	N/A	N/A
New Hampshire: Temporary Care and Control of Children at a Hospital or Safe Haven (2003)	N/A	The parent is not required to reveal identifying information. The child welfare department assumes temporary care and control of the infant.	N/A	N/A
New Jersey Safe Haven Infant Protection Act (2000)	The Division of Youth and Family Services has twenty-one days to terminate the parental rights of the mother. During that time, the mother can change her mind and reclaim her baby. DYFS files for termination of parental rights no later than twenty-one days after the day the division assumed care, custody, and control of the child.	The parent is not required to provide identifying or medical information. Relinquishment to a safe haven is an affirmative defense to prosecution for abandonment. The Division of Youth and Family Services is not required to attempt to reunite the child with the parents or to search for relatives of the child as a placement or permanency option, or to implement other placement requirements that give preference to relatives if the division does not have information as to the identity of the child, the child's mother, or the child's father. The division places the child with potential adoptive parents as soon as possible. The missing child registry must be searched to ensure that the child has not been reported missing or kidnapped.	Yes	Yes

Appendix I   State Infant Safe Haven Laws, Part II—*(Continued)*

State law	Post-abandonment time lines	Protections for the parents/effect on parental rights	Evaluation report to state government on outcomes required	Public information campaign
New Mexico Safe Haven for Infants Act (2001)	The parent has thirty days to seek reunification with the child.	The parent is not required to provide identifying information. However, any information that is disclosed remains confidential. There is no prosecution for abandonment or abuse. The Children, Youth and Families Department has immediate custody of the child. If the child is determined to be an Indian child, placement preferences apply. There will be no presumption of abuse or neglect against the person seeking reunification. DNA testing is required for reunification.	N/A	Yes
New York Safe Haven (2000)	N/A	Relinquishment to a safe haven is an affirmative defense to prosecution for abandonment or endangering the welfare of a child.	N/A	Yes (requirement added later)
North Carolina Safe Haven Law (2001)	Parents can lose their rights if the child remains abandoned for sixty days or more.	The parent is not required to provide any information and is not prosecuted for abandonment or failure to support.	N/A	Yes (but no funding provided)
North Dakota Safe Haven Law (2001)	N/A	The hospital provides the parent or the parent's agent with a numbered identification bracelet to link the parent or the agent to the abandoned infant. However, possession of an identification bracelet does not entitle the bracelet holder to take custody of the abandoned infant on demand. If an individual possesses a bracelet linking him or her to an abandoned infant and parental rights have not been terminated, possession of the bracelet creates a presumption that the individual has standing to participate in a protection services action but does not create a presumption of maternity, paternity, or custody. Neither the parent nor the parent's agent is required to provide information, nor may the parent or the parent's agent be prosecuted for abuse, neglect, or abandonment.	N/A	N/A

Ohio Safe Haven Law (2000)	The child welfare agency must move for temporary custody within twenty-four hours or the next working day.	The parent has the right to remain anonymous and is not subject to prosecution for the act of relinquishment. The child is regarded as a deserted or neglected child. A parent seeking reunification must undergo DNA testing. The missing child registry must be searched to ensure that the child has not been reported missing or kidnapped.	N/A	N/A
Oklahoma Safe Haven Law (2001)	N/A	The parent may remain anonymous. There is no prosecution for abandonment or neglect. The Department of Human Services provides information about reunification and counseling. The missing child registry must be searched to ensure that the child has not been reported missing or kidnapped.	N/A	Yes
Oregon: An Act relating to the Safe Surrender of Newborn Children (2001)	N/A	The parent is not required to provide identifying information about him- or herself or the child. Relinquishment of the child to a safe haven is an affirmative defense to prosecution for abandonment. The child is considered abandoned, and the Department of Human Services has protective custody of the child.	N/A	Yes
Pennsylvania Safe Haven (2002)		The parent is not criminally liable if the criteria for safe haven relinquishment are met. The safe haven staff must immediately notify the appropriate county children's services agency so that proceedings may be initiated, if appropriate.	Yes	Yes
Rhode Island Safe Haven for Infants (2003)	Petition for termination of parental rights begins within ninety days unless the parent asserts a claim for the child within that time. The Department of Children, Youth and Families has temporary protective custody of the child. If no one asserts a claim to be the parent of the infant within ninety days after the DCYF obtains temporary custody of the infant, proceedings to terminate the parental rights are initiated on the legal basis of abandonment.	Any information provided is kept confidential, and immunity from prosecution for abandonment is provided.	N/A	Yes

Appendix I   State Infant Safe Haven Laws, Part II—(*Continued*)

State law	Post-abandonment time lines	Protections for the parents/effect on parental rights	Evaluation report to state government on outcomes required	Public information campaign
South Carolina Safe Haven for Abandoned Babies Act (Daniel's Law) (2000; amended 2006)	The Department of Social Services has legal custody of the child. Within forty-eight hours, the Department of Social Services files a petition to dispense with reasonable efforts to find parents and terminate parental rights. A parent wishing to reunite with the child must assert parental rights at the first permanency planning hearing.	The parent is not required to disclose his or her identity. Any identifying information that is disclosed must be kept confidential. The parent is provided with immunity from prosecution for any criminal offense as long as the child has suffered no harm. Abandonment is considered conclusive evidence that the requirements for termination of parental rights have been met. The missing child registry must be searched to ensure that the child has not been reported missing or kidnapped.	N/A	Yes
South Dakota Safe Havens (2001)	After fourteen days, the child becomes a ward of the state and the relinquishing parent's rights are terminated. The non-relinquishing parent has thirty days to file for custody. Sixty days after the emergency medical service provider or licensed child-placing agency takes possession of the child, a parental rights termination hearing is held in circuit court.	The parent is not required to provide any information. Relinquishment to a safe haven is not considered a crime if the child is unharmed. Due regard is given to the Indian Child Welfare Act, if applicable.	N/A	N/A

Tennessee Safe Haven (2001)	Within ten days of receiving a child, the Department of Children's Services begins to give notice once a week for four consecutive weeks in a newspaper or other general circulation publication of the county in which the infant was received and in any other county in which there is reason to believe the child's parents may be found. Termination of parental rights is based on voluntary delivery of a child and failure of the mother to visit or seek contact with the child for thirty days after the date of relinquishment, and failure to seek contact with the child through the department or to revoke the voluntary delivery within thirty days after notice, which is cumulatively no less than ninety days from the date the child was relinquished.	Any information that is received is kept confidential, and immunity for criminal prosecution is provided if the child is delivered unharmed. A mother who voluntarily delivers an infant may revoke such voluntary delivery by applying to a court that is qualified to receive a surrender no later than thirty days after public notice of the child's relinquishment. The state's putative father registry must be searched. The Department of Children's Services assumes custody of the child.	N/A	Yes
Texas Baby Moses Law (1999)	The Department of Family and Protective Services assumes custody of the child, who is treated as a child taken into possession without a court order, and files suit to seek termination of the parent-child relationship no later than forty-five days after the department assumes the care, control, and custody of the child.	Parent may remain anonymous. Relinquishment to a safe haven is an affirmative defense to prosecution for abandoning or endangering a child. The Department of Family and Protective Services is not required to conduct a search for the relatives of a child for whom the department assumes care, control, and custody. If a non-relinquishing parent is not identified, relinquishment of the child is considered grounds for termination of parental rights of both the relinquishing and non-relinquishing parents. The missing child registry must be searched to ensure that the child has not been reported missing or kidnapped.	N/A	N/A
Utah Newborn Safe Haven (2001)	The child is placed in a potential adoptive home, and within ten days, a petition to terminate parental rights is filed. The father has two weeks to come forward and establish paternity.	The person who relinquishes the child may retain complete anonymity. Relinquishment to a safe haven is an affirmative defense to any criminal liability for abandonment or neglect. Child welfare agency must search putative father registry. DNA testing is required for reunification. The missing child registry must be searched to ensure that the child has not been reported missing or kidnapped.	N/A	N/A

Appendix I   State Infant Safe Haven Laws, Part II—*(Continued)*

State law	Post-abandonment time lines	Protections for the parents/effect on parental rights	Evaluation report to state government on outcomes required	Public information campaign
Vermont Baby Safe Haven Law (2006)	N/A	N/A	Yes	Yes
Virginia Safe Haven (2003)	The Department of Social Services institutes proceedings to terminate parental rights.	Relinquishment to a safe haven is an affirmative defense to prosecution for abuse or neglect of a child, cruelty to a child, or endangering a child.	N/A	N/A
Washington: An Act Relating to the Safety of Newborn Children (2002)	N/A	The anonymity of the parent is protected, and the parent is not subject to criminal liability for abandonment. The Division of Children and Family Services assumes custody of the child.	N/A	N/A
West Virginia: Emergency Possession of Certain Abandoned Children (2000)	N/A	The parent has the right to remain anonymous. Relinquishment to a safe haven is an affirmative defense to prosecution. The Bureau for Children and Families assumes custody of the child, and the child is eligible for adoption as an abandoned child.	N/A	N/A
Wisconsin Assembly Bill 54: Taking a Newborn Child into Custody (2001)	N/A	The parent has the right to remain anonymous. The parent and any person who assists the parent in the relinquishment are provided immunity from civil and criminal liability for abandonment or neglect, as well as for exercising the right to remain anonymous. The court may grant involuntary termination of parental rights on the grounds that custody has been relinquished.	N/A	N/A
Wyoming Safety for a Newborn Child (2003)	If neither parent seeks the return of the child within three months, the Department of Family Services files a petition for termination of parental rights.	The parent may remain anonymous. Relinquishment does not in and of itself constitute child abuse. Relinquishment to a safe haven is an affirmative defense to any potential criminal liability for abandonment or neglect. The local child protective agency assumes care and custody of the child and places the child in a potential adoptive home. A putative father registry search is required.	Yes	N/A

Appendix J

State ICPC Office Phone Numbers

State	Telephone Number	State	Telephone Number
Alabama	334-242-1468	Montana	406-444-5917
Alaska	907-465-2105	Nebraska	402-471-9245
Arizona	602-235-9134 ext. 7102	Nevada	775-684-4418
Arkansas	501-682-8556	New Hampshire	603-271-4708
California	916-651-8111	New Jersey	609-292-3188
Colorado	303-866-2998	New Mexico	505-827-8457
Connecticut	860-550-6392	New York	518-473-1591
Delaware	302-633-2698/2683	North Carolina	919-733-9465
District of Columbia	202-727-7755	North Dakota	701-328-3581 701-328-4152
Florida	850-922-6656	Ohio	614-466-9274
Georgia	404-657-3567 404-657-3564	Oklahoma	405-522-1599
Hawaii	808-586-5699	Oregon	503-945-6685
Idaho	208-334-5700 208-334-5652	Pennsylvania	717-772-5505
Illinois	217-785-2680	Rhode Island	401-254-7077
Indiana	317-232-4769	South Carolina	803-898-7637
Iowa	515-281-5730	South Dakota	605-773-3227
Kansas	785-296-0918	Tennessee	615-532-5618
Kentucky	502-564-2147	Texas	512-438-4153
Louisiana	225-342-4034	Utah	801-538-4364
Maine	207-287-5060	Vermont	802-241-2141
Maryland	410-767-7506	Virginia	804-726-7581
Massachusetts	617-748-2375	Washington	360-902-7987
Michigan	517-373-6918	West Virginia	304-558-1260
Minnesota	651-296-2725	Wisconsin	608-266-8501
Mississippi	601-359-4986	Wyoming	307-777-3570
Missouri	573-751-2981		

Allowable Birth Parent Expenses

State	Allowable birth parent expenses
Alabama*	Maternity-related medical and hospital expenses, necessary living expenses
Alaska*	Expenses incurred in connection with birth, medical and hospital care, and adoption-related services
Arizona*	Reasonable and necessary expenses, including medical and hospital costs, counseling fees, legal and agency fees, up to $1,000 for living expenses (unless approved by court), and other expenses approved by court
Arkansas*	Expenses incurred in connection with birth, medical and hospital care, adoption-related services, and legal services
California*	Reasonable maternity-related expenses, including medical and hospital costs, fees for adoption-related services, legal fees, counseling fees, and reasonable living expenses (birth parent is required to provide written request for any payment expenses)
Colorado*	Medical and legal fees as approved by court
Connecticut	Counseling fees (including transportation), living expenses up to $1,500, reasonable telephone expenses, reasonable maternity clothing expenses
Delaware*	Court and legal fees only
District of Columbia	Not specified in statute
Florida*	Reasonable living expenses (rent, food, basic phone service, utilities, transportation, insurance, clothes), medical and hospital costs, fees for adoption-related services, legal fees, and other court-approved expenses
Georgia*	Pregnancy-related medical and hospital costs, expenses related to placement and adoption
Hawaii	Not specified in statute
Idaho*	Legal and medical expenses, reasonable living and maternity expenses during the pregnancy and up to six weeks postpartum (financial assistance cannot exceed $2,000 unless court approved)
Illinois*	Reasonable living expenses (lodging, food, clothes) where need is demonstrated, medical and hospital costs, and court-approved legal fees
Indiana*	Reasonable attorney fees, hospital and medical costs, counseling expenses, travel and maternity clothing expenses, living expenses during second and third trimesters and up to six weeks postpartum, wages lost as a result of medical complications, additional court-approved living expenses up to $1,000

Iowa*	Legal costs for termination of parental rights and adoption, costs of pregnancy- and birth-related medical care for mother and child, living expenses (room, board, food, medical-related transportation), counseling fees, and expenses related to foster care for child
Kansas*	Reasonable and customary legal and professional fees, medical costs for mother and child, living expenses, and adoption-related incidentals (excessive expenses prohibited)
Kentucky*	Court-approved legal fees, cost of placement services, and expenses of birth parents
Louisiana*	Reasonable medical and hospital costs (including pharmaceuticals, travel, and similar needs) for mother and child, living expenses up to forty-five days postpartum, counseling and training fees, legal fees, and other court-approved fees
Maine*	Legal fees for consent and expenses for prenatal and postnatal counseling; prenatal, birth, and postnatal medical costs; transportation to related services; foster care for child; reasonable living expenses; and fees to placement agency
Maryland*	Reasonable and customary fees for hospital and medical and legal services
Massachusetts	Not specified in statute
Michigan*	Medical, hospital, nursing, and pharmaceutical expenses of mother and child (unless covered by mother's insurance or Medicaid); adoption-related counseling; living expenses up to six weeks postpartum; and legal fees
Minnesota	Reasonable expenses for counseling, medical, legal, and adoption-related services, which must be paid directly to service provider; expenses for transportation, meals, and lodging; and reasonable living expenses up to six weeks postpartum (not including lost wages, gifts, educational expenses, and similar expenses)
Mississippi*	Court-approved legal fees and counseling, medical, and hospital fees
Missouri*	Hospital, medical, and physician expenses; expenses for counseling services within a reasonable time before and after placement; necessary assessment fees; reasonable legal, court, travel, and administrative expenses; reasonable living expenses (food, shelter, utilities, transportation, clothing); and other court-approved expenses
Montana*	Medical and prenatal care, foster care, counseling, and travel and temporary living expenses; legal fees; and reasonable adoption-related expenses (cannot cover expenses for education, vehicle, salary, wages, vacations, permanent housing, or eleven or more hours of counseling)
Nebraska	Not specified in statute
Nevada*	Medical and necessary living expenses
New Hampshire*	Reasonable counseling, medical, and legal fees; expenses for adoption-related services, which must be paid directly to service provider; expenses for transportation, meals, and lodging; and reasonable living expenses up to six weeks postpartum (not including gifts over $50, educational expenses, and any payments for monetary gain)
New Jersey*	Medical, hospital, counseling, and other birth-related expenses; living expenses up to four weeks postpartum; and legal fees

New Mexico*	Medical, hospital, nursing, and pharmaceutical expenses; travel expenses; expenses for counseling services; legal and court fees; living expenses up to six weeks postpartum; and any other court-approved expenses
New York*	Reasonable and actual nursing, medical, hospital, and legal fees; reasonable expenses for housing, maternity clothes, and clothing for child; and transportation expenses
North Carolina*	Medical, hospital, nursing, and pharmaceutical expenses; travel expenses; expenses for counseling services; legal and court fees; and living expenses up to six weeks postpartum
North Dakota*	Fees for pre-placement counseling, adoption assessment, placement of child, and foster care; other fees related to pre-adoption and legal services, which must be paid directly to service provider; prenatal and medical expenses not covered by insurance; transportation, lodging, and meal expenses; and living expenses up to six weeks postpartum (not including gifts, educational expenses, vacations, or similar expenses)
Ohio*	Physician, hospital, and other medical facility expenses; attorney and court fees; expenses for temporary maintenance and medical care; expenses related to foster care; and guardian ad litem fees
Oklahoma*	Reasonable attorney fees, medical expenses, counseling expenses up to six months after placement, travel and transportation expenses, and additional court-approved funds needed for initial payments in excess of $500 (no payments beyond two months post-placement)
Oregon*	Legal, medical, living, and travel expenses
Pennsylvania*	Medical and hospital costs, foster care expenses, and fees for adjustment counseling and training services
Rhode Island	Not specified in statute
South Carolina*	Necessary and actual medical costs and reasonable living expenses for a reasonable amount of time (all expenses must have a corresponding receipt)
South Dakota*	Court-approved expenses only
Tennessee*	Fees for reasonable hospital and medical services related to birth; reasonable counseling and legal fees; and reasonable and actual expenses for housing, food, maternity clothes, child's clothing, utilities, and transportation from ninety days prior to birth and thirty days after birth or surrender
Texas	Legal and medical expenses for adoption-related counseling (necessary pregnancy-related expenses paid by placement agency)
Utah*	Actual and reasonable legal expenses, maternity expenses, related medical and hospital costs, and necessary living expenses
Vermont*	Medical, hospital, nursing, pharmaceutical, and similar costs; fees for counseling services before and after birth; living expenses up to six weeks postpartum; legal fees, court costs, and administrative fees; fees for transportation to services; and other court-approved services and expenses

Virginia*	Medical expenses and insurance premiums related to pregnancy and hospitalization; fees for mental health counseling for birth mother and father; reasonable and necessary expenses for food, clothing, and shelter if birth mother is unable to work during pregnancy; expenses for any court appearances (including but not limited to food, lodging, and transportation); legal fees; and expenses for any service-related transportation
Washington*	Prenatal, hospital, and medical expenses; attorney fees; and court costs
West Virginia*	Reasonable and customary legal, medical, and hospital expenses and other expenses incurred during pregnancy, birth, and adoption proceedings, and any other court-approved expenses
Wisconsin*	Pre-adoptive and post-adoptive counseling for birth parents, reasonable maternity clothing expenses, local transportation expenses, medical and hospital care expenses for mother and child, legal fees, living expenses up to $1,000 when necessary to protect health and welfare of mother or fetus, fees for birthing classes, and gifts valued at under $50
Wyoming	Not specified in statute

*A full accounting of any payments made for birth parent expenses may be required by court or at judge's discretion.

Appendix L

Timeframes for Consent and Revocation of Parental Rights

State	Timeframe for birth mother to consent to terminate rights	Timeframe for birth father to consent to terminate rights	Timeframe to revoke termination of parental rights after consent is signed
Alabama	Before (requires reaffirmation after birth) or after birth	Before (requires reaffirmation after birth) or after birth	Within five days for any reason; within fourteen days with court approval
Alaska	Anytime after birth	Anytime after birth	Within ten days; after ten days with court approval
Arizona	Seventy-two hours after birth	Seventy-two hours after birth	Irrevocable
Arkansas	Anytime after birth	Anytime after birth	Within ten days
California	Anytime after mother's discharge from hospital	Anytime after mother's discharge from hospital	Within thirty days for independent adoption; irrevocable for agency adoption
Colorado	Anytime after birth	Anytime after birth	Within ninety days
Connecticut	Forty-eight hours after birth	Forty-eight hours after birth	Prior to finalization
Delaware	Anytime after birth	Anytime before or after birth	Within sixty days
District of Columbia	Seventy-two hours after birth	Seventy-two hours after birth	Within ten days
Florida	Forty-eight hours after birth	Anytime before or after	Irrevocable for children under six months old; within three days for children six months or older
Georgia	Anytime after birth	Anytime after birth	Within ten days
Hawaii	Following the sixth month of pregnancy (requires reaffirmation after birth) or after birth	Before (requires reaffirmation after birth) or after birth	Irrevocable after placement with prospective adoptive parents without court approval
Idaho	Anytime after birth	Anytime after birth	Unspecified in statute
Illinois	Seventy-two hours after birth	Anytime before or after birth	Irrevocable

Indiana	Anytime after birth	Anytime after birth	Within thirty days
Iowa	Seventy-two hours after birth	Seventy-two hours after birth	Within ninety-six hours of execution of termination by court
Kansas	Twelve hours after birth	Anytime before or after birth	Irrevocable
Kentucky	Seventy-two hours after birth	Seventy-two hours after birth	Within twenty days of approved placement or execution of consent
Louisiana	Five days after birth	Anytime before or after birth	Irrevocable
Maine	Anytime after birth	Anytime after birth	Within three days
Maryland	Anytime after birth	Anytime after birth	Within thirty days
Massachusetts	Four days after birth	Four days after birth	Irrevocable
Michigan	After birth only during a scheduled appearance before a judge	After birth only during a scheduled appearance before a judge	Irrevocable after placement
Minnesota	Seventy-two hours after birth	Seventy-two hours after birth	Within ten working days
Mississippi	Seventy-two hours after birth	Seventy-two hours after birth	Irrevocable
Missouri	Forty-eight hours after birth	Forty-eight hours after birth	Prior to consent review and acceptance by judge
Montana	Seventy-two hours after birth	Seventy-two hours after birth	Irrevocable after issuance of termination order
Nebraska	Forty-eight hours after birth	Forty-eight hours after birth	Irrevocable
Nevada	Seventy-two hours after birth	Anytime before or after birth	Irrevocable
New Hampshire	Seventy-two hours after birth	Seventy-two hours after birth	Prior to final hearing
New Jersey	Seventy-two hours after birth	Anytime before or after birth	Irrevocable after valid surrender to agency
New Mexico	Forty-eight hours after birth	Forty-eight hours after birth	Irrevocable after final decree
New York	Anytime after birth	Anytime after birth	Irrevocable in independent adoption after consent given in court; within thirty days for agency adoption
North Carolina	Anytime after birth	Anytime before or after birth	Within seven days
North Dakota	Anytime after birth	Anytime after birth	Prior to finalization
Ohio	Seventy-two hours after birth	Seventy-two hours after birth	Irrevocable

State	Timeframe for birth mother to consent to terminate rights	Timeframe for birth father to consent to terminate rights	Timeframe to revoke termination of parental rights after consent is signed
Oklahoma	Anytime after birth	Anytime before or after birth	Irrevocable when signed before judge; within fifteen days when signed before notary public
Oregon	Anytime after birth	Anytime after birth	Irrevocable
Pennsylvania	Seventy-two hours after birth	Anytime before or after birth	Within thirty days after birth or signing, whichever occurs later
Rhode Island	Fifteen days after birth	Fifteen days after birth	Within 180 days and adoption deemed by court as not in the child's best interest
South Carolina	Anytime after birth	Anytime after birth	Irrevocable
South Dakota	Five days after birth	Five days after birth	Within thirty days of adoption finalization
Tennessee	Three days after birth	Three days after birth	Within ten days
Texas	Forty-eight hours after birth	Anytime before or after birth	Within ten days
Utah	Twenty-four hours after birth	Anytime before or after birth	Irrevocable
Vermont	Thirty-six hours after birth	Thirty-six hours after birth	Within twenty-one days
Virginia	Ten days after birth	Ten days after birth	Within fifteen days
Washington	Before (requires reaffirmation forty-eight hours after birth) or after birth	Before (requires reaffirmation forty-eight hours after birth) or after birth	Irrevocable after court approval of consent
West Virginia	Seventy-two hours after birth	Seventy-two hours after birth	Irrevocable
Wisconsin	After birth and hearing is held within thirty days filing of petition	After birth and hearing is held within thirty days filing of petition	Irrevocable after court approval of consent
Wyoming	Anytime after birth	Anytime after birth	Irrevocable

Appendix M

States with Presumed or Putative Father Registries

State	Presumed or Putative Father Registry	State	Presumed or Putative Father Registry
Alabama	Yes	Montana	Yes
Alaska	No	Nebraska	Yes
Arizona	Yes	Nevada	No
Arkansas	Yes	New Hampshire	Yes
California	No	New Jersey	No
Colorado	No	New Mexico	Yes
Connecticut	No	New York	Yes
Delaware	Yes	North Carolina	No
District of Columbia	No	North Dakota	No
Florida	Yes	Ohio	Yes
Georgia	Yes	Oklahoma	Yes
Hawaii	No	Oregon	No
Idaho	Yes	Pennsylvania	No
Illinois	Yes	Rhode Island	No
Indiana	Yes	South Carolina	No
Iowa	Yes	South Dakota	No
Kansas	No	Tennessee	Yes
Kentucky	No	Texas	Yes
Louisiana	Yes	Utah	No
Maine	No	Vermont	No
Maryland	No	Virginia	No
Massachusetts	No	Washington	No
Michigan	No	West Virginia	No
Minnesota	Yes	Wisconsin	No
Mississippi	No	Wyoming	Yes
Missouri	Yes		

Appendix N Most Frequently Used Sending Countries to the United States

Country (member of Hague Convention?)	Child characteristics	Age requirements	Marital status and other requirements	Restrictions regarding other children	Travel requirement	Country placement authority	Legal status of adoption	Post-placement reports requirement
China (yes)	Children six months to thirteen years old, older children, sibling groups, and children with special needs	Adoptive parents must be between thirty and forty-nine years old.	Couples must be married at least two years and have no more than two divorces between them. If previously divorced, they must now be married for at least for five years. Adoptive parents must have a minimum net worth $80,000, a body mass index under 40, and a minimum of a high school education.	No more than four minor children	Yes	China Center of Adoption Affairs	Finalized	Post-placement report at six and twelve months
Taiwan (no)	Children six months to thirteen years old, older children, sibling groups, and children with special needs	Adoptive parents must be at least twenty years older than the child, and no older than fifty-five years old.	Couples must be married at least five years. Singles may apply for older children only.	No more than four minor children	Interview with American Institute in Taiwan is required.	Children's Bureau, Ministry of Interior	Finalized	Quarterly written reports with photographs for one year post-adoption; annual reports for a minimum of seven years
Colombia (yes)	Newborns, toddlers, older children, sibling groups, and children with special needs	Adoptive parents must be at least twenty-five years old. Adoptive parents thirty-seven and older are referred to children over three years old.	Couples must be married for more than three years. Singles may apply for children over the age of seven only.	No restrictions specified	Both parents are required to spend a minimum of days in the country and appear before a judge for adoption decree.	Colombian Family Welfare Institute	Finalized	Post-placement report at six months

Ethiopia (no)	Children three months to thirteen years old, older children, sibling groups, and children with special needs	Adoptive parents must be at least twenty-five years old. Adoptive parents cannot be more than forty years older than the child.	Couples must be married at least two years. Singles are not encouraged to apply. The Ethiopian government prefers that couples be married for at least five years.	No restrictions	No	Adoption Team in the Children and Youth Affairs Office, under the Ministry of Women's Affairs	Finalized	Post-placement reports at three months, six months, and one year after the adoption; annual reports until the child reaches the age eighteen
Guatemala (yes)	Infants, toddlers, older children, sibling groups, and children with special needs	Adoptive parents must be at least twenty-five years old. Applicants over fifty must be flexible regarding the age of the child.	The Hague Convention has implications for adoption from Guatemala; please check with the Department of State.	No restrictions	No	Social Services Agency Bienestar Social	Finalized	Post-placement supervision and reports required for six months
Haiti (no)	Infants, toddlers, older children, sibling groups, and children with special needs	One adoptive parent must be at least thirty-five years old.	No requirement	No more than three birth children	No	Haitian Ministry of Social Affairs' Institut du Bien Etre Social et de Recherches	Finalized	Post-placement reports with photos required after arrival; after three, six, nine, and twelve months; and annually for two years
India (yes)	Children at least eight months old, toddlers, older children, sibling groups, and children with special needs	Adoptive parents must be between thirty and fifty-five years old. The combined ages of adoptive parents wishing to adopt an infant, must be under forty-five years old.	Proof of infertility or secondary infertility may be required in certain Indian states.	No more than three children	Yes, adoptive parents should anticipate that two to three months will be needed to complete all formalities in India, barring any particularly unusual delays.	Central Adoption Resource Agency	Guardianship bestowed to parents; finalized in the United States	Post-placement reports bi-annually for two years

Appendix N   Most Frequently Used Sending Countries to the United States—*(Continued)*

Country	Children available	Adoptive parent age	Other requirements	Number restrictions	Travel requirement	Authority	Finalization	Post-placement reports
Kazakhstan (no)	Children at least six months old, toddlers, older children, sibling groups, and children with special needs	Adoptive parents must be between twenty-five and fifty years old, and at least sixteen years older than the child.	Couples must be married at least two years. Single women may also apply. There is no pre-referral of the child. Referral of the child occurs in Kazakhstan.	No restrictions specified	Both parents must stay for a minimum of sixty days.	Ministry of Education, Committee on Guardianship and Care	Finalized	Post-placement reports with photos required after arrival, and at six, twelve, and twenty-four months; annual reports until the child reaches the age of eighteen
South Korea (no)	Children six months of age and older, toddlers, older children, sibling groups, and children with special needs (adoptive parents cannot request a particular gender)	Adoptive parents must be between twenty-five and forty-three years old.	Couples must be married at least three years. A minimum family income of $35,000 is required. Adoptive parents may weigh no more than 30 percent over the normal weight for their height.	No more than four children	No	Ministry of Health and Social Welfare	Guardianship bestowed to parents; finalized in the United States	Post-placement reports required during finalization period
Liberia (no)	Generally children four years of age and older, children with special needs	Adoptive parents must be at least twenty-five years old.	No requirement	No restrictions specified	No	Ministry of Justice	Finalized	Unspecified
Mexico (yes)	Children four months old and older, toddlers, older children, sibling groups, and children with special needs. If the child is over fourteen years old, he or she must consent to the adoption.	Adoptive parents must be at least twenty-five years old, and at least seventeen years older than the child.	No requirement	No restrictions specified	Both parents must travel and may have to stay up to three months or longer. Length of the adoptive parent's stay is at the discretion of Mexican judge.	State System for the Full Development of the Family	Finalized	Unspecified
Philippines (yes)	Children six months to fifteen years old, older children, sibling groups, and children with special needs	Adoptive parents must be between twenty-seven and forty-five years old, and at least sixteen years older than the child to be adopted.	Couples must be married at least three years with no more than one divorce per person. Singles are reviewed on a case-by-case basis and may be matched with an older or special-needs child.	No restrictions specified	Yes	Department of Social Welfare and Development and the Inter-country Adoption Board.	Guardianship bestowed to parents; finalized in the United States	Post-placement reports with photos required after arrival, and after three and six months

	Children eligible	Parent requirements		Number of children	Trips required	Agency/Ministry	Status	Post-placement reports
Russian Federation (yes)	Children six months of age and older, toddlers, older children, sibling groups, and children with special needs	Adoptive parents must be at least twenty-five years old, and between sixteen and forty-five years older than the child to be adopted.	No requirement	No restrictions specified	Two trips are required. Both parents must travel for the first trip.	Ministry of Education and Science of the Russian Federation	Finalized	Post-placement reports with photos required after arrival and after six, twelve, twenty-four, and thirty-six months
Ukraine (no)	Children 12 months of age and older, toddlers, older children, sibling groups, and children with special needs	Adoptive parents must be at least eighteen years old, and between fifteen and forty-five years older than the child.	Couples are given priority over single applicants. Ukraine limits the total number of all intercountry adoptions processed during the calendar year. Referral of child occurs in Ukraine.	No restrictions specified	Yes	State Department for Adoptions and Protection of Rights of the Child	Finalized	Post-placement reports with photos required after six, twelve, and twenty-four months; annual reports until the child reaches the age of eighteen
Vietnam (no)	Infants and children up to fifteen years old, older children, sibling groups, and children with special needs (children over nine years old must provide written consent to the adoption)	At least one of the adoptive parents must be at least twenty years older than the child. Adoptive parents should be between the ages of twenty-five and fifty years old. Older parents may be reviewed on case-by-case basis.	No requirement	No more than five children	Yes	Ministry of Justice's Department of International Adoptions	Finalized	Post-placement reports every six months for the first three years; annual reports until the child reaches the age of eighteen

Appendix O

State Readoption Requirements

State	Readoption required	Full recognition of intercountry adoption decrees
Alabama	Not specified in statute	Not specified in statute
Alaska	Not specified in statute	Yes
Arizona	Not specified in statute	No
Arkansas	Not specified in statute	Yes
California	No	Not specified in statute
Colorado	Yes	Not specified in statute
Connecticut	Yes	Not specified in statute
Delaware	No	Yes
District of Columbia	Not specified in statute	Not specified in statute
Florida	Not specified in statute	Yes
Georgia	No	Yes
Hawaii	Yes	Yes
Idaho	No	Yes
Illinois	Not specified in statute	Yes
Indiana	Not specified in statute	Yes
Iowa	Not specified in statute	Yes
Kansas	Yes	No
Kentucky	Not specified in statute	Not specified in statute
Louisiana	Yes	No
Maine	Yes	No
Maryland	No	Yes
Massachusetts	No	Yes
Michigan	Not specified in statute	Yes
Minnesota	No	Yes
Mississippi	Not specified in statute	Not specified in statute
Missouri	Not specified in statute	Yes
Montana	Not specified in statute	Yes
Nebraska	Not specified in statute	Not specified in statute
Nevada	Not specified in statute	Not specified in statute

New Hampshire	No	Yes
New Jersey	No	Yes
New Mexico	Not specified in statute	Yes
New York	Yes	No
North Carolina	No	Yes
North Dakota	Not specified in statute	Yes
Ohio	No	Yes
Oklahoma	No	Yes
Oregon	Not specified in statute	Yes
Pennsylvania	Yes	No
Rhode Island	Not specified in statute	Not specified in statute
South Carolina	Yes	No
South Dakota	Not specified in statute	Not specified in statute
Tennessee	No	Not specified in statute
Texas	No	Yes
Utah	No	Yes
Vermont	Not specified in statute	Yes
Virginia	Not specified in statute	Not specified in statute
Washington	Not specified in statute	Not specified in statute
West Virginia	No	Yes
Wisconsin	No	Yes
Wyoming	Not specified in statute	Not specified in statute

Early Intervention Oversight Agencies

State	Early Intervention Oversight Agency
Alabama	Early Intervention Program Department of Rehabilitation Services 2129 East South Boulevard P.O. Box 11586 Montgomery, AL 36111-0586 Phone: 334-215-5043 TTY: 800-499-1816 Fax: 334-215-5046 Web site: http://www.rehab.state.al.us/
Alaska	State of Alaska/DHSS Office of Children's Services, Suite 934 P.O. Box 240249 Anchorage, AK 99524-0249 Phone: 907-269-3423 Fax: 907-269-3497 Web site: http://health.hss.state.ak.us/ocs/InfantLearning/default.htm
Arizona	Arizona Early Intervention Program Department of Economic Security 3839 North Third Street, Suite 304 Site Code #801 A-6 Phoenix, AZ 85012 Phone: 602-532-9960 or 888-439-5609 (in Arizona) Fax: 602-200-9820 Web site: http://www.de.state.az.us/azeip/default.asp
Arkansas	Department of Human Services Division of Developmental Disabilities Children's Services P.O. Box 1437, Slot N504 Little Rock, AR 72203-1437 Phone: 501-682-8703 or 501-682-8695 Fax: 501-682-8890 Web site: http://www.arkansas.gov/dhhs/ddds/FirstConn/index.html
California	Early Start Children and Family Services Branch Department of Developmental Services 1600 Ninth Street, MS 3-12 Sacramento, CA 95814 Phone: 916-654-2773 or 800-515-2229 Fax: 916-654-3255 Web site: http://www.dds.ca.gov/EarlyStart/ESHome.cfm

Colorado	CDHS-Division for Developmental Disabilities 3824 West Princeton Circle Denver, CO 80236 Phone: 303-866-7657 Fax: 303-866-7680 Web site: http://www.earlychildhoodconnections.org/
Connecticut	Birth to Three System Department of Mental Retardation 460 Capitol Avenue Hartford, CT 06106-1308 Phone: 860-418-6147 or 800-505-7000 (for referrals) Fax: 860-418-6003 Web site: http://www.birth23.org/
Delaware	Division of Management Services Department of Health and Social Services Main Administration Building, Room 204 1901 North Dupont Highway New Castle, DE 19720 Phone: 302-255-9135 Fax: 302-255-4407 Web site: http://www.dhss.delaware.gov/dhss/dms/epqc/birth3/directry.html
District of Columbia	Early Care and Education Administration Infants and Toddlers with Disabilities Division 717 Fourteenth Street, NW, Suite 1200 Washington, DC 20002 Phone: 202-727-5853 Fax: 202-727-9709 Web site: http://dhs.dc.gov/dhs/cwp
Florida	Children's Medical Services Early Steps State Department of Health 4052 Bald Cypress Way SE, Bin A06 Tallahassee, FL 32399-1707 Phone: 850-245-4444 ext. 4221 or 800-654-4440 Fax: 850-921-5241 Web site: http://www.cms-kids.com/
Georgia	Office of Children with Special Needs, Babies Can't Wait Program Division of Public Health, Family Health Branch Department of Human Resources 2 Peachtree Street NE, Suite 11-206 Atlanta, GA 30303-3186 Phone: 404-657-2721 or 888-651-8224 Fax: 404-657-2763 Web site: http://health.state.ga.us/programs/bcw/index.asp
Hawaii	Early Intervention Section State Department of Health Pan Am Building 1600 Kapiolani Boulevard, Suite 1401 Honolulu, HI 96814 Phone: 808-973-9656 Fax: 808-973-9655 Web site: http://www.hawaii.gov/health/family-child-health/eis/

Idaho	Children's Developmental Services State Department of Health and Welfare 450 West State Street, Fifth Floor P.O. Box 83720 Boise, ID 83720-0036 Phone: 208-334-5523 or 800-926-2588 Fax: 208-334-6664 Web site: http://www.healthandwelfare.idaho.gov/portal/alias__Rainbow/ lang__en-US/tabID__3369/DesktopDefault.aspx
Illinois	Department of Human Services Division of Community Health and Prevention Bureau of Early Intervention 222 South College, Second Floor Springfield, IL 62704 Phone: 217-782-1981 or 800-323-4769 (in Illinois) Fax: 217-524-6248 Web site: http://www.dhs.state.il.us/ei/
Indiana	First Steps Bureau of Child Development Division of Family and Children 402 West Washington Street #W-386, MS02 Indianapolis, IN 46204 Phone: 317-233-9229 or 800-441-7837 (in Indiana) Fax: 317-232-7948 Web site: http://www.state.in.us/fssa/first_step/index.html
Iowa	Early ACCESS (IDEA/Part C) Iowa Department of Education Bureau of Children, Family, and Community Services Grimes State Office Building, Third Floor Des Moines, IA 50319-0146 Phone: 515-281-5437 or 800-779-2001 Fax: 515-242-6019 Web site: http://www.state.ia.us/earlyaccess/
Kansas	Children's Developmental Services State Department of Health and Environment 1000 Southwest Jackson, Suite 220 Topeka, KS 66612-1274 Phone: 785-296-6135 or 800-332-6262 (in Kansas) Fax: 785-296-8626 Web site: http://www.kdheks.gov/its/
Kentucky	Early Childhood Development Branch Department for Public Health 275 East Main Street, HS2WC Frankfort, KY 40621 Phone: 502-564-3756 ext. 3800 Fax: 502-564-8389 Web site: http://chfs.ky.gov/dph/firststeps.htm

Louisiana	Early Steps Louisiana's Early Intervention System 1010 Common Street, Room 1147 New Orleans, LA 70112 Phone: 504-599-1072 or 866-327-5978 (in Louisiana) Fax: 504-599-1082 Web site: http://www.oph.dhh.state.la.us/childrensspecial/ earlyinterventionservices/index.html
Maine	Early Childhood Special Education Department of Education State House Station #146 Augusta, ME 04333 Phone: 207-624-6660 or 800-355-8611 Fax: 207-624-6661 Web site: http://www.maine.gov/education/speced/cds/index.htm
Maryland	Infant/Toddler/Preschool Services Division of Special Education and Early Intervention Services State Department of Education 200 West Baltimore Street Baltimore, MD 21201 Phone: 410-767-0261 or 800-535-0182 (in Maryland) Fax: 410-333-2661 Web site: http://www.marylandpublicschools.org/MSDE/divisions/ earlyinterv/infant_toddlers/message.htm
Massachusetts	State Department of Public Health 250 Washington Street, Fourth Floor Boston, MA 02108-4619 Phone: 617-624-5901 or 617-624-5070 Central directory for early intervention: 800-905-8437 Fax: 617-624-5927 Web site: http://www.mass.gov/dph/fch/ei.htm
Michigan	Early On Michigan Office of Early Childhood Education and Family Services State Department of Education P.O. Box 30008 Lansing, MI 48909-7508 Phone: 517-335-4865 or 800-327-5966 Fax: 517-373-7504 Web site: http://www.1800earlyon.org/
Minnesota	State Department of Education Special Education Policy 1500 Highway 36 West Roseville, MN 55113-4266 Phone: 651-582-8883 or 800-728-5420 Fax: 651-582-8494 Web site: http://children.state.mn.us/mde/Learning_Support/Special_ Education/Birth_to_Age_21_Programs_Services/Early_Childhood_ Special_Education/index.html

Mississippi	First Steps State Department of Health Early Intervention A-107 570 East Woodrow Wilson P.O. Box 1700 Jackson, MS 39215-1700 Phone: 601-576-7816 or 800-451-3903 (in Mississippi) Fax: 601-576-7540 Web site: http://www.msdh.state.ms.us/msdhsite/index.cfm/41074.html
Missouri	Early Intervention Services Department of Education P.O. Box 480 Jefferson City, MO 65102-0480 Phone: 573-751-3559 Fax: 573-526-4404 Web site: http://dese.mo.gov/divspeced/FirstSteps/index.html
Montana	Developmental Disabilities Program Community Services Bureau Department of Public Health and Human Services P.O. Box 4210 Helena, MT 59604-4210 Phone: 406-444-5647 Fax: 406-444-0230 Web site: http://www.dphhs.mt.gov/dsd/
Nebraska	Special Education Office State Department of Education 301 Centennial Mall South P.O. Box 94987 Lincoln, NE 68509-4987 Phone: 402-471-2463 Fax: 402-471-5022 Web site: http://www.nde.state.ne.us/edn/
Nevada	Nevada Department of Human Resources Division of Health Bureau of Early Intervention Services 3427 Goni Road, Suite 108 Carson City, NV 89706 Phone: 775-684-3464 or 800-522-0066 Fax: 775-684-3486 Web site: http://health2k.state.nv.us/BEIS/
New Hampshire	Family Centered Early Supports and Services Bureau of Developmental Services Department of Health and Human Services 105 Pleasant Street Concord, NH 03301 Phone: 603-271-5122 or 800-852-3345 (in New Hampshire) Fax: 603-271-5166 Web site: http://www.dhhs.nh.gov/DHHS/BDS/family-early-support.htm

New Jersey	Early Intervention Program Division of Family Health Services Department of Health and Senior Services P.O. Box 364 Trenton, NJ 08625-0364 Phone: 609-777-7734 Fax: 609-292-0296 Web site: http://nj.gov/health/fhs/eis/index.shtml
New Mexico	Long Term Services Division State Department of Health 1190 St. Francis Drive P.O. Box 26110 Santa Fe, NM 87502-6110 Phone: 505-827-0103 or 877-696-1472 Fax: 505-827-2455 Web site: http://www.health.state.nm.us/ddsd/fit/index.html
New York	Early Intervention Program State Department of Health Corning Tower Building, Room 287 Empire State Plaza Albany, NY 12237-0660 Phone: 518-473-7016 or 800-577-2229 (in New York City) Fax: 518-473-8673 Growing Up Healthy 24-Hour Hotline: 800-522-5006 for information on a variety of topics including the Early Intervention Program Web site: http://www.health.state.ny.us/community/infants_children/ early_intervention/index.htm
North Carolina	Early Intervention Branch Head Women's & Children's Health Section Division of Public Health 1916 Mail Service Center Raleigh, NC 27699-1916 Phone: 919-707-5535 Fax: 919-870-4834 Web site: http://www.ncei.org/ei/index.html
North Dakota	Developmental Disabilities Unit Department of Human Services 1237 West Divide Avenue, Suite 1A Bismarck, ND 58501 Phone: 701-328-8936 or 800-755-8529 (in North Dakota) Fax: 701-328-8969 Web site: http://www.nd.gov/humanservices/services/disabilities/ earlyintervention/
Ohio	Bureau of EI Services State Department of Health 246 North High Street, Fifth Floor P.O. Box 118 Columbus, OH 43266-0118 Phone: 614-644-9164 or 800-755-4769 Fax: 614-728-9163 Web site: http://www.ohiohelpmegrow.org/

Oklahoma	Special Education Office State Department of Education Oliver Hodge Memorial Education Building, Fourth Floor 2500 North Lincoln Boulevard Oklahoma City, OK 73105-4599 Phone: 405-521-4880 Fax: 405-522-3503 Web site: http://sde.state.ok.us/home/
Oregon	Early Childhood Programs State Department of Education 255 Capitol Street NE Salem, OR 97310-0203 Phone: 503-378-3600 ext. 52338 Fax: 503-373-7968 Web site: http://www.ode.state.or.us/search/results/?id=252
Pennsylvania	Division of Program Implementation Office of Child Development Department of Public Welfare P.O. Box 2675 Harrisburg, PA 17105-2675 Phone: 717-783-7213 or 800-692-7288 Fax: 717-772-0012 Web site: http://www.dpw.state.pa.us/Child/EarlyIntervention/
Rhode Island	Department of Human Services Center for Child and Family Health 600 New London Avenue Cranston, RI 02920 Phone: 401-462-0318 Fax: 401-462-6253 Web site: http://www.dhs.ri.gov/dhs/famchild/early_intervention.htm
South Carolina	Division of Children & Youth with Special Health Care Needs SC DHEC P.O. Box 101106 Columbia, SC 29211 Phone: 803-898-0789 Fax: 803-898-0613 Web site: http://www.scdhec.net/health/mch/cshcn/programs/babynet/
South Dakota	Office of Special Education Department of Education Kneip Building 700 Governors Drive Pierre, SD 57501-2291 Phone: 605-773-3678 or 800-305-3064 Fax: 605-773-3782 Web site: http://doe.sd.gov/oess/Birthto3/

Tennessee	Early Childhood Services/Division of Special Education State Department of Education Andrew Johnson Tower, Seventh Floor 710 James Robertson Parkway Nashville, TN 37243-0375 Phone: 615-741-3537 or 615-741-2851 or 888-212-3162 Fax: 615-532-9412 Web site: http://www.state.tn.us/education/speced/TEIS/
Texas	Texas Early Childhood Intervention Program Department of Assistive and Rehabilitative Services Brown-Heatly State Office Building 4900 North Lamar Austin, TX 78751-2399 Phone: 512-424-6754 or 800-250-2246 Fax: 512-424-6749 Web site: http://www.dars.state.tx.us/ecis/index.shtml
Utah	Baby Watch Early Intervention State Department of Health P.O. Box 144720 Salt Lake City, UT 84114-4720 Phone: 801-584-8441 or 800-961-4226 Fax: 801-584-8496 Web site: http://www.utahbabywatch.org
Vermont	Family, Infant and Toddler Program DCF-2 North 103 South Main Street Waterbury, VT 05671-2901 Phone: 802-241-3622 Fax: 802-241-1220 Web site: http://www.dcf.state.vt.us/cdd/programs/prevention/fitp/index.html
Virginia	Infant and Toddler Connection of VA Department of MH/MR/SA Services P.O. Box 1797 Richmond, VA 23218-1797 Phone: 804-371-6592 Central directory for Early Intervention: 800-234-1448 Fax: 804-371-7959 Web site: http://www.infantva.org/
Washington	Infant Toddler Early Intervention Program Department of Social and Health Services 640 Woodland Square Loop SE P.O. Box 45201 Olympia, WA 98504-5201 Phone: 360-725-3516 Fax: 360-725-3523 Web site: http://www1.dshs.wa.gov/iteip/

West Virginia	Early Intervention Program
	Office of Maternal and Child Health
	Department of Health and Human Resources
	350 Capital Street, Room 427
	Charleston, WV 25301
	Phone: 304-558-6311; 304-558-3071; or 866-321-4728
	Fax: 304-558-4984
	Web site: http://www.wvdhhr.org/birth23/
Wisconsin	Family Centered Services and Systems Administration
	Bureau of Developmental Disabilities
	1 West Wilson Street, Room 418
	P.O. Box 7851
	Madison, WI 53707-7851
	Phone: 608-266-7469 or 800-642-7837
	Fax: 608-261-6752
	Web site: http://dhfs.wisconsin.gov/bdds/birthto3/
Wyoming	Division of Developmental Disabilities
	Early Intervention Council
	186 East Qwest Building
	6101 Yellowstone Road
	Cheyenne, WY 82002
	Phone: 307-777-6972 or 800-996-4769
	Fax: 307-777-6047
	Web site: http://ddd.state.wy.us/Documents/mitch1.htm

Glossary

Active adoption registry. Adoption registry that does not require that both parties consent to the release of information

Adoption assistance. Financial support for adoptive parents of children with special needs adopted from the public foster care system

Adoption assistance agreement. Document detailing adoption assistance benefits that will be given

Adoption decree. Legal document that provides full parental rights over the child who has been adopted

Adoption facilitator. Individual, other than an adoption agency representative or attorney, who assists with the process of matching adoptive parents with birth parents

Adoption insurance. Insurance to protect adoptive parents from financial loss if the birth parents choose not to go through with the adoption process

Adoption memory book. Scrapbook or collection of materials and photographs documenting the life of a child and his or her family's growth through adoption (also called a life book)

Adoption petition. Formal request to the court by prospective adoptive parents wishing to adopt a child

Adoption registry. Index in which birth parents and individuals who were adopted may post names and contact information for reunification purposes (also called a reunion registry)

Adoption resource exchanges. Organizations found in each state that find, train, and support families who wish to adopt children, typically from public foster care

Adoption subsidy. Monthly financial assistance funds that are awarded to adoptive parents to help them care for children with special needs who are adopted through the public foster care system

Adoption tax credit. The IRS provision that allows adoptive parents to deduct adoption benefits received from their annual adjusted gross income (also called tax exclusion for adoption benefits)

Adoption Taxpayer Identification Number (ATIN). A temporary identification number issued by the Internal Revenue Service for a child who is residing with the adoptive parents but whose final domestic adoption is pending that allows parents to claim child as a dependent before the adoption is finalized

Affidavit. Sworn written statement that is signed and witnessed by an authorized official, such as a notary public

Agency-assisted adoption. Adoption in which an agency refers children to prospective adoptive parents

Agency-identified adoption. Adoption in which both prospective adoptive parents and birth parents who are considering making an adoption plan for a child work together through the same agency

Aid to Families with Dependent Children. Federal/state financial aid program that until 1997 provided transitional financial assistance to needy families

Apostille seal.   Seal issued by a Secretary of State's notary public for official use of documents submitted to sending countries, in accordance with the Hague Convention

Attachment.   Emotional connection formed between child and caregivers; also refers to a framework of organized behavior patterns resulting from social interactions with caregivers

Attention deficit disorder.   Neurological condition that causes distractibility, forgetfulness, and impulsiveness

Attention-deficit/hyperactivity disorder.   Neurological condition that involves the symptoms of attention deficit disorder in addition to hyperactivity

Authentication.   Official confirmation of documents and information in intercountry adoptions

Central Authority.   A country's regulatory body, as established by the Hague Convention on Intercountry Adoption, that provides an authoritative point of contact for prospective adoptive parents to receive reliable and accurate information on the adoption process and is also responsible for addressing complaints involving violations of convention standards

Certification.   Verification by the Department of State that documents have been notarized appropriately

Child abuse.   Intentional physical, emotional, or mental harm done caused by an adult to a child

Child neglect.   Failure of a caregiver to provide a sufficient level of physical, mental, and/or emotional care for a child

Closed adoption.   Adoption in which contact information is not exchanged and there is no direct communication between birth parents and adoptive parents

Communication agreement.   An agreement for continued contact between adoptive and birth families that is arranged before the finalization of an adoption plan

Concurrent planning.   Work toward a goal of family reunification while an alternative permanency plan is developed

Conduct disorder.   General term describing a number of emotional or behavioral issues in youths

Consent.   Permission or agreement to a course of action; regarding adoption, a birth parent's agreement to terminate parental rights so that adoption proceedings may take place

Cooperative adoption.   See Open adoption

Co-parent adoption.   The legal recognition of an unmarried partner of a parent, which provides that individual with full legal parental rights to the child (also called second-parent adoption)

Co-parenting.   Parenting arrangement in which duties are shared by two or more individuals who have a relationship with the child

Criminal offender record information form.   Document that gives the agency or social worker who is conducting the home study permission to request all criminal case data for the prospective adoptive parent, including convictions, non-convictions, and pending cases

Custodial parent.   Parent with whom the child primarily resides

Custody.   Legal determination regarding who has legal control of a minor child

Developmental disability.   A physical, mental, or emotional disability affecting a child or adolescent

Disclosure.   Act of revealing previously unknown information

Domestic adoption.   Adoption in which the child to be adopted and the adoptive parents reside in the same country

Domestic infant adoption.   Adoption of a newborn or infant by adoptive parents in the same country

Dossier.   File containing legal information and documents required for international adoptions

Down syndrome.   A genetic disorder in which a person's cells contain an extra copy of the twenty-first chromosome, which causes varying degrees of cognitive difficulties and physical disabilities, and in which the individual presents with characteristic facial features

Facilitator.   See Adoption facilitator.

Family preservation.   Program in which support services are offered to the birth families of children in public foster care with the goal of keeping the family intact

Fetal alcohol syndrome.   Disorder presenting in children that is caused by maternal consumption of alcohol during pregnancy and can result in a range of mental and physical issues

Finalization.   Legal completion of an adoption, resulting in the issuance of an adoption decree

Foster care.   The temporary placement of a child with a family or individual other than the child's birth parents as a result of neglect, abuse, or abandonment

Guardianship.   Position of responsibility for the management of a child's care and property by a court-appointed individual without termination of the parents' rights, as would be required in the case of adoption

Guardian ad litem.   Court-appointed individual whose duty it is to represent the best interests of a child, born or unborn

Hague Convention on the Protection of Children and Co-operation in Respect of Intercountry Adoption.   An international treaty signed by over sixty-six nations, including the United States, to address the terms of and protections offered through intercountry adoption

Home study.   Document that consists of information including a report of a home observation and interviews conducted by a licensed social worker with prospective adoptive parents to determine their fitness to be foster or adoptive parents

I-171H Notice of Favorable Determination concerning Application for Advance Processing of an Orphan Petition.   Document that allows prospective adoptive parents to continue with adoption proceedings of a child who is not a citizen of the United States

I-600 Petition to Classify Orphan as an Immediate Relative.   Petition to the U.S. Citizenship and Immigration Services to issue a visa for a specific child adopted from a country outside of the United States that is filed by adoptive parents

I-600A Application for Advance Processing of an Orphan Petition.   Request to the U.S. Citizenship and Immigration Services by adoptive parents for advanced processing of a visa application for a child who has not yet been identified, or when the prospective adoptive parents must travel to the child's native country

ICAMA.   See Interstate Compact on Adoption and Medical Assistance (ICAMA).

ICPC.   See Interstate Compact on the Placement of Children (ICPC).

IEP.   See Individualized Education Plan (IEP).

Independent adoption.   Adoption that takes place without the involvement of an adoption agency, public or private (also called private adoption)

Indian Child Welfare Act of 1978.   Act that regulates the placement and adoption of Native American children

Individualized Education Plan (IEP).   A formal plan designed to delineate educational objectives for children with diagnosed learning disabilities

Infertility.   A condition of the female or male reproductive system that makes it impossible for the individual to conceive, or for a woman to carry a pregnancy to term; often diagnosed after one year of unprotected, well-timed intercourse or multiple unsuccessful pregnancies

Intercountry adoption.   Adoption of a child from one country by an individual or couple from another country

Interethnic Adoption Provision Act.   An amendment to the Multiethnic Placement Act that was passed in 1996 and prevents the use of an individual's color, race, or national origin to restrict adoption placements

Interstate Compact on Adoption and Medical Assistance (ICAMA).   Legal contract or agreement between member states that provides children with special needs who are adopted in one state with continued medical benefits upon moving to another state

Interstate Compact on the Placement of Children (ICPC).   Interstate contract that regulates adoptions across states

IR-3 visa.   Visa for orphans who had a complete and finalized adoption in the country of origin

IR-4 visa.   Visa for orphans whose prospective adopting parents were granted legal custody or legal guardianship by the sending country for purposes of emigration and adoption

Irrevocable consent.   Consent to make an adoption plan that has been signed by a birth parent and can no longer be withdrawn

Jurisdiction.   Authority to act within a defined legal area

Kinship placement.   Placement of a child for adoption or foster care with a biological relative

Legal risk placement.   Situation in which a child is placed with a family prior to becoming legally free for adoption, with the understanding that the family will adopt the child upon termination of parental rights

Legally free.   Legal status of a child who is available for adoption due to termination of parental rights

Life book.   Memory book or scrapbook composed of materials and photographs documenting the life of a child and his or her family's growth through adoption

Mediated information sharing.   A level of openness in adoption in which communication between the birth parents and the adoptive parents is controlled by an adoption attorney or an employee of the adoption agency (e.g., letters between the parties to the adoption are sent to the attorney or agency, which then forwards them to the recipients without identifying information)

Mongolian spots.   Darker patches of skin pigmentation typically found in children with dark skin that may be deep brown, slate gray, or blue-black with indistinct edges and may resemble bruises

Multiethnic Placement Act of 1994.   Statute that bars the use of color, race, or national origin of a child or prospective adoptive parent to impede a child's placement

National Association of Black Social Workers (NABSW).   Association that directs its efforts toward establishing a world in which people of African ancestry live free from racial domination, economic exploitation, and cultural oppression, and whose members seek to preserve families of African ancestry and to strategically develop the capacity of people of African ancestry to thrive

National Association of Social Workers.   Largest organization of social workers in the world, whose members advocate services for children and families and strive to support families and ensure children's safe and healthy development

National Indian Child Welfare Association. Organization whose efforts support compliance with the Indian Child Welfare Act of 1978 and benefit Indian children and families by providing research to support public policy, advocacy, information, and training regarding issues of Indian child welfare to state child welfare agencies and other interested organizations, agencies, and professionals

Neglect. See Child neglect.

Non-identifying information. Health information or personal history data that does not include names, birth dates, addresses, telephone numbers, or other information that may be used to identify an individual

Notary public. Individual with the authority to act as an unbiased witness to endorse official documents

Open adoption. Adoption in which some extent of contact and communication is maintained between adoption parties after finalization (also called cooperative adoption, communication agreement, and post-adoption contact agreement)

Original birth certificate. Birth certificate issued at birth, before an adoption is finalized

Orphan. A child who is available for adoption due to parental death, termination of parental rights, or consent by birth parents to an adoption plan

Orphanages. Facilities that house children who can no longer live with their birth family as a result of death, abuse, or neglect (this term is no longer used in the United States)

Otitis media. Inflammation of the middle ear resulting in an ear infection

Parental rights. Legal responsibilities and benefits that are associated with raising a child

Parent-identified adoption. Adoption in which prospective adoptive parents network with others to identify birth parents who are interested in making an adoption plan for their child

Parent profile. Usually a letter and photo album that are prepared by prospective adoptive parents as a way to introduce themselves to birth parents who are considering making an adoption plan for their children

Passive adoption registry. Adoption registry that requires that both parties consent to the release of information

Paternity. The parental relationship between a father and his child

Permanency planning. Planning for family reunification or for termination of parental rights so that a child may be adopted

Photolisting book. Listing of children who are legally free for adoption

Post-adoption contact agreement. See Communication agreement.

Post-placement period. Period of time between the placement of a child with a family or individual and the finalization of the adoption

Post-placement report. Report documenting the current family situation that is prepared by a social worker prior to the finalization of an adoption and in which the worker records observations regarding the adoptive parents and the child and makes recommendations concerning whether an adoption should be finalized

Post-placement revocation. The withdrawal of consent for adoption by the birth parents prior to finalization, but after placement of the child

Post-traumatic stress disorder. Psychological condition resulting from anxiety produced by highly traumatic experiences

Pre-adoption certification. The process, primarily the home study, by which prospective adoptive parents are approved for the purpose of a child's adoption placement

Prenatal substance exposure.   Maternal drug or alcohol usage during pregnancy, which increases the risk of developmental disabilities in the fetus

Private adoption.   Adoption in which the services of a private adoption agency are used

Private adoption agency.   State-licensed institution that is authorized to facilitate home studies, adoptions, related services, and outreach

Psychological parent.   The individual, not necessarily related by birth, who has assumed parental responsibility for a child and with whom the child has bonded

Psychological presence.   A phenomenon commonly experienced by birth mothers who have made adoption plans for their children, in which the birth mother experiences the child's presence or frequently thinks about the child both on special occasions and during routine daily activities

Putative father.   Unmarried male who claims to be the father of a child for whom paternity is in question

Putative father registry.   Registry for unmarried males who claim paternity for a child in question, and whose claims have not been proved

Reactive attachment disorder.   Condition that occurs when a youth who has experienced severe deprivation or trauma is unable to establish trusting relationships and emotional bonds with caregivers and others

Readoption.   State finalization of an intercountry adoption that was previously finalized in a foreign country

Receiving state.   In an interstate adoption, the state in which the child will reside once the adoption placement has been made

Relinquishment.   Voluntary termination of parental rights by a birth parent in order to allow an adoption to take place

Residential treatment.   Treatment that is provided on a continuous basis within a institutional setting and is intended to help residents overcome severe emotional and behavioral issues that affect their everyday lives and threaten their safety or the safety of others

Respite care.   Temporary relief from some or all of the responsibilities of caregiving

Reunion registry.   See Adoption registry.

Rumination.   Regurgitation of food in order to either rechew and swallow it or spit it out, which may lead to malnourishment

Second-parent adoption.   See Co-parent adoption.

Sending country.   The country of origin of a child adopted through intercountry adoption

Sending state.   In an interstate adoption, the state in which the child lived prior to the adoption placement

Special needs.   A broad term that may be used to describe a child with mental, physical, or emotional disabilities, or to a child who is difficult to place, such as sibling groups and children who are older

Stepparent adoption.   Adoption of a child by a nonbirth-related individual who marries one of the child's birth parents

Supplemental Security Income.   Federal income supplement for blind, disabled, or senior people with little income

Surrender.   Consent to waive parental rights and allow an adoption plan to be made.

Tax exclusion for adoption benefits.   See Adoption tax credit.

Teratogens.   Agents that can cause malformations of an embryo or fetus

Termination of parental rights.   Decision by a court to terminate a parent's rights to a child; may or may not be voluntary

Title IV-E.   Federal assistance program operated under the Social Security Act that provides reimbursement to states for the costs of the individual entitlement for qualified children who have been removed from their homes and placed in foster homes or other types of out-of-home care under a court order or voluntary placement agreement

Title XX.   Federal assistance program under the Social Security Act in which funds are allocated for social services provided at state discretion related to child welfare; also known as the Social Services Block Grant

Transcultural adoptions.   Adoption in which the adoptive parents' race or ethnicity differs from that of the child

Transracial adoption.   Adoption in which the adoptive parents' race differs from that of the child

United States Citizenship and Immigration Services (USCIS).   Federal agency responsible for the enforcement of laws regarding admission into and continued dwelling of foreign citizens in the United States

Waiting child.   Child who is legally free for adoption

References

Adoption and Foster Care Reporting and Analysis System. (2007). *Trends in foster care and adoption—FY 2000–FY 2005.* Retrieved January 10, 2008, from http://www.acf.hhs.gov/programs/cb/stats_research/afcars/trends.htm

American Academy of Pediatrics Committee on Early Childhood, Adoption and Dependent Care. (1991). Initial medical evaluation of an adopted child. *Pediatrics, 88,* 642–644.

American Academy of Pediatrics Committee on Early Childhood, Adoption and Dependent Care. (1994). Health care of children in foster care. *Pediatrics, 93,* 335–338.

American Academy of Pediatrics Committee on Early Childhood, Adoption and Dependent Care. (2000). Developmental issues for young children in foster care. *Pediatrics, 106,* 1145–1150.

American Academy of Pediatrics Committee on Early Childhood, Adoption and Dependent Care. (2002). Health care of children in foster care. *Pediatrics, 109,* 536–541.

American Academy of Pediatrics Committee on Psychosocial Aspects of Child and Family Health. (1997). *Guidelines for health supervision II.* Elk Grove, IL: Author.

American Academy of Pediatrics Committee on Psychosocial Aspects of Child and Family Health. (2002). Coparent or second-parent adoption by same-sex parents [Electronic version]. *Pediatrics, 109*(2), 339–344.

Askren, H. A., & Bloom, K. C. (1999). Postadoptive reactions of the relinquishing mother: A review. *Journal of Obstetric, Gynecologic, and Neonatal Nursing, 28*(4), 395–400.

Avery, R. (2004). *Strengthening and preserving adoptive families: A study of TANF-funded post adoption services in New York State.* Ithaca, NY: Cornell University, Department of Policy Analysis and Management.

Barth, R. P., & Berry, M. (1988). *Adoption and disruption: Rates, risks, and responses.* New York: Aldine de Gruyter.

Benson, P. L., Sharma, A. R., & Roehlkepartain, E. C. (1994). *Growing up adopted: A portrait of adolescents and their families.* Minneapolis, MN: Search Institute.

Bohman, M., & Sigvardsson, S. (1990). Outcome in adoption: Lessons from longitudinal studies. In D. M. Brodzinsky & M. D. Schechter (Eds.), *The psychology of adoption* (pp. 93–106). New York: Oxford University Press.

Bowlby, J. (1969). *Attachment and loss.* 2 vols. New York: Basic Books.

Brodzinsky, A. B. (1990). Surrendering an infant for adoption: The birthmother experience. In D. M. Brodzinsky & M. D. Schechter (Eds.), *The psychology of adoption* (pp. 295–315). New York: Oxford University Press.

Brodzinsky, D. M. (1987). Adjustment to adoption: A psychosocial perspective. *Clinical Psychology Review, 7*(1), 25–47.

Brodzinsky, D. M. (1993). Long-term outcome in adoption. *The Future of Children, 3*(1), 153–166.

Brodzinsky, D. M., & Schechter, M. D. (Eds.). (1990). *The psychology of adoption.* New York: Oxford University Press.

Brodzinsky, D. M., Schechter, M. D., & Henig, R. M. (1992). *Being adopted: The lifelong search for self.* New York: Doubleday.

Brodzinsky, D. M., Singer, L., & Braff, A. M. (1984). Children's understanding of adoption. *Child Development, 55*(3), 869–878.

Brodzinsky, D. M., Smith, D. W., & Brodzinsky, A. B. (1998). *Children's adjustment to adoption: Developmental and clinical issues.* Thousand Oaks, CA: Sage.

Bundy, A. C., Lane, S. J., Fisher, A. G., & Murray, E. (2002). *Sensory integration: Theory and practice.* Philadelphia: F. A. Davis.

Carr, M. J. (2000). Birthmothers and subsequent children: The role of personality traits and attachment history. *Journal of Social Distress and the Homeless, 9*(4), 339–348.

Centers for Disease Control and Prevention. (2006, May 2). *Fetal alcohol spectrum disorders.* Retrieved January 22, 2008, from http://www.cdc.gov/ncbddd/fas/fasask.htm

Centers for Disease Control and Prevention. (2007, July 18). *Birth defects: Frequently asked questions.* Retrieved January 22, 2008, from http://www.cdc.gov/ncbddd/bd/faq1.htm#chanceofBD

Centers for Medicare and Medicaid Services. (2008). *Medicaid early & periodic screening & diagnostic treatment benefit: Overview.* Retrieved January 28, 2008, from http://www.cms.hhs.gov/MedicaidEarlyPeriodicScrn/

Chernoff, R., Combs-Orme, T., Risley-Curtiss, C., & Heisler, A. (1994). Assessing the health status of children entering foster care. *Pediatrics, 93*(4), 594–601.

Child Welfare Information Gateway. (2004a). *Factsheet for families: Stepparent adoption.* Retrieved February 20, 2008, from http://www.childwelfare.gov/pubs/f_step.cfm

Child Welfare Information Gateway. (2004b). *Infant safe haven laws.* Retrieved July 17, 2007, from http://www.childwelfare.gov/systemwide/laws_policies/statutes/safehaven.cfm

Child Welfare League of America. (1988). *Standards for health care services for children in out-of-home care.* Washington, DC: Author.

Children's Aid Society. (2008). *History: The orphan trains.* Retrieved February 19, 2008, from http://www.childrensaidsociety.org/about/history

Chippindale-Bakker, V., & Foster, L. (1996). Adoption in the 1990s: Sociodemographic determinants of biological parents choosing adoption. *Child Welfare, 75,* 337–355.

Chisholm, K. (1998). A three-year follow-up of attachment and indiscriminate friendliness in children adopted from Romanian orphanages. *Child Development, 69,* 1092–1106.

Chung, E. K., Webb, D., Clampet-Lundquist, S., & Campbell, C. (2001). A comparison of elevated blood lead levels among children living in foster care, their siblings, and the general population. *Pediatrics, 107,* e81.

Cicchetti, D., & Beeghly, M. (Eds.). (1990). *The self in transition: Infancy to childhood.* Chicago: University of Chicago Press.

Cicchetti, D., Toth, S. L., & Lynch, M. (1995). Bowlby's dream comes full circle: The application of attachment theory to risk and psychopathology. In T. H. Ollendick & R. J. Prinz (Eds.), *Advances in clinical child psychology* (Vol. 17, pp. 1–75). New York: Plenum Press.

Cicchini, M. (1993). *The development of responsibility: The experience of birth fathers in adoption.* Mount Lawley, West Australia: Adoption Research and Counseling Service.

Clapton, G. (2007). The experiences and needs of birth fathers in adoption: What we know now and some practice implications. *Practice, 19*(1), 61–71.

Cline, F. (1990). Understanding and treating the severely disturbed child. In P. V. Grabe (Ed.), *Adoption resources for mental health professionals* (pp. 137–150). London: Transaction Publishers.

Cocozzelli, C. (1989). Predicting the decision of biological mothers to retain or relinquish their babies for adoption: Implications for open placement. *Child Welfare, 68*(1), 33–44.

Cohen, N. J. (2005). Adoption. In M. Rutter & E. T. Taylor (Eds.), *Child and adolescent psychiatry* (4th ed., pp. 373–381). London: Blackwell.

Cohen, N. J., Coyne, J., & Duvall, J. (1993). Adopted and biological children in the clinic: Family, parental, and child characteristics. *Journal of Child Psychology and Psychiatry, 34,* 555–562.

Combs-Orme, T., Chernoff, R. G., & Kager, V. A. (1991). Utilization of health care by foster children: Application of a theoretical model. *Children and Youth Services Review, 15*(2), 113–129.

Cournos, F. (1999). A psychiatrist recalls life as a foster child. *Psychiatric Services, 50*, 479–480.

Cystic Fibrosis Foundation. (2007, June). *About cystic fibrosis: What you need to know.* Retrieved January 22, 2008, from http://www.cff.org/AboutCF/

Deykin, E. Y., Campbell, L., & Patti, P. (1984). The postadoption experience of surrendering parents. *American Journal of Orthopsychiatry, 54*, 271–280.

Deykin, E. Y., Patti, P., & Ryan, J. (1988). Fathers of adopted children: A study of the impact of child surrender of birthfathers. *American Journal of Orthopsychiatry, 58*, 240–248.

Diamond, D., Diamond, M., & Jaffe, J. (1999). Infertility, pregnancy loss, and other reproductive traumas: A developmental perspective. *San Diego Psychological Association Newsletter, 8*(2), 1–3.

Dunn, P. M. (2003). Gregor Mendel, OSA (1822–1884), founder of scientific genetics. *Archives of Disease in Childhood: Fetal and Neonatal Edition, 88*(6), F537–F539.

Dworkin, R. J., Harding, J. T., & Schreiber, N. B. (1993). Parenting or placing: Decision making by pregnant teens. *Youth and Society, 25*, 75–92.

Fahlberg, V. (1991). *A child's journey through placement.* Indianapolis, IN: Perspectives Press.

Fenster, J. (2002). Transracial adoption in black and white: A survey of social worker attitudes. *Adoption Quarterly, 5*(4), 33–58.

Flaherty, E. G., & Weiss, H. (1990). Medical evaluation of abused and neglected children. *American Journal of Diseases in Children, 144*, 330–334.

Fratter, J. (1996). *Adoption with contact: Implications for policy and practice.* London: British Agencies for Adoption and Fostering.

Fravel, D. L., McRoy, R. G., & Grotevant, H. D. (2000). Birth mother perceptions of the psychologically present adopted child: Adoption openness and boundary ambiguity. *Family Relations, 49*, 425–433.

Freundlich, M., & Wright, L. (2003). *Post-permanency services.* Washington, DC: Casey Family Programs Center for Resource Family Support.

Glennen, S. (2002). Language development and delay in internationally adopted infants and toddlers: A review. *American Journal of Speech-Language Pathology, 11*, 333–339.

Glidden, L. M. (2000). Adopting children with developmental disabilities: A long-term perspective. *Family Relations, 49*, 397–405.

Goldberg, A. E., Downing, J. B., Harp, A. G., & Sauck, C. C. (2006). *Choices, challenges, and tensions: Perspectives of lesbian prospective adoptive parents.*

Grotevant, H. D., & McRoy, R. (1998). *Openness in adoption: Exploring family connections.* Thousand Oaks, CA: Sage.

Groze, V. (1994). Clinical and nonclinical adoptive families of special-needs children. *Families in Society, 75*(2), 90–104.

Groze, V. (1996). *Successful adoptive families.* Westport, CT: Praeger.

Gunnar, M. R., Bruce, J., & Grotevant, H. D. (2000). International adoption of institutionally reared children: Research and policy. *Development and Psychopathology, 12*, 677–693.

Hague Conference on Private International Law. (1961). *Convention abolishing the requirement of legalization for foreign public documents.* Retrieved February 20, 2008, from http://www.hcch.net/index_en.php?act=conventions.text&cid=41

Harden, B. J. (2004) Safety and stability for foster children: A developmental perspective. *The Future of Children, 14*(1), 31–47.

Harter, S. (2006). The self. In N. Eisenberg, W. Damon, & R. M. Lerner (Eds.), *Handbook of child psychology: Vol. 3. Social, emotional, and personality development* (6th ed., pp. 505–570). Hoboken, NJ: Wiley.

Hartup, W. W. (1992). Peer relations in early and middle childhood. In V. B. Van Hasselt & M. Hersen (Eds.), *Handbook of social development: A lifespan perspective* (pp. 257–281). New York: Plenum.

Henry, M. J., Pollack, D., & Lazare, A. (2006). Teaching medical students about adoption and foster care. *Adoption Quarterly, 10*(1), 45–62.

Herman, E. (2003). *The history of adoption project timeline.* Retrieved July 19, 2007, from http://darkwing.uoregon.edu/~adoption/timeline.html

Herr, K. M. (1989). Adoption vs. parenting decisions among pregnant adolescents. *Adolescence, 24,* 795–799.

Hochstadt, N. J., Jaudes, P. K., Zimo, D. A., & Schachter, J. (1987). The medical and psychosocial needs of children entering foster care. *Child Abuse & Neglect, 11*(1), 53–62.

Hollingsworth, L. D. (2003). International adoption among families in the United States: Considerations of social justice. *Social Work, 48,* 209–217.

Horwitz, S. M., Simms, M. D., & Farrington, R. (1994). Impact of developmental problems on young children's exits from foster care. *Developmental and Behavioral Pediatrics, 15,* 105–110.

Hughes, B. (1995). Openness and contact in adoption: A child-centred perspective. *British Journal of Social Work, 25,* 729–747.

Internal Revenue Service. (2008a). *Adoption taxpayer identification number.* Retrieved February 20, 2008, from http://www.irs.gov/individuals/article/0,,id=96452,00.html

Internal Revenue Service. (2008b). *Topic 607—adoption credit.* Retrieved February 20, 2008, from http://www.irs.gov/taxtopics/tc607.html

Johnson, D. (2000). Medical and developmental sequelae of early childhood institutionalization in Eastern European adoptees. In C. A. Nelson (Ed.), *The effects of early adversity on neurobehavioral development* (pp. 113–162). Mahwah, NJ: Lawrence Erlbaum.

Johnson, S. C., & Solomon, G. E. (1997). Why dogs have puppies and cats have kittens: The role of birth in young children's understanding of biological origins. *Child Development, 68,* 404–419.

Johnston, P. I. (2001). *Adoption is a family affair: What relatives and friends must know.* Indianapolis, IN: Perspectives Press.

Jones, M. B. (2000). *Birthmothers: Women who have relinquished babies for adoption tell their stories.* Chicago: Chicago Review Press.

Juffer, F., & van IJzendoorn, M. H. (2005). Behavior problems and mental health referrals of international adoptees. *Journal of the American Medical Association, 293,* 2501–2515.

Keck, G. C., & Kupecky, R. M. (1995). *Adopting the hurt child: Hope for families with special needs kids.* Colorado Springs, CO: Pinon Press.

Kim, W. J. (1995). International adoption: A case review of Korean children. *Child Psychiatry and Human Development, 25*(3), 141–155.

Klee, L., Kronstadt, D., & Zlotnick, C. (1997). Foster care's youngest: A preliminary report. *American Journal of Orthopsychiatry, 67,* 290–299.

Kohler, J., Grotevant, H. D., & McRoy, R. G. (2002). Adopted adolescent's preoccupation with adoption: The impact on adoptive family relationships. *Journal of Marriage and Family, 64*(1), 93–104.

Krueger-Jago, M. J., & Hanna, F. J. (1997). Why adoptees search: An existential treatment perspective. *Journal of Counseling and Development, 75*(3), 195–202.

Lauderdale, J., & Boyle, J. (1994). Infant relinquishment through adoption. *Image: Journal of Nursing Scholarship, 26*(3), 213–217.

Lee, J. S., & Twaite, J. A. (1997). Open adoption and adoptive mothers: Attitudes toward birthmothers, adopted children, and parenting. *American Journal of Orthopsychiatry, 67,* 576–584.

Leslie, L., Gordon, J. N., Lambros, K., Premji, K., Peoples, J., & Gist, K. (2005). Addressing the developmental and mental health needs of young children in foster care. *Developmental and Behavioral Pediatrics, 26*(2), 140–151.

Leslie, L., Hurlburt, M., Landsverk, J., Rolls, J., Wood, P., & Kelleher, K. (2003). Comprehensive assessments for children entering foster care: A national perspective. *Pediatrics, 112,* 134–142.

Leslie, L., Landsverk, J., Ezzet-Lofstrom, R., Tschann, J., Slymen, D., & Garland, A. (2000). Children in foster care: Factors influencing outpatient mental health service use. *Child Abuse and Neglect, 24*(4), 465–476.

Logan, J., & Smith, C. (2005). Face-to-face contact post adoption: Views from the triangles. *British Journal of Social Work, 35*(1), 3–35.

Low, J. M., Moely, B. E., & Willis, A. S. (1989). The effects of perceived parental preferences and vocational goals on adoption decisions: Unmarried pregnant adolescents. *Youth and Society, 20,* 342–354.

MacAskill, C. (2002). *Safe contact: Children in permanent placement and contact with their birth relatives.* Dorset, UK: Russell House.

Mack, K. (2006). Survey examines post adoption services among private agencies. *Children's Bureau Express, 7*(8), 15.

Maurice, C. (1993). *Let me hear your voice: A family's triumph over autism.* New York: Knopf.

Maynard, J. (2005). Permanency mediation: A path to open adoption for children in out-of-home care. *Child Welfare, 84,* 507–526.

McRoy, R. G., Grotevant, H. D., & Ayers-Lopez, S. (1994). *Changing practices in adoption.* Austin, TX: Hogg Foundation for Mental Health.

McRoy, R. G., Grotevant, H. D., & White, K. L. (1988). *Openness in adoption: New practices, new issues.* New York: Praeger.

Miall, C. E. (1987). The stigma of adoptive parent status: Perceptions of community attitudes toward adoption and the experience of informal social sanctioning. *Family Relations, 36,* 34–39.

Namerow, P. B., Kalmuss, D., & Cushman, L. F. (1997). The consequences of placing versus parenting among young unmarried women. *Marriage & Family Review, 25*(3–4), 175–197.

National Association of Black Social Workers. (1994). *Position statement: Preserving African-American families.* Detroit, MI: Author.

National Association of Black Social Workers. (2003). *Position paper: Preserving families of African ancestry.* Washington, DC: Author. Retrieved July 11, 2007, from http://www.nabsw.org/mserver/PreservingFamilies.aspx?menuContext=757

National Association of Social Workers. (2003). *Social work speaks: NASW policy statements, 2003–2006* (6th ed., pp. 144–151). Washington, DC: Author.

National Indian Child Welfare Association. (2008). *Indian Child Welfare Act (ICWA) compliance.* Retrieved February 19, 2008, from http://www.nicwa.org/Indian_Child_Welfare_Act/

Neil, E. (1999, August). *The "contact after adoption" study.* Poster session presented at the International Conference on Adoption Research, University of Minnesota.

Neil, E. (2003). Understanding other people's perspectives: Tasks for adopters in open adoption. *Adoption Quarterly, 6*(3), 3–30.

Newton, R. R., Litrownik, A. J., & Landsverk, J. A. (2000). Children and youth in foster care: Disentangling the relationship between problem behaviors and numbers of placements. *Child Abuse and Neglect, 24,* 1363–1374.

Nickman, S. L., & Lewis, R. G. (1994). Adoptive families and professionals: When experts make things worse. *Journal of the American Academy of Child & Adolescent Psychiatry, 33,* 753–755.

O'Hara, M. T., Church, C. C., & Blatt, S. D. (1998). Home-based developmental screening of children in foster care. *Pediatric Nursing, 24*(2), 113–117.

Pasztor, E. M., Hollinger, D. S., Inkelas, M., & Halfon, N. (2006). Health and mental health services for children in foster care: The central role of foster parents. *Child Welfare, 85,* 33–57.

Pearce, J. W., & Pezzot-Pearce, T. D. (2001). Psychotherapeutic approaches to children in foster care: Guidance from attachment theory. *Child Psychiatry & Human Development, 32,* 19–44.

Perry, B. D. (2001). Bonding and attachment in maltreated children: Consequences of emotional neglect in childhood. *Child Trauma Academy Press, Parent and Caregiver Education Series, 1*(4). Retrieved December 27, 2006, from http://www.childtrauma.org/ctamaterials/default.asp

Peters, B. R., Atkins, M. S., & McKay, M. M. (1999). Adopted children's behavior problems: A review of five explanatory models. *Clinical Psychology Review, 19*(3), 297–328.

Piaget, J. (1990). *The child's conception of the world*. New York: Littlefield Adams. (Originally published 1929)

Pollack, K., & Hittle, L. (2003). *Baby abandonment: The role of child welfare systems*. Retrieved February 26, 2008, from http://www.cwla.org/programs/baby/babyaboutpage.htm

Racusin, R., Maerlender, A. C., Sengupta, A., Isquith, P. K., & Straus, M. (2005). Psychosocial treatment of children in foster care: A review. *Community Mental Health Journal, 41*, 199–221.

Resnick, M. D., Blum, R. W., Bose, J., Smith, M., & Toogood, R. (1990). Characteristics of unmarried adolescent mothers: Determinants of child rearing versus adoption. *American Journal of Orthopsychiatry, 60*, 577–584.

Risly-Curtiss, C., & Kronenfeld, J. J. (2001). Health care policies for children in out-of-home care. *Child Welfare 80*, 325–350.

Robinson, E. B. (2000). *Adoption and loss: The hidden grief*. Christies Beach, South Australia: Clova.

Roby, J. L., & Matsumura, S. (2002). If I give you my child, aren't we family?: A study of birthmothers participating in Marshall Islands-U.S. adoptions. *Adoption Quarterly, 5*(4), 7–31.

Roby, J. L., Wyatt, J., & Pettys, G. (2005). Openness in international adoption: A study of U.S. parents who adopted children from the Marshall Islands. *Adoption Quarterly, 8*(3), 47–71.

Rosenthal, J. A. (1993). Outcomes of adoption of children with special needs. *The Future of Children, 3*(1), 77–88.

Rubin, D., Alessandrini, E., Feudtner, C., Mandell, D., Localio, A. R., & Hadley, T. (2004). Placement stability and mental health costs for children in foster care. *Pediatrics, 113*, 1336–1341.

Rutter, M. (1998). Developmental catch-up, and deficit, following adoption after severe global early privation. *Journal of Child Psychology and Psychiatry, 39*, 465–476.

Schooler, J. E., & Norris, B. L. (2002). *Journeys after adoption: Understanding lifelong issues*. Westport, CT: Bergin & Garvey.

Siegel, D. (1993). Open adoption of infants: Adoptive parents' perceptions of advantages and disadvantages. *Social Work, 38*, 15–23.

Siegel, D. (2003). Open adoption of infants: Adoptive parents' feelings seven years later. *Social Work, 48*(3), 409–419.

Simms, M. D., Dubowitz, H., & Szilagyi, M. A. (2000). Health care needs of children in the foster care system. *Pediatrics, 106*(Suppl. 4), 909–917.

Simms, M. D., Freundlich, M., Battistelli, E. S., & Kaufman, N. D. (1999). Delivering health and mental health care services to children in family foster care after welfare and health care reform. *Child Welfare, 78*(1), 166–183.

Simone, M. (1996). Birth mother loss: Contributing factors to unresolved grief. *Clinical Social Work Journal, 24*(1), 65–76.

Sorosky, A. D., Baran, A., & Pannor, R. (1976). The effects of the sealed record in adoption. *American Journal of Psychiatry, 133*, 900–904.

Sroufe, L. A. (1995). *Emotional development: The organization of emotional life in the early years*. Cambridge: Cambridge University Press.

Stams, G. J., Juffer, F., Rispens, J., & Hoksbergen, R. A. (2000). The development and adjustment of 7-year-old children adopted in infancy. *Journal of Child Psychology and Psychiatry, 41*, 1025–1037.

Stams, G. J., Juffer, F., & van Ijzendoorn, M. H. (2002). Maternal sensitivity, infant attachment, and temperament in early childhood predicts adjustment in middle childhood: The case of adopted children and their biologically unrelated parents. *Developmental Psychology, 38*, 806–821.

Steinberg, G., & Hall, B. (2000). *Inside transracial adoption*. Indianapolis, IN: Perspectives Press.

Stroud, J. E., Stroud, J. C., & Staley, L. M. (1997). Understanding and supporting adoptive families. *Early Childhood Education Journal, 24*(4), 229–235.

Takayama, J. I., Wolfe, E., & Coulter, K. P. (1998). Relationship between reason for placement and medical findings among children in foster care. *Pediatrics, 101*, 201–207.

Terr, L. (1991). Childhood traumas: An outline and overview. *American Journal of Psychiatry,* *148,* 10–20.

Terwogt, M. M., Stegge, H., & Rieffe, C. (2003). Children's understanding of inherited resemblance: The case of two parents. *International Journal of Behavioral Development, 27*(4), 366–374.

Thomas, C., Beckford, V., Lowe, N., & Murch, M. (1999). *Adopted children speaking.* London: British Association for Adoption & Fostering.

Tizard, B., & Rees, J. (1975). The effect of early institutional rearing on the behavior problems and affectional relationships of four-year-old children. *Journal of Child Psychology and Psychiatry, 16,* 61–73.

U.S. Department of Health and Human Services. (2001). *1998 national estimates of the number of boarder babies, abandoned infants and discarded infants.* Washington, DC: Author.

U.S. Department of Health and Human Services. (2003). *National survey of child and adolescent well-being (NSCAW). One year in foster care: Wave 1. Data analysis report.* Washington, DC: Author. Retrieved July 12, 2007, from http://www.acf.hhs.gov/programs/opre/abuse_neglect/nscaw/reports/nscaw_oyfc/oyfc_report.pdf

U.S. Department of State. (2008). *Immigrant visas issued to orphans coming to the U.S.: Top countries of origin.* Retrieved February 20, 2008, from http://travel.state.gov/family/adoption/stats/stats_451.html

U.S. General Accounting Office. (2003). *HHS could play a greater role in helping child welfare agencies recruit and retain staff* (GAO-03-357). Washington, DC: Author.

Vig, S., Chinitz, S., & Shulman, L. (2005). Young children in foster care: Multiple vulnerabilities and complex service needs. *Infants & Young Children, 1*(2), 147–160.

Vroegh, K. S. (1997). Transracial adoptees: Developmental status after 17 years. *American Journal of Orthopsychiatry, 67,* 568–575.

Walsh, J. M. (1999). *Adoption and agency: American adoptions of Marshallese children.* Retrieved February 19, 2007, from http://www.yokwe.net/modules.php?op=modload&name=News&file=article&sid=597

Warren, S. B. (1992). Lower threshold for psychiatric treatment for adopted adolescents. *Journal of the American Academy of Child Psychiatry, 31,* 512–517.

Warren, K. C., & Johnson, R. W. (1989). Family environment, affect, ambivalence and decisions about unplanned adolescent pregnancy. *Adolescence, 24,* 505–522.

Watkins, M., & Fisher, S. M. (1993). *Talking with young children about adoption.* New Haven, CT: Yale University Press.

Weinman, M. L., Robinson, M., Simmons, J. T., Schreiber, N. B., & Stafford, B. (1989). Pregnant teens: Differential pregnancy resolution and treatment implications. *Child Welfare, 68,* 45–55.

Wierzbicki, M. (1993). Psychological adjustment of adoptees: A meta-analysis. *Journal of Clinical Child Psychology, 22,* 447–454.

Wiley, M. O., & Baden, A. L. (2005). Birth parents in adoption: Research, practice, and counseling psychology. *The Counseling Psychologist, 33*(1), 13–50.

Wilson, S. L. (2003). Post-institutionalization: The effects of early deprivation on development of Romanian adoptees. *Child and Adolescent Social Work Journal, 20,* 473–483.

Wrobel, G. M., Ayers-Lopez, S., Grotevant, H. D., McRoy, R. G., & Friedrick, M. (1996). Openness in adoption and the level of child participation. *Child Development, 67,* 2358–2374.

Wyatt, D. T., Simms, M. D., & Horwitz, S. M. (1997). Widespread growth retardation and variable growth recovery in foster children in the first year of placement. *Archives of Pediatric and Adolescent Medicine, 151,* 813–816.

Zamostny, K. P., O'Brien, K. M., Baden, A. L., & Wiley, M. O. (2003). The practice of adoption: History, trends, and social context. *The Counseling Psychologist, 31*(6), 651–678.

Suggested Readings

American Psychiatric Association. (1994). *Diagnostic and statistical manual of mental disorders* (4th ed.). Washington, DC: Author.

Baker, D. L., Schuette, J. L., & Uhlmann, W. R. (Eds.). (1998). *A guide to genetic counseling*. New York: Wiley-Liss.

Bennett, R. L. (1999). *A practical guide to the genetic family history*. New York: Wiley-Liss.

Berry, M. (1993). Adoptive parents' perceptions of, and comfort with, open adoption. *Child Welfare, 72*, 231–253.

Berry, M. (1993). Risks and benefits of open adoption. *The Future of Children, 3*(1), 125–138.

Blanton, T. L., & Deschner, J. (1990). Biological mothers' grief: The postadoptive experience in open versus confidential adoptions. *Child Welfare, 69*, 525–535.

Blatt, S. D., Saletsky, R. D., Meguid, V., Church, C. C., O'Hara, M. T., Haller-Peck, S. M., et al. (1997). A comprehensive, multidisciplinary approach to providing health care for children in out-of-home care. *Child Welfare, 76*, 331–347.

Bolling, I. M. (2003). *Adoption trends in 2003: Infant abandonment and safe haven legislation*. Retrieved July 19, 2007, from http://www.ncsconline.org/WC/Publications/KIS_Adopt_Trends03Haven.pdf

Borchers, D. (2003). Families and adoption: The pediatrician's role in supporting communication. *Pediatrics, 112*, 1437–1441.

Brodzinsky, D. M. (1993). *Being adopted: The lifelong search for self.* New York: Anchor.

Brodzinsky, D. M., & Palacios, J. (2005). *Psychological issues in adoption: Research and practice.* Westport, CT: Praeger.

Brodzinsky, D. M., & Pinderhughes, E. (2002). Parenting and child development in adoptive families. In M. Bornstein (Ed.), *Handbook of parenting: Vol. 1. Children and parenting* (3rd ed., pp. 279–312). Hillsdale, NJ: Lawrence Erlbaum.

Cavanaugh, K., & Pollack, D. (1997). Liability protections for foster parents. *Kansas Journal of Law and Public Policy, 6*(3), 78–88.

Center for Adoption Research. (2006). *Adoption in Massachusetts: Private and public agency placements and practices in 2004.* Retrieved July 18, 2007, from http://www.umassmed.edu/adoption/reports.aspx

Child Welfare Information Gateway. (2003). *Openness in adoption: A bulletin for professionals.* Retrieved December 27, 2006, from http://www.childwelfare.gov/pubs/f_openadoptbulletin.cfm

Cushman, L. F., Kalmuss, D., & Namerow, P. B. (1997). Openness in adoption: Experiences and social psychological outcomes among birth mothers. *Marriage & Family Review, 25*(1–2), 7–18.

Fratter, J. (1991). Parties in the triangle. *Adoption and Fostering, 15*(4), 91–98.

Freundlich, M. (1997). The future of adoptions for children in foster care: Demographics in a changing socio-political environment. *Journal of Children and Poverty, 3*(2), 33–62.

Freundlich, M. (1999). *Open cooperative adoption: The impact of current laws on negotiated relinquishments.* Retrieved December 27, 2006, from http://www.adoptioninstitute.org/policy/abaopen.html

Gediman, J. S., & Brown, L. P. (1991). *Birth bond: Reunions between birthparents and adoptees.* Far Hills, NJ: New Horizon.

Gilmore, U., Oppenheim, E., & Pollack, D. (2004). Delays in the adoption and foster home interstate study process. *University of California–Davis Law School Journal of Juvenile Law and Policy, 8*(1), 55–94.

Grotevant, H., & McRoy, R. (1997). The Minnesota/Texas adoption research project: Implications of openness in adoption for development and relationships. *Applied Developmental Science, 1*(4), 166–184.

Grotevant, H., McRoy, R., Elde, C. L., & Fravel, D. L. (1994). Adoptive family system dynamics: Variations by level of openness in the adoption. *Family Process, 33*(2), 125–146.

Guttman, J. (1999). *The gift wrapped in sorrow: A mother's quest for healing.* Palm Springs, CA: JMJ.

Halfon, N., & Klee, L. (1987). Health services for California's foster children: Current practices and policy recommendations. *Pediatrics, 80*, 183–191.

Halfon, N., Mendonca, A., & Berkowitz, G. (1995). Health status of children in foster care: The experience of the Center for the Vulnerable Child. *Archives of Pediatric Adolescent Medicine, 149*, 386–392.

Hall, B., & Steinberg, G. (n.d.). *Are you prepared for transracial adoption?* Retrieved August 16, 2006, from http://www.bcadoption.com/articles_pf.asp?pageid=38&Offset=25&AK=ShowAll&HC=1&AD=131

Hansen, M., & Pollack, D. (2005). Unintended consequences of bargaining for adoption assistance payments. *Family Court Review, 43*, 494–510.

Hansen, M., & Pollack, D. (2006). The regulation of intercountry adoption. *Brandeis Law Journal, 45*(1), 105–128.

Hansen, M., & Pollack, D. (2006). The subtleties of race and recruitment in foster care and adoption. *California NASW News, 32*(8), 6.

Henderson, D. B. (2002). Challenging the silence of the mental health community on adoption issues. *Journal of Social Distress and the Homeless, 11*(2), 131–141.

Human Rights Campaign Foundation. (n.d.). *Parenting.* Retrieved March 13, 2008, from http://www.hrc.org/issues/parenting.asp

Javier, R. A., Baden, A. L., Biafora, F. A., & Camacho-Gingerick, A. (2007). *Handbook of adoption: Implications for researchers, practitioners, and families.* Thousand Oaks, CA: Sage.

Jenista, J. A. (2006). *Infectious disease and the internationally adopted child.* Retrieved February 25, 2008, from http://www.comeunity.com/adoption/health/infectious-disease.html

Kohler, J., Grotevant, H. D., & McRoy, R. G. (2002). Adopted adolescents' preoccupation with adoption: The impact on adoptive family relationships. *Journal of Marriage and Family, 64*(1), 93–104.

Marsh, J., & Pollack, D. (2002). Constitutional rights of foster parents to adopt foster children. *Adoption & Fostering, 26*(1), 71–73.

McKenzie, J. K., McKenzie, J. L., & Jackson, R. (2006). *Wherever my family is: That's home! Adoption services for military families.* Retrieved July 11, 2007, from http://www.adoptuskids.org/images/resourceCenter/militaryGuide.pdf

McLaughlin, S. D., Pearce, S. E., Manninen, D. L., & Winges, L. D. (1988). To parent or relinquish: Consequences for adolescent mothers. *Social Work, 33*(4), 320–324.

McRoy, R. G. (1999). *Special needs adoptions: Practice issues.* New York: Garland.

Miller, L. C. (2005). *The handbook of international medicine: A guide for physicians, parents, and providers.* New York: Oxford University Press.

National Center for Lesbian Rights. (2003). *Second parent adoptions: A snapshot of current law.* Retrieved October 31, 2006, from http://www.nclrights.org/publications/2ndparentadoptions.htm

Nickman, S. L., Rosenfeld, A. A., Fine, P., MacIntyre, J. C., Pilowsky, D. J., Howe, R. A., et al. (2005). Children in adoptive families: Overview and update. *Journal of the American Academy of Child & Adolescent Psychiatry, 44*, 987–995.

Nussbaum, R. L., McInnes, R. R., & Willard, H. F. (2001). *Thompson & Thompson genetics in medicine.* Philadelphia: W. B. Saunders.

Pertman, A. (2000). *Adoption nation: How the adoption revolution is transforming America.* New York: Basic Books.

Pollack, D. (2002). The capacity of a mentally retarded parent to consent to adoption. *Child Law Practice, 21*(1), 10–12.

Pollack, D. (2005). Intercountry adoption: Who are the good guys? *Policy & Practice, 63*(1), 28.

Pollack, D. (2006). Child trafficking and international adoption. *Adoption Today, 8*(5), 39.

Pollack, D., Bleich, M., Reid, C., & Fadel, M., (2004). Classical religious perspectives of adoption law. *Notre Dame Law Review, 79*(2), 693–753.

Russell, M. (1996). *Adoption wisdom.* Santa Monica, CA: Broken Branch Production.

Schaefer, C. (1991). *The other mother.* New York: Soho.

Schweitzer, H., & Pollack, D. (2006). Ethical and legal dilemmas in adoption social work. *Family Court Review, 44*(2), 258–269.

Sharma, A. R., McGue, M. K., & Benson, P. L. (1996). The emotional and behavioral adjustment of United States adopted adolescents. Part II: Age at adoption. *Children and Youth Services Review, 18*(1–2), 101–114.

Silverstein, D. N., & Roszia, S. K. (1999). Openness: A critical component of special needs adoption. *Child Welfare, 78*, 637–651.

Swire, M. R., & Kavaler, F. (1977). The health status of foster children. *Child Welfare, 56*, 635–653.

Takayama, J. I., Bergman, A. B., & Connell, F. A. (1994). Children in foster care in the state of Washington: Health care utilization and expenditures. *Journal of the American Medical Association, 271*, 1850–1855.

U.S. General Accounting Office. (1995). *Child welfare: Complex needs strain capacity to provide services* (GAO/HEHS-95-208). Washington, DC: Author. Retrieved December 27, 2006, from http://www.gao.gov/archive/1995/he95208.pdf

U.S. General Accounting Office. (1995). *Foster care: Health needs of many young children are unknown and unmet* (GAO/HEHS-95-114). Washington, DC: Author. Retrieved July 12, 2007, from http://www.gao.gov/archive/1995/he95114.pdf

Whalen, T., & Pollack, D. (2007). Decision tools to benefit children needing adoption. *Human Systems Management, 26*(1), 35–45.

Wicks-Nelson, R., & Israel, A. C. (2006). *Behavior disorders of childhood* (6th ed.). Upper Saddle River, NJ: Prentice Hall.

Wolfe, D. A., & Mash, E. J. (Eds.). (2006). *Behavioral and emotional disorders in adolescents.* New York: Guilford Press.

Selected Resources

Adoption Community of New England
45 Lyman Street #2
Westborough, MA 01581
Phone: 508-366-6812 or 800-932-3678
Fax: 508-366-6813
E-mail: info@adoptioncommunityofne.org
Web site: http://adoptioncommunityofne.org/

Adoption Information Center of Illinois
120 West Madison Street, Suite 800
Chicago, IL 60602
Phone: 312-346-1516
Fax: 312-346-0004
Web site: http://www.adoptinfo-il.org/

AdoptUsKids
Children's Bureau Collaboration
Adoption Exchange Association
8015 Corporate Drive, Suite C
Baltimore, MD 21236
Phone: 888-200-4005
E-mail: info@adoptuskids.org
Web site: http://www.adoptuskids.org/
Photolistings by state:
    http://www.adoptuskids.org/resourceCenter/photolistings/statePhotolistings.aspx

American Academy of Adoption Attorneys
P.O. Box 33053
Washington, DC 20033
Phone: 202-832-2222
E-mail: info@adoptionattorneys.org
Web site: http://www.adoptionattorneys.org/

American Academy of Pediatrics Section on Adoption and Foster Care
E-mail: adoption@aap.org
Web site: http://www.aap.org/sections/adoption

American Adoption Congress
P.O. Box 42730
Washington, DC 20015
Web site: http://www.americanadoptioncongress.org/mission.php

American Bar Association
Center on Children and the Law
740 15th Street, NW
Washington, DC 20005
Phone: 202-662-1720 or 800-285-2221
Fax: 202-662-1755
E-mail: ctrchildlaw@abanet.org
Web site: http://www.abanet.org/child/

Jane Aronson
International Pediatric Health Services, PLLC
151 East 62nd Street, Suite 1A
New York, NY 10065
Phone: 212-207-6666
E-mail: orphandoctor@aol.com
Web site: http://www.orphandoctor.com

Association for Research in International Adoption
E-mail: tmcg@uab.edu
Web site: http://www.adoption-research.org

Bastard Nation: The Adoptee Rights Organization
P.O. Box 1469
Edmond, OK 73083-1469
Phone/Fax: 415-704-3166
E-mail: members@bastards.org
Web site: http://www.bastards.org/

Casey Family Programs National Center for Resource Family Support
E-mail: contactus@casey.org
Web site: www.casey.org

Center for Adoption Research
University of Massachusetts
333 South Street
Shrewsbury, MA 01545
Phone: 508-856-5397
E-mail: car@umassmed.edu
Web site: http://www.umassmed.edu/adoption/index.aspx

Centers for Disease Control and Prevention
1600 Clifton Road
Atlanta, GA 30333
Phone: 404-639-3311 or 800-CDC-INFO
TTY: 888-232-6348
Health Information for International Travel 2008:
    http://wwwn.cdc.gov/travel/contentYellowBook.aspx

Child Welfare Information Gateway
Children's Bureau/ACYF
1250 Maryland Avenue, SW
Eighth Floor
Washington, DC 20024
E-mail: info@childwelfare.gov
Phone: 800-394-3366 or 703-385-7565
Fax: 703-385-3206
State Adoption Exchange Web sites:
    http://www.childwelfare.gov/pubs/reslist/rl_dsp_website.cfm?typeID=81&rate_chno=AZ-0003E

Child Welfare League of America
2345 Crystal Drive, Suite 250
Arlington, VA 22202
Phone: 703-412-2400
Fax: 703-412-2401
Web site: http://www.cwla.org/

ComeUnity
International Adoption Health and Medicine
Web site: http://www.comeunity.com/adoption/health/index.html

Concerned United Birthparents
P.O. Box 503475
San Diego, CA 92150-3475
Fax: 858-712-3317
E-mail: info@CUBirthparents.org
Web site: http://www.cubirthparents.org/

Congressional Coalition on Adoption Institute
311 Massachusetts Avenue, NE
Washington, DC 20002
Phone: 202-544-8500
Fax: 202-544-8501
E-mail: info@ccainstitute.org
Web site: http://www.ccainstitute.org/

Dave Thomas Foundation for Adoption
4150 Tuller Road, Suite 204
Dublin, OH 43017
Phone: 800-275-3832
Fax: 614-766-3871
E-mail: info@davethomasfoundation.org
Web site: http://www.davethomasfoundationforadoption.org/

Evan B. Donaldson Adoption Institute
120 E. 38th Street
New York, NY 10016
Phone: 212-925-4089
Fax: 775-796-6592
E-mail: info@adoptioninstitute.org
Web site: http://www.adoptioninstitute.org/index.php

Families with Children from China
Web site: http://www.fwcc.org/

Family Equality Council
P.O. Box 206
Boston, MA 02133
Web site: http://www.familyequality.org/

Flying with Kids: Air Travel Tips for Families Flying with a Baby or Small Child
Web site: www.flyingwithkids.com

Immunization Action Coalition
1573 Selby Avenue, Suite 234
St. Paul, MN 55104
Phone: 651-647-9009
Fax: 651-647-9131
E-mail: admin@immunize.org
International Adoption: http://www.immunize.org/adoption/

Institute for Adoption Information
409 Dewey Street
Bennington, VT 05201
Phone: 802-442-2845
E-mail: info@adoptioninformationinstitute.org
Web site: http://www.adoptioninformationinstitute.org/

International Soundex Reunion Registry
P.O. Box 371179
Las Vegas, NV 89137
Phone: 775-882-7755 or 888-886-ISRR
Web site: http://www.isrr.net/

Joint Council on International Children's Services
117 South St. Asaph Street
Alexandria, VA 22314
Phone: 703-535-8045
Fax: 703-535-8049
E-mail: jcics@jcics.org
Web site: http://www.jcics.org/

Korean American Adoptee Adoptive Family Network
P.O. Box 5585
El Dorado Hills, CA 95762
Phone: 916-933-1447
E-mail: kaanet@kaanet.com
Web site: http://www.kaanet.com/

National Abandoned Infants Assistance Resource Center
School of Social Welfare, UC Berkeley
1950 Addison Street, Suite 104
Berkeley, CA 94704-1182
Phone: 510-643-8390
Web site: http://aia.berkeley.edu/

National Adoption Center
1500 Walnut Street, Suite 701
Philadelphia, PA 19102
Phone: 800-TO-ADOPT
Web site: http://www.adopt.org/whoweare/index.html

National Adoption Day
Phone: 202-572-2993
E-mail: info@nationaladoptionday.org
Web site: http://www.nationaladoptionday.org/

National Center for Adoption Law and Policy
Capitol University Law School
303 E. Broad Street
Columbus, OH 43215
Phone: 614-236-6730
Fax: 614-236-6958
E-mail: adoptionctr@law.capital.edu
Web site: http://www.law.capital.edu/adoption/

National Council for Adoption
225 N. Washington Street
Alexandria, VA 22314-2561
Phone: 703-299-6633
Fax: 703-299-6004
E-mail: ncfa@adoptioncouncil.org
Web site: http://www.adoptioncouncil.org/

National Foster Parent Association
7512 Stanich Avenue #6
Gig Harbor, WA 98335
Phone: 253-853-4000 or 1-800-557-5238
Web site: http://www.nfpainc.org

National Indian Child Welfare Association
5100 SW Macadam Avenue, Suite 300
Portland, OR 97239
Phone: 503-222-4044
Fax: 503-222-4007
Web site: http://www.nicwa.org/

National Resource Center for Foster Care and Permanency Planning
Hunter College School of Social Work
129 E. 79th Street
New York, NY 10021
Phone: 212-452-7053
Web site: http://www.hunter.cuny.edu/socwork/nrcfcpp/

North American Council on Adoptable Children
970 Raymond Avenue, Suite 106
St. Paul, MN 55114
Phone: 651-644-3036
Fax: 651-644-9848
E-mail: info@nacac.org
Web site: http://www.nacac.org/

Pact: An Adoption Alliance
4179 Piedmont Avenue, Suite 101
Oakland, CA 94611
Phone: 510-243-9460
Fax: 510-243-9970
Web site: http://www.pactadopt.org
E-mail: info@pactadopt.org

U.S. Department of State
Intercountry Adoption Booklet:
   http://travel.state.gov/family/adoption/intercountry/intercountry_473.html
Intercountry Adoption News:
   http://travel.state.gov/family/adoption/intercountry/intercountry_482.html

Zero to Three: National Center for Infants, Toddlers and Families
2000 M Street NW, Suite 200
Washington, DC 20036
Phone: 202-638-1144
Fax: 202-638-0851
E-mail: 0to3@presswarehouse.com
Web site: http://www.zerotothree.org/site/PageServer

Western Office
350 South Bixel, Suite 150
Los Angeles, CA 90017
Phone: 213-481-7279

Index